UNTITLED

Billy Allen (death row prisoner)

There are moments, though rare, when my emotions will escape from the prison in which I've kept them prisoner. Their cries, some of pain, frustration, anger, and fear, will then erupt onto the canvas, paper, or whatever material that's been chosen as the arena for them to be heard. The colors scream of the emotions that I have longed to set free! The brush stokes, some calm, bold, others wildly controlled, leave an undeniable impression of a soul that has suffered, is somewhat shattered, not yet broken, but barely holding together!

My name is Billie Allen and my art is what I call "Painting With Tears: The Art Of Innocence!" It is the story that you never hear as one fights to hold on while trying to get the justice they have been denied! These pieces and more were created from a cell on Federal Death Row, where I fight to prove my innocence. To hear more about my story and to see more artwork, please feel free to visit freebillieallen.com and twitter.com/freebilliealle1.

Billie Allen 26901-044
P.O. Box 33
Terre Haute, IN. 47808
freebillieallen.com

ADVANCE PRAISE

"*Abolishing Carceral Society* is an immense contribution to contemporary struggles for freedom. The pieces in this collection provoke new questions that inform resistance strategies, and deepen our understandings of the systems we are seeking to abolish and the social relations we are working to transform. This collection will be a profoundly useful tool in classrooms and activist groups. The conversation happening in *Abolition* is essential reading for those participating in the thorny, complex debates about how we dismantle structures of state violence and domination. The writers and artists whose work makes up the inaugural issue of *Abolition*, rigorously explore the most pressing questions emerging in liberation struggles."

—Dean Spade, author of *Normal Life: Administrative Violence, Critical Trans Politics and the Limits of Law.*

"*Abolishing Carceral Society* is a wonderful mix of provocative ideas married with art, to help us consider a world without prisons, policing, and surveillance. Many of the submissions, however, are less concerned with dismantling what exists than they are with taking seriously that abolition is a project interested in building and in practical organizing. This comes through particularly in David Turner's essay, among others. *Abolishing Carceral Society* asks us some questions that we sometimes prefer to ignore, like 'What does it mean to transform human relations?' This inaugural issue from *Abolition* pushes us to ask a number of questions that are important to moving us toward an abolitionist horizon."

—Mariame Kaba, founder of Project NIA, and cofounder of Chicago Freedom School, Chicago Taskforce on Violence Against Girls & Young Women, and Love & Protect.

"*Abolition* is a crucial contribution to radical social movements. While fighting against prisons and the death penalty as instruments of class rule, the journal amplifies the voices of the incarcerated, actively engages with organizers on the ground, and builds bridges across multiple movements. The first issue, *Abolishing Carceral Society*, presents incisive interventions in the current debates about prison abolition and abolitionism as a political principle. It is a bold beginning for what will become an essential forum for all insurgent thinkers."

—Silvia Federici, author of *Revolution at Point Zero: Housework, Reproduction, and the Feminist Struggle* and *Caliban and the Witch: Women, the Body, and Primitive Accumulation.*

"From slavery to prisons, abolition has always been a project of courage and breadth. *Abolishing Carceral Society* brings to bear the reflective, transformative urgency needed to confront today's violent world order. Of the struggle, by the struggle, and for the struggle: this auspicious collection offers not answers but pathways down which contemporary abolitionists travel en route to a future freedom. Check out their words, scope their visions—heed their calls."

—Dan Berger, author of *Captive Nation: Black Prison Organizing in the Civil Rights Era.*

"*Abolition: A Journal of Insurgent Politics* continues the radical, democratic tradition started by abolitionists to speak truth to power. In these dismal political times, it is a matter of the greatest urgency to create and sustain a counter-public sphere and an alternative print culture to sustain and expand American democracy. This remarkable and inspiring advocacy journal is poised to do precisely that for democratic activists as well as the broader lay public."

—Manisha Sinha, author of *The Slave's Cause: A History of Abolition.*

"The Abolition Collective embodies the kind of work anybody interested in justice should aspire to reproduce. Astute, rigorous, and uncompromising, the collective seeks to bring radical perspectives to a wide readership within and beyond academe. With the publication of its inaugural issue we are treated to the very best of revolutionary analysis. Anybody interested in upending a carceral and colonial order will find plenty of inspiration here. Something we all need and do well to pass along."

—Steven Salaita, author of *Inter/Nationalism: Decolonizing Native America and Palestine.*

"The Abolition Journal project offers a unique, revolutionary lens through which to view, analyze and fight against capitalism and patriarchy on the terrain of the prison-industrial complex. It aims to combine an abolitionist message with a democratic production process that prioritizes participation of those directly affected by incarceration. What a welcome and needed approach! I am confident the project will help intellectuals build ties of solidarity across race, class, gender, nationality, and other borders that block liberation and in its finest moments will help teach us, as Mumia says, to 'fight with light in our eyes.'"

—James Kilgore, author of *Understanding Mass Incarceration: A People's Guide to the Key Civil Rights Struggle of Our Time.*

"*Abolition: Journal of Insurgent Politics* is a bold journal mapping new roads out of the inferno in which we live. As the editors' Manifesto tells us, 'abolition' is a key strategy out of our carceral, slave-like society—the prison being the pivotal place for the perpetuation of an unjust political system. But the journal also sheds light on the many ways in which we're imprisoned beyond the prison's walls. With scholarly articles, poems and artwork, in a beautifully designed text, it asks us to open our eyes and support a liberation struggle against jails and jailers."

—George Caffentzis, author of *In Letters of Blood and Fire: Work, Machines, and the Crisis of Capitalism* and *No Blood For Oil: Essays on Energy, Class Struggle and War, 1998-2017.*

"What is the most damage we can do—given our biographies, abilities, and commitments—to the racial order and rule of capital?"

Adapted from Joel Olson

ABOLISHING CARCERAL SOCIETY

ABOLITION: A JOURNAL OF INSURGENT POLITICS

Abolition Collective, editors

ACKNOWLEDGEMENTS

The Abolition Journal's publication working group for this first issue included: Kevin Bruyneel, Jaskiran Dhillon, Andrew Dilts, Paula Ioanide, Brian Lovato, Eli Meyerhoff, and Dylan Rodríguez. While the publication group worked hard as managing coeditors to facilitate review and conceptualize themes for the first issue, Eli Meyerhoff and Andrew Dilts offered critical leadership and disproportionate labor in making it come to life. The art working group who reviewed and selected the art for the journal included LJ Amsterdam, Jaskiran Dhillon, Eli Meyerhoff, and Amanda Priebe. Reviewers from within and beyond Abolition's editorial review board gave invaluable feedback on articles in the issue. We thank Michelle Beckett for her copy-editing expertise. Our editors at Common Notions, Malav Kanuga and Natsumi Paxton, have been wonderfully encouraging and patient. Thank you as well to Neelufar Franklin, Morgan Buck, Josh MacPhee, and Ash Goh at Common Notions.

ABOUT ABOLITION

Abolition: A Journal of Insurgent Politics is a collectively-run project supporting radical scholarly and activist ideas, poetry, and art, publishing and disseminating work that encourages us to make the impossible possible, to seek transformation well beyond policy changes and toward revolutionary abolitionism.

We seek submissions from both incarcerated people and from people outside the prison walls. To submit to *Abolition*, email: abolitionjournal@gmail.com.

We are developing our capacity to work across carceral walls, and we encourage currently incarcerated people to send us their writings, submissions, and thoughts about this publication. We will try to respond to mail as quickly as possible. Given that we are a small collective, our limited capacity may mean our replies might be slightly delayed. Please note that at this time, we are not able to offer legal support.

We thank you for your patience in advance, and we hope to continue to spread the publication in spaces of abolitionist and insurgent thought and work.

Abolition: A Journal of Insurgent Politics
1321 N. Milwaukee Avenue
PMB 460
Chicago, IL 60622

Abolishing Carceral Society
Abolition: A Journal of Insurgent Politics

Edited by Abolition Collective
This edition © 2018 Common Notions

ISBN: 978-1-942173-08-3
LCCN: 2018907923

Common Notions
314 7th Street
Brooklyn, NY 11215
commonnotions.org
info@commonnotions.org

Design and typesetting by Morgan Buck and Josh MacPhee
Antumbra Design | antumbradesign.org

Printed in the USA by the employee-owners of Thomson-Shore
thomsonshore.com

CONTENTS

INTRODUCTION

IT IS DIFFICULT TO INTRODUCE THIS FIRST ISSUE OF THE JOURNAL, because the collective and journal together are self-consciously provisional and evolving projects. In keeping with our manifesto (itself an openly revisable and changing document) this project seeks to radically dismantle and transform the world in which we find ourselves. It seeks to theorize, organize, and directly act in ways to make the impossible possible. It works as part of, and in solidarity with, radical movements that identify their work and aspirations as abolitionist.

As put succinctly by Keeanga-Yamahtta Taylor, reflecting on the fortieth anniversary of the Combahee River Collective Statement, "Political analysis outside of political movements and struggles becomes abstract, discourse driven, and disconnected from the radicalism that made it powerful in the first place."[1] The truth of this statement and the legacy of radical activism and constant and fearless critical reflection on that action drives the artwork, articles, poetry, and interventions in this inaugural issue of *Abolition: A Journal of Insurgent Politics*. This issue is many years in the making, and is just one part of the work undertaken by members of the Abolition Collective.

Many of us who make up the collective are organizers in abolitionist movements already, and where we are not, we individually and collectively aspire to be accomplices rather than allies.[2] You will find contributions that reach far and wide to movements

---

1. Keeanga-Yamahtta Taylor, *How We Get Free: Black Feminism and the Combahee River Collective*. (Haymarket Books, 2017).
2. Indigenous Action Media, "Accomplices Not Allies: Abolishing the Ally Industrial Complex," May 4, 2014, available at indigenousaction.org.

and actions that operate within the broad frame of abolitionist politics and everyday life. We do not seek to define in advance what these projects will look like, nor do we delimit in advance what will count as an abolitionist project. Yet not everything can or should be assumed to be abolitionist merely by invoking the name. We insist not solely on the ruthless criticism of everything existing, but more directly to a radical and transformative politics, predicated on the end of this oppressive world and the building of a more liberatory one.

In another sense, we can introduce this journal and its inaugural issue in a very straightforward way, by differentiating it from the kind of academic journals which have become instruments to institutions of domination and oppression. We are a journal that seeks to directly confront the terms of knowledge production while at the same time carving out tactics of subterfuge and survival. In our attempts to struggle *against* and *beyond* academia, this first issue seeks to *practice* what we have set forth in our manifesto. As such, readers will not find a singular theme within abolitionist politics. On the contrary, what unites the essays, poems, artworks, and interventions of this inaugural issue is the *way* in which the journal has operated: collectively, horizontally, and in a radically democratic mode.

So, to be clear: *Abolition: A Journal of Insurgent Politics* strives to be completely open access, available both online and in print, and accessible in as many senses of that term as possible. And when our reach is limited by what is possible, we will work to recognize that failure and be accountable for it, never resting with our current reach. This issue has been produced collaboratively, stealing labor-time from universities. We have organized our editorial review without official support from universities or other neoliberal institutions of "higher education" or the university-as-such.[3] In practice, this means that while we engage in a process of "peer review," we insist on a different understanding of what is meant by "peer" (recognizing that while seemingly a term implying egalitarianism between "peers," such equality

---

3. Undercommoning Collective, "Undercommoning within, against and beyond the University-as-Such," *ROAR Magazine*, 2016, available at roarmag.org.

historically reproduces hierarchies of domination). Our peers are in the streets, comrades in arms, and movement actors for whom these questions are anything but "academic" or "ideal curiosities." Submissions for *Abolition* are evaluated and critiqued by experts and movement actors on the ground.

This inaugural issue is our opening foray into this practice. It is the first artifact of learning to engage with each other on these terms, within and against the neoliberal university. It is ruthlessly critical in orientation, dedicated to destroying oppressive institutions, understanding the entanglement between (and within) different systems of oppression, and generating creative visions for transforming the world.

For color versions of the artworks in this issue, please see abolitionjournal.org/art.

MANIFESTO OF
THE ABOLITION JOURNAL

ABOLITIONIST POLITICS IS NOT ABOUT WHAT IS POSSIBLE, BUT ABOUT making the impossible a reality. Ending slavery appeared to be an impossible challenge for Sojourner Truth, Denmark Vesey, Nat Turner, John Brown, Harriet Tubman, and others, and yet they struggled for it anyway. Today we seek to abolish a number of seemingly immortal institutions, drawing inspiration from those who have sought the abolition of all systems of domination, exploitation, and oppression—from Jim Crow laws and prisons to patriarchy and capitalism. The shockingly unfinished character of these struggles can be seen from some basic facts about our present. The eighty-five richest people in the world have as much wealth as the poorest half; more African American men are in prison, jail, or parole than were enslaved in 1850; we have altered the chemical composition of our atmosphere threatening all life on this planet; women and trans people are significantly more likely than cisgender men to be victims of sexual and domestic violence; rich nations support military interventions into "developing" countries as cover for neocolonial resource exploitation. Recognizing that the institutions we fight against are both interconnected and unique, we refuse to take an easy path of reveling in abstract ideals while accepting mere reforms in practice. Instead, we seek to understand the specific power dynamics within and between these systems so we can make the impossible possible; so we can bring the entire monstrosity down.

We must ask questions that are intimately connected with abolitionist movements if we are to understand these dynamics in ways that are strategically useful. How do those in power use differences of race, gender, sexuality, nationality, and class to divide and exploit us? How do we build bridges across these divides through our organizing? Activists on the ground ask such questions often, but rarely do those within universities become involved. Instead, academia has more often been an opponent to abolitionist movements, going back to the coconstitution of early universities with colonialism and slavery, and the development of racial science and capitalist ideologies. Academic journals have functioned to maintain a culture of conformity, legitimated with myths of "political neutrality" and "meritocracy." At the same time, colleges and universities have always been terrains of struggle, as radical organizers have found ways to expropriate their resources: from W.E.B. DuBois's abolitionist science at Fisk University to the Black Campus Movement of the sixties. Inspired by them, we refuse to abandon the resources of academia to those who perpetuate the status quo.

Instead, we are creating a new project, centered around *Abolition: A Journal of Insurgent Politics*—for research, publishing, and study that encourage us to make the impossible possible, to seek transformation well beyond policy changes and toward revolutionary abolitionism.

Our journal's title has multiple reference points in a tense relation with one another. "Abolition" refers partly to the historical and contemporary movements that have identified themselves as "abolitionist": those against slavery, prisons, the wage system, animal and earth exploitation, racialized, gendered, and sexualized violence, and the death penalty, among others. But we also refer to *all* revolutionary movements, insofar as they have abolitionist elements—whether the abolition of patriarchy, capitalism, heteronormativity, ableism, colonialism, the state, or white supremacy. Rather than just seeking to abolish a list of oppressive institutions, we aim to support studies of the entanglement of different systems of oppression, not to erase the tensions between different movements, but to create spaces for collective experimentation with those tensions. Instead of assuming one homogenous subject as our audience (e.g., "abolitionists of the world unite!"), we write for multiple, contingent, ambivalent subjectivities—for people coming from different places, living and struggling in different circumstances, and in the process of figuring out who we are and untangling these knots to fight for a more just and liberated world. With Fanon, we are "endlessly creating" ourselves.

Abolition takes cues from the abolition-democracy espoused by figures like W.E.B. Du Bois, Angela Davis, and Joel Olson. Our orientation toward academic insurgency builds upon the struggles of the Black campus movement against the White University, the American Indian movement against the Colonial University, feminist and queer movements against the Hetero-Patriarchal University, and anarchist and communist movements against the Capitalist University. As efforts to revolutionize academia originated and drew their lifeblood from movements outside and across the boundaries of academic institutions, today we recognize that our journal's radical aspirations must be similarly grounded. We must therefore facilitate collaborations of radical academics *with and in support of* movements that are struggling against oppressive regimes and for the creation of alternative futures. Recognizing that the best movement-relevant intellectual work is happening both in the movements themselves and in the communities with whom they organize (e.g., in dispossessed neighborhoods and prisons), the journal aims to support scholars whose research amplifies such grassroots intellectual activity.

In tension with struggles *against* and *beyond* academia, we recognize the desires of academics to survive *within* it, for the access to resources that inclusion can offer. Rather than accepting such desires as eternal necessities, we foresee that the success of abolitionist projects will change the availability of resources for intellectual activity as well as what we understand as a "resource." To help academics grapple with transgressing academia's boundaries, our journal aims to provide some legitimacy within the dominant value practices of academia (e.g., publication requirements for hiring, tenure, and promotion), while simultaneously pushing the limits of those practices. All of our publications will be accessible, free, and open access, refusing the paywalls of the publishing industry. We will also produce hard-copy versions for circulation to communities lacking internet access. Yet, we are not abandoning peer review—sharing writing with respected comrades and giving each other feedback before wider circulation—which can be useful for movements to strengthen and amplify their intellectual activities. As peer review is ultimately based on relationships of trust, we ask why academics on the opposite side of our struggles are our "peers." Instead, we commit to building relationships with activist-intellectuals for whom a new kind of peer review can serve as an insurgent tool to expropriate academia's resources for knowledge production.

"Abolition" as a concept, process, and reality becomes the common ground upon which we meet, struggle, and join together in solidarity.

The Abolition Collective

LONG LIVE JOHN AFRICA![1]

Mumia Abu-Jamal

IF WE ARE TO ADOPT THE NAME OF ABOLITIONIST, LET US DO SO openly, mindfully, and aware of its great and true significance.

For, guild history has rewritten the texts, and penned what Black historian Lerone Bennett has called "theology" rather than truth to depict some figures of the past, to create a past that never lived.

We all know of Lincoln, for we were taught of him as children: "The Great Emancipator." Bennett's view is that he was (as were most men of his era) a white supremacist who was "forced into glory" (the title of his book, by the way). He was many things, but he wasn't an abolitionist.

In his prepresidential speech before Cooper Union in New York, he gave a contemptuous tone to his comments about "abolitionists," and he took great pains to separate himself from a group seen as mad by the elites.

John Brown, perhaps the noblest white figure of his age, is but a madman on Lincoln's tongue.

But any considered vista of history shows us that this small, focused, and brave group sent vibrations of honor through the annals of time, and gave us new ways of reliving the abolitionist creed in new eras of U.S. history.

Both Howard Zinn and Staughton Lynd, some of the most-loved and most-respected historians of the sixties, saw the youth of the civil rights movement as the *new abolitionists*.

Abolitionists are, simply put, those beings who look out upon their time and say, "No."

---

1. This essay is part of a series of "Abolition Statements" from members of the Abolition Collective and Editorial Review Board. For the rest of the statements, see abolitionjournal.org.

They want to abolish state policies that they cannot abide. Slavery. Mass incarceration. The death penalty. Juvenile life. Solitary confinement. Police terrorism.

Those goals are worthy of the name. Only the fire and will seem to be lacking.

Let us recover their vision—and build new ones that soar towards the bright morning of Freedom.

And yet—and yet—before we hug ourselves in isolated, sweet self-contentment, let us ponder our history, and one of its most potent turning points.

Our revered abolitionist ancestor, Frederick Douglass, as the Civil War was dying down, in favor of the ending of slavery, he warned his abolitionist brethren and sisters to beware of thinking that the battle was over. In his typical, lyrical, southern-informed proverb, he told them,

> Slavery has been fruitful in giving itself names. It has been called 'the peculiar institution', 'the social system', and the 'impediment.' It has been called by a great many names, and it will call itself by yet another name; and you and I and all of us had better wait and see what new form this old monster will assume, in what new skin this old snake will come forth next.

It is our abolitionist duty to hear Douglass well, as we tackle monsters we dare to think are new, but are, in actuality, "old wine in new bottles." If he had been heeded, perhaps Reconstruction could've been extended, instead of its miserable ten years. Instead, too many abolitionists took off their fighting clothes, and went back home, satisfied that the good fight had been won.

Let us fight with light in our eyes, that we see what is before us; and not succumb to New Jim Crows, ever again.

In the Spirit of the Ancestors,
Mumia Abu-Jamal

MAKE RACISTS AFRAID AGAIN

Zola Montreal

Zola is the name for my street art projects that I consider as a part of my contribution to activism for social change. I am a queer settler (French-Canadian descent) working in an anti-oppressive framework. My political upbringing was through the Quebec student movement, and I am now involved in different affinity groups and collectives addressing indigenous solidarity, and art and activism.

The ongoing street art project under the Zola pseudonym focuses on the iconic character of the masked protester as a romantic allegory for street politics. Both demonized by liberals and idealized by insurrectionists, masked protesters are no one and every one at the same time. In this "case study," I am concerned with representing the diversity of folks who engage in this radical tactic, and with shifting the male stereotype of the frontlines fighter. Putting up portraits of anonymous protesters on city walls is also a way to create more space for radical politics, by and for activists, in a way that reminds daily commuters of ongoing social struggles.

One of the things I value most in my art/activism is mutual trust. I am primarily accountable to the communities, groups and people I work with. I have worked with: Tadamon!, Solidarity Across Borders, Non-Status Women's Collective, Librairie Racines, Missing Justice, Montreal Anarchist Bookfair Collective and Art and Anarchy exhibit, Ni Québec Ni Canada, Aamjiwnaang and Sarnia Against Pipelines, Unist'ot'en camp, and more. I have been involved in collectives such as ANTI375!, Howl! Arts Collective, Decolonizing Street Art, OFFMurales and Maille à Part. Recently, I've been published with *Certain Days: Freedom for Political Prisoners Calendar*, AK Press, Mentoring Artists for Women's Art, and I've participated in a few local zines, etc.

zolamtl.tumblr.com
instagram.com/zola_mtl
zolamtl.storenvy.com

DISMANTLE AND TRANSFORM:

ON ABOLITION, DECOLONIZATION, AND INSURGENT POLITICS

A conversation between Harsha Walia and Andrew Dilts

Andrew Dilts (AD): I want to start by asking about "No One is Illegal" and your involvement with it.[1] You talk about this a lot in your book, *Undoing Border Imperialism* (AK Press, 2013). For people who haven't read the book, could you explain how you became involved with that organization?

Harsha Walia (HW): My work around migrant justice is based on personal experiences and fifteen years as an organizer. I grew up in a family of migrants with an even longer history of displacement. Partition in South Asia was a very violent process. The colonially-imposed border between what is now known as India and Pakistan led to over fourteen million people being killed or displaced. It is known by the United Nations as one the largest mass displacements and migrations in human history. And when I came to Turtle Island, I lived as a migrant for many years, part of it with precarious legal status. This familial history of displacement, migration, labor exploitation and race—all the issues discussed in the book—are very personal for me. So after 9/11 when we witnessed massive roundups, surveillance, increasing deportations, and new antimigrant and antiterror laws being passed, that became my entry point into organizing within the migrant justice movement and No One Is Illegal.

AD: I want to ask you about the proliferation of security check points and border check points, because in your analysis, you describe how the border does not exist at the exterior of any nation.

---

1. For more info on No One Is Illegal, see noii-van.resist.ca.

Is it right to say that borders are almost entirely *inside* of nations and that the production of illegal persons is happening not at historical or geographic borders but as a *practice* of bordering?

HW: The border extends far beyond the geographic border. The practice of bordering is being both internalized and externalized as power and modes of control are increasingly diffused. The border is externalized through interdiction, which is the interception of migrants before the border by disallowing migrants to board airplanes and making their journeys more perilous. In Europe, this outsourcing of border regimes has resulted in the drowning deaths of tens of thousands of migrants over the past decade.

The internalization of borders is happening in so-called public institutions—schools, hospitals, transit—that are operating as checkpoints and either denying migrants access and often acting as border guards to detain and report people to immigration authorities. The temporary foreign worker program also operates as a domesticated border and form of incarceration both literally and figuratively. Migrant workers often have their documents confiscated and are held captive to work under conditions of indentured servitude. For live-in caregivers in Canada, for example, historically Caribbean women and now Filipina women came to work as domestic workers and the rates of sexual violence are incredibly high because vulnerable migrant women are being forced to live with predominantly white middle-class employers. The internalized form of control and bordering that is inherent to such state-sanctioned indentured labor programs is the new template for global migration, or "managed migration" as the elites call it.

AD: I want to look deeper into the internal workings of an organization like NOII which is all volunteer-based. As you argue in the book, part of resisting the nonprofit industrial complex is trying to not fall into these traps of fundraising cycles where you lose power and self-determination. So one of the tensions that comes up a lot, however, is the expectation of doing a whole lot of labor without much (or any) compensation for it. How have you all navigated the tensions of making sure people can survive while they're doing this work?

HW: It's something we definitely struggle with. There have been a few instances in the past where members in the collective didn't have full legal immigration status and weren't able to "legally" work, and so we put aside the little bit of money for those folks to be compensated for their labor in the collective. But we don't have any specific policy since we are not a formal nonprofit, and our collective members and capacity is constantly changing.

We also support through other forms of labor by, for example, always providing childcare or supporting each other emotionally in times of stress. So trying to build more resilient networks in everyday acts of living. NOII has no paid staff and we do have to find other ways to financially support themselves, which immensely affects our collective capacity. But the flipside of monetizing our labor is to strengthen relational forms of labor—by helping each other move, making meals when people are sick, supporting with childcare etc. We reduce our reliance on the state by relying on each other. Of course our capacities—both individual and institutional—to make this possible are incredibly limited and marginalized communities are constantly forced to be in contact with the state and its bureaucracies, whether it is the immigration system, prison, child apprehension system, food banks, welfare, courts, etc. It is imperfect and adhoc but I have immense respect for the intention and care of building community as a form of labor within political practice.

AD: In an interview you did with Glen Coulthard, you asked him a question about state engagement versus disengagement.[2] I want to ask you the same question: How do we determine when and how to turn away?

HW: I think the disengagement versus engagement dichotomy is false, just as the reform versus revolution debate is reductive. Even if our long-term vision is turned away from the state, in the short term we may have to engage with the state—things like dealing with the courts or calling the cops to address gender violence etc. Part of the reason someone may decide to rely on the police is

---

2. Interview available at rabble.ca.

because our community accountability mechanisms are dismal. I asked Glen that question because I don't think it's a simple answer. Despite my vision to disengage with the state, the reality is that I end up engaging with the state every day especially when supporting marginalized women.

I am not suggesting that engagement versus disengagement with the state is simply a temporal distinction, as many alternatives to the state do exist in the immediate. It is more of a practical and contextual consideration for me. The main principle I work around in these individual instances is the principle of self-determination. If I am supporting someone facing deportation or partner violence, what do they need? Are there effective alternatives to the state that exist that I can suggest or do they feel the need to engage with the state in order to reduce harm or to access safety?

AD: As a general answer that seems really helpful because that answer makes it concrete immediately in terms of specific needs and specific situations. And it pushes back on the traditional "reform versus revolution" version of the question. In prison abolition work, I hear the language of "reformist reforms" versus "non-reformist reforms" being used more and more, and I'm wondering if that language makes sense based on the concrete situations you're invoking here: a reform that reinforces the system versus a reform that requires a different system.

HW: Yes, I think so. Arguably every reform entrenches the power of the state because it gives the state the power to implement that reform. But from an ethical orientation towards emancipation, I think a guiding question on non-reformist reforms is: Is it increasing the possibility of freedom? In the context of detention centers and prisons, there are tangible differences between various kinds of reforms.

Locally, we are in the period of a state inquest after the tragic death of a Mexican migrant woman Lucia Vega Jimenez in immigration detention.[3] There are now a number of reform-based

---

3. "Lucia Vega Jimenez found hanging in CBSA shower stall," *CBC News*, Jan. 29, 2014, available at cbc.ca. See also, "NOII Statement: Inquest into Lucia Vega Jimenez Death in CBSA Custody," Oct 7, 2014, available at noii-van.resist.ca.

recommendations on the table coming from legal organizations, NGO's and state-based agencies. Our allies and us put forward our vision for an end to all deportations and detentions, and then we supported those specific necessary reforms that detainees over the years have talked about that would increase their access to the outside world—for example, increased access to phones, computers, and legal advice.

Conversely, one of the proposed reforms that we did not support was a GPS electronic bracelet as an alternative to incarceration. This is forcing people to incarcerate their own body and their home becomes their cages. Another reform we opposed was more cameras in prisons. Even though it was pitched under the guise of "keeping detainees safe," surveillance is less about safety and more about invasion of privacy and increased social control. So that was how we decided—is the reform increasing the possibility of freedom or is it incarceration and control in another form?

AD: Let me go straight into the book for a moment: one of the things that I really love about the book, and one of the reasons that I teach it too, is that every chapter of this book includes a series of narratives from individuals who are from racialized groups, and almost all are women-identified folks. In the beginning of the book, you call this a political act. So, first: what is it that you are thinking of as *politics*, and as *action*, such that the inclusion of those voices counts as a *political act*? And second: what does it mean in both the activism and the writing to place those voices at the center rather than at the periphery?

HW: Part of my hesitation in agreeing to write the book was the impact it would have on collective organizing. We know how harmful it is when one individual becomes seen as the "expert" voice of a movement, and writing is one of the key ways that happens. I wanted to be accountable to that concern as it is a legitimate political concern. At the same time, I am also aware of how we need to be writing and sharing our stories and movement histories, and to not cede that terrain of knowledge production to others who often usurp or misrepresent our histories and theories.

The process of how to envision and write this book took longer than writing the book. From the beginning, I reached out to as many comrades as possible and including the narratives and roundtable was a deliberate effort to lift up movement as a collective. This action is also a political affirmation—movements can produce our own theory, enact group-centered space because there is no liberation in isolation, assess movement victories and challenges in a multitude of ways, and push against the competition and tokenism that often happens to and amongst racialized women by actively centering those voices throughout the entire book.

AD: How do you think about solidarity and allyship? Or, alternately, as described in "Abolishing the Ally Industrial Complex," about accomplices rather than allies?[4]

HW: I think allies and accomplices have become identities in and of themselves, when in fact they are meant to be verbs—to signify ways of being and of doing, of relationship and relationality. It is impossible for any one person to be "an ally" because we all carry multitudes of experiences and oppressions and privileges. Most people are simultaneously oppressed and simultaneously privileged, and even those are always specific and contextual.

My paid work is in one of the poorest neighborhoods in the country. Unsurprisingly, this is a disproportionately racialized neighborhood but there are many older cisgendered white men. A straight white cisgendered man who is homeless faces a harsher material reality than me on a daily basis—with minimal to no access to food, shelter, health care, or income. Reductively, one would say that I have class privilege in relationship to him. But it goes beyond that. Even taking into account that I might be able to count off more forms of oppression, the entirety of my material reality is more secure.

For me that is where intersectionality falls short; it has become a static analysis and one of fixed categories that leads to oppressed/ally dichotomies. Anti-oppression analysis becomes rigid

---

4. "Accomplices Not Allies: Abolishing the Ally Industrial Complex," available at indigenousaction.org.

in its categorizations when the question becomes who is more oppressed, rather than engaging in a dialogue of *how* oppression, which is relational and contextual, is specifically manifesting. Oppression develops a strange quantifiable logic, a commodity that can be stocked up on. This isn't to say I don't believe in anti-oppression allyship, but rather that I question its reductionism in place of a fluid, contextual and relational practice.

Another example is within No One Is Illegal. We are a collective of mainly racialized women and trans folks, but we rarely see ourselves as a group that seeks out others with more privilege to be allies to us. It is more often the inverse; we strive to be allies to and supportive of other struggles—whether it's refugee or non-status people facing deportation or grassroots Indigenous land defenders. Those are the relationship we strive to strengthen, and not ones that reinforce our supposed "victim" or oppressed status. That comes from an understanding that movements are about responsibilities, and allyship is about ethical and consensual relationships.

AD: I want to go back to what you were saying about the state. Another thing you do in the book that is really helpful is in tracing the language of "No One is Illegal," and making the point that *states are in fact illegal.* Part of what *centers* settler colonialism is, in fact, a whole series of gross violations of law. So can you say more about the language of illegality and how it shapes your work?

HW: I think no one is illegal, or no human being is illegal, is a profound idea; the idea that we cannot criminalize a person simply for existing. We live in a world where we call people "illegal" and this happens because we have normalized the idea that the act of crossing a border is a so-called criminal act. The criminalization of migration represents a profound injustice where the state, like corporations, attains the status of personhood that is supposedly being violated or trespassed, thus rendering human beings as non-status. To be a non-status or undocumented person is to be a non-person of sorts, especially in the state-sanctioned legal sense of citizenship. This is then further racialized as migrants of color are cast as "terrorists" and "threats" etc. So no human being is illegal is the affirmation that, as Eduardo Galeano has said, "the world was born yearning to be a home for everyone."

In the context of settler colonial states like Canada, a necessary corollary to No One Is Illegal has been the assertion of Canada Is Illegal. Settler-colonial states are founded on the racist doctrine of discovery and *terra nullius*, which denies and erases the presences of Indigenous peoples and nations. Conquest in Canada was designed to ensure forced displacement of Indigenous peoples from their territories, the destruction of autonomy and self-determination in Indigenous self-governance, and the assimilation of Indigenous peoples' cultures and traditions. For the No One Is Illegal movement to assert this truth about Canada also means that we must be in alliance with Indigenous self-determination and to remember our responsibilities to support Indigenous nationhood.

It is also important to share where this framework of "No One Is Illegal, Canada Is Illegal" stems from, as it is a reflection of how this journey is embodied and enacted. Ten years ago we were supporting logistics like childcare and food preparation for an international indigenous youth gathering, and through this process were entering into dialogue about our histories and struggles. There was a march on the last day of the gathering and we heard the MC start chanting, "No one is illegal. Canada is illegal." This was an incredible moment— articulating a vision that the settler-colonial state and its laws are illegal and illegitimate, not displaced and migrating human beings. Also this chant was a genuine expression and gesture of relationship and solidarity.

AD: The terms "decolonization" and "abolition" are being used more and more in analysis and radical action, and it feels like we're at a moment where that language is ascendant, but also in danger of losing its specific meaning. How would you articulate the meaning of a concept or a practice of abolition, decolonization or insurgence?

HW: To me, abolition and decolonization are strong and necessary frameworks, though we have to be cognizant of the critiques about their co-option in ways that no longer root them in the specificity of Black and Indigenous struggles. Decolonization has become a metaphor for everything—like decolonize the academy or decolonize your mind—without necessarily centering anticolonial struggle, Indigenous nationhood, and the repatriation of land. Here I would point to the crucial work of Eve Tuck and K. Wayne Yang in "Decolonization is not a metaphor," and Robyn Maynard's piece "#Blacksexworkerslivesmatter: White-Washed 'Anti-Slavery' and the Appropriation of Black Suffering."[5] So the politics of decolonization and abolition must be foundational to all our movements in a way that centers, rather than erases, the historic and ongoing legacies of struggle emerging from these communities.

I tend to use the framework of a transformative politics, one that weaves in a range of critiques and articulations and that understands that the violence of the system is not an aberration. Prisons, reservations, borders, sweatshops, pipelines, gentrification, and drone warfare are all interrelated systems of exploitation and control. Movements today are re-articulating how capitalism, colonialism, white supremacy, cisheteropatriarchy, imperialism, and oppression are systems that must end. This is an overall vision oriented towards revolutionary transformation.

Transformative politics allow us to not only move beyond our silos but also help us understand how these interrelated systems of violence are at times weaponized against each other. For example, one of the main justifications for the occupation of Afghanistan was this allegedly feminist logic of liberating Afghan women. Similarly, one of the many logics of the prison industrial complex is to protect women from sexual violence. Transformative politics provides a critical lens through which to interrogate how prisons and military occupations actually reproduce rather than resolve gender violence. Battered women and gender non-conforming people are a growing part of the prison industrial complex, and women are constantly reporting rape in military bases around the world. Furthermore, military occupations and increased policing over incarcerate Indigenous, Black, migrant, trans and homeless

---

5. Eve Tuck and K. Wayne Yang, "Decolonization is not a metaphor,"
Decolonization: Indigeneity, Education & Society 1, no. 1 (2012). Robyn Maynard,
"#Blacksexworkerslivesmatter: White-Washed 'Anti-Slavery' and the Appropriation of
Black Suffering," *The Feminist Wire*, Sept. 9, 2015, available at thefeministwire.com.

communities. Therefore transformative politics makes visible how struggles can be appropriated in the service of empire—which is what pink-washing is all about.

Finally, I think transformative politics also provide a window into our own movements and communities. Anti-authoritarians have been great at theorizing "dismantling the system," but there is less emphasis on the importance of building alternative institutions. It is no coincidence that the work of growing alternative relations and networks has largely been invisible in our movements because it is gendered labor. Both the dominant political economy and the microcosm of our movements are subsidized by the labor of those who provide childcare, cook meals, do secretarial work and provide emotional support. Even recognizing these as forms of labor is an uphill battle; we are able to articulate critiques of capital and labor in the wage economy but continue to invisibilize care work in the unwaged economy. A transformative politics requires us to rethink, reimagine and reorient work and its relationship to gender and dis/ability—what is the work that makes all other work possible? How do we foster social relations across generations and communities based on interdependence, resilience, vulnerability, and solidarity? Connection is, after all, the antithesis of commodification and at the heart of a truly transformative politics.

Recorded February 5, 2015.
Edited for length and clarity, January 2016.
Thank you to Colin Arnold and Alexia Barbaro
for transcription and editorial assistance.

AFTER MY PA CUT THE GRASS

Yvette Mayorga

Yvette Mayorga's project Borderland Series (2014–2015) employs confection, industrial materials, and the American board game Candy Land as a conceptual framework to juxtapose the borderlands of the United States and Mexico. The spaces in the "Candy Lands" of her work relate to notions of Utopia, exemplifying the immigrant's vision of the American Dream. Candy Land signifies an America filled with the possibility of happiness while Mexico becomes the land of lost hope. Informed by the politics of the border, the events that happen on it and the transnational narratives that arise after crossing it, Yvette tackles issues of race, identity, gender, and Latin stereotypes using the visual tropes of celebration. The monuments/towers, built from accumulated candy, frosting found objects exemplify the excess associated with the American Dream. They stand as living shrines to real life individuals, such as Selena Quintanilla, her mother, and her sister. She received her BFA from University of Illinois at Urbana-Champaign and is currently an MFA candidate at The School of the Art Institute of Chicago. Yvette has exhibited in galleries and museums including the Krannert Art Museum at University of Illinois, The National Museum of Mexican Art, and EXPO Chicago Art Fair.

SHIFTING CARCERAL LANDSCAPES

DECARCERATION AND THE RECONFIGURATION OF WHITE SUPREMACY

Colleen Hackett and Ben Turk

THE PRISON STATE IN THE UNITED STATES IS UNDERGOING YET another reconfiguration. Under a combination of popular pressure, fiscal limitations, and stubbornly ungovernable populations, the system of mass incarceration is widely understood as unsustainable in its current form. This critical understanding has gained the attention of policy-makers and political elites, who have adopted the cause of decarceration. The top-down goals, priorities, and framings of these reformers depart significantly and problematically from the decarceration movements that precede them. Mainstream democrats as well as hardcore conservatives have come together in a much-lauded bipartisan coalition to reform mass incarceration. Archconservatives like Newt Gingrich and the Koch Brothers contend with the high cost of prisons that burden state and federal budgets while Democrats like Hillary Clinton and Bernie Sanders frame their discontent with mass incarceration and especially privatized prisons as unjust, but emphasize the importance of strategic coalition with fiscal conservatives while adding a flavor of pandering to their Black and Latinx constituencies.

Many in the pre-existing decarceration movement applaud this shift, welcoming the involvement of policy makers and rightfully feeling validated in their own work by these small steps toward justice. Others are more hesitant, raising critiques of the elites and warning against collaboration with forces that strengthen and reinforce carceral logics.[1] These critiques have contributed

---

1. Ruth Wilson Gilmore, "The Worrying State of the Anti-Prison Movement," *The Social Justice Journal*, February 23, 2015, available at socialjusticejournal.org; Mariame Kaba, "Prison Reform's in Vogue and Other Strange Things...," *Truthout*, March 21, 2014, available at truthout.org.

to expanding the abolition movement. Radicals from other tendencies as well as newly aware activists are giving more attention to the antiprison struggle. As a result, the United States has seen a resurgence of militant direct action coordinated across prison fences. On September 9, 2016, to commemorate the forty-fifth anniversary of the Attica prison rebellions, prisoners staged a nationally coordinated work stoppage and protest while militants on the outside across the country attacked prison profiteers, blocked traffic, and demonstrated in solidarity at prisons and jails.[2] We want to join in critiquing elitist decarceration strategies through top-down reformist policies, while also questioning the viability and sustainability of abolitionist-supported decarceration efforts. Specifically, we will focus on how embedded white supremacy can continue to operate through various structural mechanisms and institutions while possibly even expanding and diffusing racialized social control.

The system of carcerality in the United States is one that extends beyond the prison walls. We borrow a definition of the carceral from philosopher Michel Foucault that refers to an institution, a system, or a body of knowledge that renders people as objects and exercises control over and through them.[3] Carcerality is a system that confines, entraps, and incapacitates, whether that be through the criminal legal system or by other means. This system of control in the United States has always been a function of a social order founded on white supremacy. In its most basic articulation, "white supremacy is the presumed superiority of white racial identities . . . in support of the cultural, political and economic domination of non-white groups."[4] The agents of whiteness and white supremacy—usually status quo whites—invent and assume racialized differences, often based on spectacular stereotypes of

2. Isabelle Nastasia, "Live Updates from the National Prisoner Strike," *Mask Magazine*, 2016, available at maskmagazine.com; It's Going Down, "Prisoners Launch Hunger-Strike Inside Merced's Concrete Hell," IDGCast (podcast), September 15, 2016, available at itsgoingdown.org.

3. Michel Foucault, *The Birth of the Clinic: An Archaeology of Medical Perception* (New York: Vintage Books, 1994); *Discipline and Punish: The Birth of the Prison* (New York: Vintage Books, 1995).

4. Anne Bonds and Joshua Inwood, "Beyond White Privilege: Geographies of White Supremacy and Settler Colonialism," *Progress in Human Geography* 40, no. 6 (2015): 5–6.

people of color. Some historical misrepresentations include the murderous savage, the illegal and criminal alien, the bestial, inhuman slave, or the diseased drug addict. These crude caricatures are used to solidify the myth of white superiority and to also mobilize white anxieties in order to build apparatuses that control or disappear people of color (or both). The ideology of white supremacy has fueled and *continues* to fuel countless iterations of sustained racial domination through extermination, displacement, confinement, and assimilation. From the colonization of Turtle Island and the disappearing of Native bodies through genocide, forcible relocation, and cultural appropriation, to the Japanese internment camps and anti-Asian immigration laws, or to the annexation of Mexican lands and mass detention and deportations of undocumented Latinxs, white supremacy assumes the biological or cultural inferiority of nonwhiteness (or both), thereby rendering resources, land, and socioeconomic capital to white settlers or those who align themselves with whiteness.[5]

The most oft-cited historic case of intentional white supremacy with matters involving the modern prison and policing infrastructures is the evolution of systemic repression of Black Americans. The police force in the South has its roots in the slave patrol, which was an organized form of extralegal terror against slaves to catch plantation escapees and to prevent revolts.[6] After the abolition of slavery, apparatuses of whiteness—including federal and state laws, along with white militias—implemented and regulated Black Codes, which, through vaguely defined vagrancy laws, channeled newly freed Black people to the prison system to extract coerced labor. The convict lease system that emerged out of the Thirteenth Amendment was simply put, "slavery by another name"[7] and similar forms of bondage remain in present day. In conjunction with the convict lease system and vigilante white terror, post-emancipation Jim Crow laws attempted to stifle Black

5. Paula Ioanide, *The Emotional Politics of Racism: How Feelings Trump Facts in an Era of Colorblindness* (Stanford, CA: Stanford University Press, 2015).

6. Tony Platt, "Crime and Punishment in the United States: Immediate and Long-Term Reforms from a Marxist Perspective," *Crime and Social Justice*, no. 18 (Winter 1982): 38–45.

7. Douglas Blackmon, *Slavery by Another Name: The Reenslavement of Black Americans From the Civil War to World War II* (New York: Anchor Books, 2009).

American civic and political growth. Yet, this codified segregation resulted in a crisis for liberal democratic sentiments, in very large part because organized people of color—both militant and nonviolent—effectively challenged the white status quo. And, although the much-lauded Civil Rights Act inspired hope among many that the country might move toward racial equity, it is now clear that the legislation forced white supremacy to shift and to become more subtle in effect. The post-civil rights form of white supremacy is most evident in policing and in the prison systems, where young Black, Native, and Latino males are substantially more likely to be profiled and shot than their white counterparts and where Black, Native, and Latinx peoples are more likely to be sentenced to prison than their white counterparts.

The mainstream recognition of this historicized understanding of and connections between anti-Blackness and the criminal legal system has varied greatly over the decades. The most recent resurgence of mainstream critiques of the prison system seem to partly stem from the popularity of Michelle Alexander's book, *The New Jim Crow.* Alexander's arguments gained traction just as the phase of mass incarceration she described was beginning to change. In her final chapter, Alexander urges us to recognize that just as slavery turned into Jim Crow, and Jim Crow into mass incarceration, mass incarceration could also evolve into a new form of racial caste system if we do not first address "the racial divisions and resentments that gave rise to mass incarceration."[8] Alexander's critiques come during a period in which the belief in the social contract of protection and equality is once again compromised. The awareness of mass incarceration and racial inequalities disrupts and shakes collective understandings of the United States as an advanced liberal democratic nation. As the political theorist Charles W. Mills asserts, "the liberal individual is supposed to be protected by the liberal state, and any infringement of his or her rights corrected for."[9] Yet, as Mills later reveals in his

---

8. Michelle Alexander, *The New Jim Crow: Mass Incarceration in the Age of Colorblindness* (New York: The New Press, 2010), 245.

9. Charles W. Mills, "Liberalism and the Racial State," in *State of White Supremacy: Racism, Governance, and the United States,* edited by Moon-Kie Jung, João H. Costa Vargas, and Eduardo Bonilla-Silva (Stanford, CA: Stanford University Press, 2011), 28.

indictment of white supremacy and racialized white liberalism, "the founding principles of justice prescribe different schedules of rights for whites and people of color,"[10] and, racism is structurally built into the sociopolitical order, unsettling the myth of democratic progress or equality. White supremacy is much more complex than individual acts of racism or overtly racist rhetoric, which is often cast as "irrational." Whiteness, as a category, shapes the definitions of and boundaries between superiority/inferiority, civility/incivility, deserving/nondeserving, and criminal/noncriminal. Further, material resources and institutional privileges are doled out according to where one "fits" in the racial order. We must understand white supremacy as a complex web of prejudicial beliefs and attitudes as well as institutionalized forms of racism (e.g., anti-immigration policies, voter ID laws, standardized testing, etc.). The institutional arrangement that prioritizes whiteness is intentional, rationalized, and collectively defines "white America" as normative.

The authors of this article are white abolitionists. We acknowledge the ways that our raced experiences limit our perspectives, particularly because our skin privileges afford us relative distance from many of the issues we write about in this piece. Despite our limitations, we want to critique the shifts and accommodations of a system that is transforming to produce new forms of racial caste, carcerality, and white supremacy. Both authors of this piece played active roles in coordinating the September 9th protests and have been working closely with prison rebels and antiprison movements for years. We've seen the shortcomings of reform and of mainstream nonprofit organizations. We've stood beside and shared space and visiting room vending machine meals with our comrades who have been left behind or ignored by reformist organizations. Our incarcerated colleagues provided much of the fodder for the analysis that follows, and we first want to acknowledge them and to thank the many people that engage in the struggle to dismantle the prison system.

Abolitionists such as Angela Davis have warned that prison reform has had a historical tendency to rearticulate and repackage

---

10. Ibid., 33.

racialized social control.[11] We must not only end the current institutions of control and carcerality but also anticipate and prevent their replacements. Therefore we wish to add to a growing abolitionist analytic that critiques the institutional embedment of white supremacy not only in the criminal legal system but also in the broader society that necessitates prisons in the first place. We will first broadly examine an array of contemporary decarceration strategies, presenting criticisms of elitist strategies grounded in the measurable failures of the recent past. We then discuss abolitionist visions of "nonreformist reforms" that include supporting certain decarceration efforts. Although these latter tactics are promising, we also wish to present a brief and limited survey of some shifts in the broader carceral landscape that pose challenges to the deceleration and decarceration of our prison population. We identify other social and economic institutions that serve to reify exclusionary logics and that further the collective disinvestment in groups deemed "unworthy" or "disposable." Alexander Lee writes in the *Abolition Now!* anthology, "We should understand that 'prison abolition' means much more than closing down prisons. . . . The real work of abolition must be done away from prisons—in shelters, health clinics, schools, and in battles over government budget allocations."[12] Similarly, we analyze how non-prison systems maintain and perpetuate racialized hierarchies. We do not view our survey as exhaustive; we anticipate and welcome scholars who will call attention to our limitations, particularly those features we as white people cannot recognize. Our goal is not to see the future or predict the entire shape of nascent white supremacist institutions but rather to identify some evolving or developing features of racial oppression that are worthy of greater attention when critiquing the carceral state. Any commitment to full decarceration and abolishing the cages that keep people, particularly people of color but also impoverished whites, from their

11. Angela Davis, *Are Prisons Obsolete?* (New York: Seven Stories Press, 2003); *Freedom Is a Constant Struggle: Ferguson, Palestine, and the Formation of a Movement* (Chicago: Haymarket Books, 2016).

12. Alexander Lee, "Prickly Coalitions: Moving Prison Abolitionism Forward," in *Abolition Now!: Ten Years of Strategy and Struggle against the Prison Industrial Complex*, edited by The CR10 Publications Collective (Oakland, CA: AK Press, 2008), 111.

families and their communities, needs to include opposition to these features.

DECARCERATION STRATEGIES:
DIFFERENTIATING BETWEEN ELITIST AND RADICAL

The new broad public awareness of mass incarceration and calls for reform emerge on a landscape already scarred by years of struggle against prison. Over the forty years following the civil rights and Black Liberation movements, the United States has pursued policies driving the incarceration rate up rapidly.[13] This progress was steepest in the mid-nineties when the Clinton dynasty employed a "third way" strategy to outmaneuver the Republican Revolution.[14] Faced with congressional gridlock promised by House Speaker Newt Gingrich's aggressive "Contract With America" campaign, President Bill Clinton signed a host of laws that targeted criminalized populations. The 1994 Violent Crime Control and Law Enforcement Act allotted federal dollars for prison expansion to states that adopted "tough on crime" policies such as "truth in sentencing" and "three strikes" rules. Clinton's Community Oriented Policing Services (COPS) program added 100,000 police to the streets of American cities. The Antiterrorism and Effective Death Penalty Act of 1996 instituted far more restrictive rules for habeas corpus appeals of convictions. In the same year, Clinton's Personal Responsibility and Work Opportunity Act gutted the social welfare safety net. These policies both allowed Clinton and other "New Democrats" to defang the Republican threat (by instituting its platform themselves) and to further entrench the legitimacy of incarceration as a response to social harm, no matter the severity.

Recent adjustments by New Democrat elites and the bipartisan coalition on mass incarceration maintain that entrenchment, even while nominally repealing the policies and rhetorically indicating "sweeping reversals" to trends in the criminal legal

13. Jeremy Travis and Bruce Western, eds., *The Growth of Incarceration in the United States: Exploring Causes and Consequences* (Washington, DC: National Academies Press, 2014).
14. Jake Johnson, "The Third Way's Last Triumph," *Jacobin*, August 17, 2016, available at jacobinmag.com.

system.[15] Attorney General Eric Holder's 2013 speech before the American Bar Association (ABA), which is often described as "ending the war on drugs," actually argued for being "both tougher and smarter on crime."[16] Beyond the rhetoric, we see a similar transition and entrenchment in policy. For example, changes enacted by the Obama administration to the federal prison system include releasing approximately six thousand prisoners and implementing reduced sentences for those convicted of nonviolent drug charges. The decrease in punishment will be applied retroactively and is projected to release nearly nine thousand more prisoners. Additionally, the heralded bipartisan Sentencing Reform and Corrections Act of 2015 (S.2123), which has passed the Senate Judiciary Committee and is predicted to successfully become law[17], promises to further relieve nonviolent drug offenders by reducing the penalties for three-strike-laws from life imprisonment to twenty-five years. But, S.2123 also discreetly increases the maximum sentence for those convicted of unlawful firearm possession and additionally implements two new mandatory minimums for interstate domestic violence and certain export offenses related to state-defined "terrorism." In this bill, and in the mainstream political conversations, decarcerating *some* hinges on increased penalties for others.

Although one side of this example looks promising, it is only affecting a small number of federal prisoners, which in total amount to 8–10 percent of the entire U.S. incarcerated population. As Maya Schenwar points out in an article for *Truthout*, "just because the public consensus has shifted against 'mass incarceration' in a general sense, doesn't mean that it will simply coast downhill from here."[18] These actions are relevant for but a sliver of the prison population, since most prisoners are in state institutions and about

15. Terry Carter, "Sweeping Reversal of the War on Drugs Announced by Atty General Holder," August 12, 2013, available at abajournal.com.

16. Jason Breslow, "Eric Holder: If Sentencing Reform Dies, 'I'd Be Ashamed,'" February 23, 2016, available at pbs.org; Eric Holder, Speech before the American Bar Association, San Francisco, CA, August 12, 2013.

17. S.2123 was reintroduced as Sentence Reform and Corrections Act of 2017 (S.1917) October 4, 2017 and ordered reported February 15, 2018.

18. Maya Schenwar, "When Prison Reform Means Expansion," *Truthout*, April 12, 2016, available at truthout.org.

half of state prisoners' primary offense was deemed "violent."[19] In addition to being slower than some would make it seem, the decarceration trend is uneven; some states are actually experiencing double-digit increases in prison population.[20]

These elitist decarceration measures, along with the rhetoric and actions of mainstream politicians, further concretize the moralistic division between nonviolent and violent "offenders." The repeated calls of salvation for nonviolent drug offenders mobilize public notions of and sentiments about "deservedness" and "dangerous others"—codes that carry both racialized and classed meanings, since African Americans are convicted on violent offenses at higher rates than whites.[21] We must not only ask which racial subjects are being released but also who is allowing the release and why certain prisoners are deemed worthy of state redemption while others are not. Those prisoners convicted on nonviolent charges that receive—and therefore deserve—state mercy are those who appeal to liberal white sympathies and who do not threaten status quo white racial interests. A white supremacist society that is interested in maintaining their "possessive investment" of generational wealth, legal-judicial institutions, and civic advantages could not, and would not, allow anything less than imprisonment for the menacing threat of disenfranchised populations who are considered violent.[22] Moreover, the obsession with the violence of a "dangerous few" and their street-level crimes masks structural violence. Reserving the label of violence for, say, a Latino youth caught carrying an unregistered firearm, obscures the immeasurable violence perpetrated by governmental and transnational capitalist forces and relieves them of the kind of disproportionate punishment that "violent offenders" receive. We maintain that the fiscally motivated movement to decarcerate a few and lockdown the rest preserves white racial interests and

19. Marie Gottschalk, *Caught: The Prison State and the Lockdown of American Politics* (Princeton, NJ: Princeton University Press, 2015).

20. Schenwar, "When Prison Reform Means Expansion."

21. Michael Tonry and Matthew Melewski, "The Malign Effects of Drug and Crime Control on Black Americans," *Crime and Justice: A Review of Research* 37, no. 1 (2008): 1–44.

22. George Lipsitz, *The Possessive Investment in Whiteness: How White People Profit from Identity Politics* (Philadelphia: Temple University Press, 1998).

colonialist nation-making processes that continuously inflict violence on impoverished communities of color.

Looking forward, the elite decarceration movement promises more of the same: changes that focus on reducing the cost of incarceration while promising increased crime control and maintaining a social order based in white supremacy. In 2009, the Pew Center for the States released a report entitled *One in 31: The Long Reach of American Corrections*. This report quotes Newt Gingrich and applauds the work of bipartisan lawmakers who are managing a shift from incarceration to "community control" systems like probation and parole. Like the rhetoric of the elite reformers, the emphasis is on the costs of corrections and on keeping "serious, chronic and violent offenders . . . behind bars, for a long time" but improving the state's "ability to better manage the 5 million offenders on probation and parole."[23] Another example of bipartisan reform efforts led by political elites is #Cut50. This organization is led by Van Jones, a policy advisor for the Obama administration, and funded by a wide range of political and funding organizations, including conservative groups like Gingrich Productions, the American Conservative Union Foundation, and the Koch Brothers. Their 2015 summit pulled in New Democrats and fiscally conservative Republicans to join in advancing a policy consensus to "highlight bipartisan solutions for reducing incarceration, lowering justice system costs and producing better public safety outcomes."[24]

These elite dilettantes of the decarceration movement have been met with justified skepticism from the existing antiprison movement and critical criminologists. Ruth Wilson Gilmore, cofounder of the abolitionist group Critical Resistance, warns against a tendency to "cozy up to the right wing" and "defining the problem as narrowly as possible in order to produce solutions that on closer examination will change little."[25] Marie Gottschalk takes "neoliberal prison reform" to task for "relying on cost-benefit analysis to

---

23. Pew Center on the States, *One in 31: The Long Reach of American Corrections* (Washington, DC: The Pew Charitable Trusts, 2009), 2.

24. Rebuild the Dream, "The Bipartisan Summit on Criminal Justice Reform 2015," December 7, 2015, available at youtube.com.

25. Gilmore, "The Worrying State of the Anti-Prison Movement."

accomplish what only a deep concern for justice and human rights can" and for "focus[ing] on devising micro interventions at the local and community levels to change the behavior of individuals."[26] California's Public Safety Realignment initiative of 2011 provides a visceral example of Gottschalk's concerns. This "top-down" initiative was designed by elites and aimed to reduce costs and incarceration rates by shifting "the responsibility for incarcerating some categories of non-violent offenders from state prisons to county jails."[27] According to the numbers from California Department of Rehabilitation and Corrections (CDCR) the realignment plan has reduced overall prison and jail populations.[28] At the same time, as critics warned, the conditions of confinement for the incarcerated sent to jails have plummeted. At the time of this writing there are mass hunger strikes underway against abuse and inhumane conditions of confinement at county jails in Merced and Santa Clara counties. In Merced, protesting prisoners were met with shotguns, dogs, and retaliation, while in Santa Clara, deputies took the protester's side against their boss after four days.[29]

Although abolitionism envisions a prison-free society, many antiprison organizers and scholars recognize the practical need for "nonreformist reforms" and pushing for abolition through gradualism. Strategically, many abolitionists support those official reformist measures that don't compromise a more radical and liberatory end goal,[30] but that do bring some relief to the leviathanic problem. Antiprison organizers view certain tactics as both strategic and nonobstructive to revolutionary movement-building, such as pushing for compassionate release of aging and terminally ill

26. Gottschalk, *Caught*.

27. Alessandro De Giorgi, "Reform or Revolution: Thoughts on Liberal and Radical Criminologies," *Social Justice* 40, nos. 1–2 (2014): 24–31.

28. California Department of Corrections and Rehabilitation, "Public Safety Realignment: State and Counties Setting a New Course, Together," accessed 2016, available at cdcr.ca.gov.

29. It's Going Down, "Prisoners Launch Hunger-Strike Inside Merced's Concrete Hell" available at itsgoingdown.org; Jennifer Wadsworth, "Santa Clara County Sheriff's Deputies Side with Inmates on Fourth Day of Hunger Strike," *San Jose Inside*, October 20, 2016, available at sanjoseinside.com.

30. Dan Berger, "Social Movements and Mass Incarceration," *Souls: A Critical Journal of Black Politics, Culture, and Society* 15, nos. 1–2 (2013): 3–18; Allegra McLeod, "Prison Abolition and Grounded Justice," *UCLA Law Review* 62 (2015): 1156–1239.

prisoners, decriminalizing low level offenses including minor possession charges or offenses against the public order, and eliminating bail requirements and pretrial detention.[31] Decarcerate PA, a Pennsylvania broad-based coalition of several organizations and individuals, exemplifies the abolitionist approach to embracing "nonreformist reforms" in its creation of three main initiatives: to impose a moratorium on the construction of new jails and prisons in the state, to decarcerate the current prison population by arresting less, convicting less, and incarcerating less, and reinvesting money and energy into the communities that have been torn apart by the prison system.[32] More specifically, Decarcerate PA has helped to push a bill to be considered by its state congress to end "death by incarceration"—alternatively known as life without the possibility of parole. House Bill 2135, still under deliberation, would allow for all prisoners the opportunity to see the parole board after serving fifteen years, no matter what their conviction or the length of their sentence,[33] with the hope that every prisoner will at least have a chance at release.

Related to Decarcerate PA's third initiative is the crucial part of abolitionist organizing that is not just a "negative" project of deconstructing harmful institutions but also a "positive" project of creating opportunities and allowing communities to flourish.[34] The neoliberalized political economy in the United States has effectively led to a "death of the social," by which governmental measures prioritize thrifty economic concerns at the expense of the social contract and social justice concerns, effectively gutting crucial welfare programs, defunding schools, and privatizing social services.[35]

---

31. Jason Lydon, "Tearing Down the Walls: Queerness, Anarchism and the Prison Industrial Complex," in *Queering Anarchism: Addressing and Undressing Power and Desire*, ed. C.B. Daring, J. Rogue, Deric Shannon, and Abbey Volcano (Oakland, CA: AK Press, 2012); Schenwar, "When Prison Reform Means Expansion"; Judah Schept, "Prison Re-Form: The Continuation of the Carceral State," July 15, 2014, available at tnsocialjustice.wordpress.com.

32. Decarcerate PA, "No More Prisons: A Call to Conscience," available at decarceratepa.info.

33. Russell Frank, "It's Time to Give Lifers A Chance At Life," October 26, 2016, available at statecollege.com.

34. McLeod, "Prison Abolition and Grounded Justice."

35. Gottschalk, *Caught*; Nikolas Rose, "The Death of the Social? Re-figuring the Territory of Government," *Economy and Society* 25, no. 3 (1996): 327–56.

Therefore, to create egalitarian conditions and subsequently thriving individuals and communities, abolitionism also prioritizes community reinvestment led by community members who are the most impacted and harmed by the prison system. This "bottom-up" approach directly combats the problems associated with elitist "top-down" measures and asserts that emancipation cannot be granted by the state or some other authority, but instead through a process of collective struggle and steering.[36] Additionally, grassroots initiatives are often less concerned with fiscal budgets than elitist strategies are. They prioritize human rights and unearthing and eradicating the racialized (and gendered and classed and ableist) violence that undergirds the carceral state. Abolitionist analyses make space for a transformational politics that trusts in the human ability to change and also in the collective ability to dismantle domination and white supremacy in all of its forms.

Abolitionists must not allow the ruling political elites, many of whom are responsible for the incarceration spike in the first place, to hijack the decarceration movement. We must recognize the ways that elitist decarceration strategies strengthen and legitimate the prison system. In addition, abolitionists should be wary of how political elites are moving toward emboldening carceral structures that augment and might even replace incarceration. The prison's accommodation of shrinking state budget allowances by adjusting incarceration levels to better correspond to public criticism does not disrupt the entrenchment of carceral white supremacy. Infrastructures of racialized social control remain and only grow more sophisticated and efficient by becoming embedded into the community. Even if we are turning toward deceleration and even decarceration of prison populations, we wish to analyze the structures that might continue to obstruct abolitionist visions of justice. Three specific structures we wish to turn our attention to are exclusionary geographies, the rehabilitative facade, and the tier system.

---

36. Davis, *Are Prisons Obsolete?*; Joy James, ed., *The New Abolitionists: (Neo)Slave Narratives and Contemporary Prison Writings* (Albany: State University of New York Press, 2005).

EXCLUSIONARY GEOGRAPHIES

The intentional preservation of white racial interests through interpersonal prejudices, public policy, and governmental action is overwhelmingly evident in the realm of housing and neighborhood formations. The overtly segregationist agendas of governmental policies officially ended by the late twentieth century, yet they have had lasting influence on the raced and classed dynamics of communities across the United States. Ending formalized discrimination without implementing any remedies does not *undo* the consequences of prejudicial decisions. As Ta-Nehisi Coates wrote in *The Atlantic*, "ending white supremacy requires the ability to do math—350 years of murderous plunder are not undone by 50 years of uneasy ceasefire."[37] For centuries, local and federal governments practiced a politics of containment and exclusion in an attempt to bar Asian peoples, Native peoples, Latinxs, Pacific Islanders, and Black Americans from sharing resources and spaces with the white publics that had been appropriated from Native dominion.

The direct involvement of governments in segregationist aims is borne from the colonialist visions that created the United States. As early colonial America established industries through the lawful use of Black labor, several federal laws condoned and accelerated the forcible displacement of Native peoples. For example, the Indian Removal Act of 1830 under the Andrew Jackson administration pushed tens of thousands of indigenous people from tribes throughout the Southeast to areas west of the Mississippi River. The most notorious of expulsions was the "Trail of Tears," which caused the premature death of nearly ten thousand Native peoples. This act paved the way for a series of Homestead Acts starting in 1862, which granted white settlers access to lands previously occupied by Native peoples, leading to conflicts between settlers and indigenous peoples. The contention over land and settlements extended to Black America soon after, following the abolition of slavery in 1863. Throughout the "free land," white racists enacted restrictive ordinances in small towns and larger cities

---

37. Ta-Nehisi Coates, "Segregation Forever," *The Atlantic*, April 18, 2014, available at theatlantic.com.

that effectively barred Black Americans (and Mexican populations) from living in white neighborhoods or even *existing* in white communities after sundown (a covenant known as a "sundown" law).

Governmental policies *in conjunction with* collective white racism continued throughout the majority of the twentieth century as well, most overtly through Federal Housing Authority actions that greatly limited opportunities for homeownership and loans to Black Americans while also endorsing banks and real estate agents to prejudicially make decisions based on an applicant's race, ethnicity, and income. Additionally, whites' preferences for self-segregation created modern suburbia, largely attributed to the "white flight" of the fifties and sixties, when thirty million Black Americans migrated from Southern locales to Northern cities.[38] At the same time, federally funded urban renewal projects destroyed 20 percent of subsidized housing units across several cities and of those, 90 percent were never replaced.[39] This created poor conditions and weak infrastructures in several inner cities, along with residential segregation and racial isolation. Overall, these racist measures that span centuries of time fuel a system of both containment of nonwhite groups and their systematic exclusion from dominant society and politics. Although the Fair Housing Act of 1968 sought to officially end discrimination in housing, these residential divisions by race persist and continue in our contemporary era, particularly because of white America's sustained disinvestment in poor and marginalized communities. The resistance against "mixed-income" housing and affordable housing projects is palpable across geographic regions and the proprietary arguments against integration disproportionately targets low-income families and families of color. This has severe consequences, considering that one's residence determines one's closeness to (or distance from) environmentally hazardous elements, quality schools, supermarkets, and other community resources.

The segmentation of U.S. residents by race and class allows for the exertion of social control to be concentrated and targeted. As Loïc Wacquant has argued, the prison system extends into and

---

38. Douglas Massey and Nancy Denton, *American Apartheid: Segregation and the Making of the Underclass* (Cambridge, MA: Harvard University Press, 1993).
39. Ibid.

enmeshes with the ghetto and this carceral containment functions to shunt people between poverty and imprisonment.[40] According to this reasoning, since incarceration has been consistently used as a response to social problems, segregated neighborhoods have likewise reflected the everyday surveillance and monitoring used within the prison system. In fact, "high rates of imprisonment and release follow persistent patterns of racialized residential segregation meaning that incarceration's aftermath comes to be similarly concentrated into the same historically marginalized spaces."[41] The racialized meanings attached to disadvantaged spaces, particularly those with concentrated poverty, are ideological fuel for white publics that believe that racial "others" are culturally deficient, dangerous, or more criminal (or all of these). These myths about cultural deficiency coincide with the widely circulated rationales for aggressive policing practices and other measures of social control. For example, we increasingly witness policing mentalities being infused into social institutions in disadvantaged neighborhoods, such as schools, community centers, neighborhood patrols, etc.

The symbiotic parasitism of the urban "ghetto" and the prison system is amplified in new ways as local governments move to decarcerate and divert people from prison. Although many local governments are vowing to use prison less, there is no promise of less reliance on policing. In fact, during Eric Holder's "Smart on Crime" speech to the American Bar Association's annual conference in 2013, he referenced a new kind of policing and crime policy. His remarks, which reflect the modern approach that many municipalities are trying to move toward, emphasize the use of "hot spot" policing. By concentrating efforts in "criminogenic" neighborhoods, policing mechanisms become redirected toward those locations deemed to contain "the most serious and hardened criminals." This type of intensive and concentrated policing already exists; for example, a damning Bureau of Justice report on

---

40. Loïc Wacquant, "Deadly Symbiosis: When Ghetto and Prison Meet and Mesh," *Punishment & Society* 3, no. 1 (2001): 95–134.

41. Patrick Lopez-Aguado, "The Collateral Consequences of Prisonization: Racial Sorting, Carceral Identity, and Community Criminalization," *Sociology Compass* 10, no. 1 (2016): 13.

racial profiling by the Baltimore City Police Department finds that just 44 percent of pedestrian stops in Baltimore occur in just two predominantly Black American districts.[42] Police terror in racialized communities and historically marginalized spaces will only be sustained and perhaps amplified through a supposed redirecting of policing tactics. There is an abundant body of cautionary literature on carceral systems of control through the prisonization of communities of color and those neighborhoods targeted as hot spots.[43] Although decarceration might be on the horizon, the criminalization of communities of color has not been substantively addressed and therefore racialized sorting and social control will continue.[44]

Even if the United States adopts a wide-sweeping plan for decarceration, we must interrogate the ways that the logics of white supremacy continue to operate in neighborhoods and city planning projects. At the same time that objectionable policing practices are being interrogated, city geographies are rapidly changing. According to Elizabeth Kneebone and Alan Berube's research for the Brookings Institute, poverty has both spread to the suburbs and concentrated into diffused clusters.[45] Urban "renewal" projects have displaced countless low-income families and families of color by pushing them from now-desirable city centers to the edge or outside of the city. This pattern is often presented as the natural and inevitable result of human migration trends, or as intentional and benevolent efforts to "deconcentrate" poverty and create "mixed-income" neighborhoods. The formal narrative of "deconcentrating poverty" produces a social amnesia of the long and painful history of racial discrimination that brought us the inner city in the first

42. Department of Justice, Investigation of the Baltimore City Police Department, 2016, Washington, DC: U.S. DOJ.

43. Massey and Denton, *American Apartheid*; Alice Goffman, *On the Run* (Chicago: University of Chicago Press, 2014); Victor Rios, *Punished: Policing the Lives of Black and Latino Boys* (New York: New York University Press, 2011); Dorothy Roberts, "Constructing a Criminal Justice System Free of Racial Bias: An Abolitionist Framework," *Columbia Human Rights Law Review* 39 (2008): 261–85; Wacquant, "Deadly Symbiosis."

44. Lopez-Aguado, "The Collateral Consequences of Prisonization."

45. Kneebone, Elizabeth and Alan Berube. *Confronting Suburban Poverty in America.* Washington, DC: Brookings Institution Press, 2014).

place as well as a denial of the continued violence that displacement requires. Poor households are intentionally pushed to the periphery through arrests and incarceration, but also through rising rents, evictions and discrimination, which creates more difficulties navigating life at the margins. Once displaced, the poor are often reconcentrated into enclaves, which can then be labeled criminogenic and treated as extensions of the prison. We find this to be a crucial issue to contend within the struggle against carcerality before, during, and after substantive decarceration efforts.

THE "REHABILITATIVE" FAÇADE

Coinciding with elitist decarceration rhetoric and strategies, state actors and prison officials seek to increase the legitimacy of the criminal legal system by adopting (or "returning to") the much-fabled rehabilitative ideal. Rehabilitative programming behind prison walls are suspect to us, but we want to focus on the ways in which officials are using rehabilitation as a label to subtly expand the scope of control into communities of color. If a criminalized person can escape the grip of a jail or prison sentence, that rarely means they are free from scrutiny or control. Courts sentence people to so-called alternatives to incarceration, while parolees are mandated to undergo some type of rehabilitative programming, all for the stated purpose of monitoring people in the community while offering them limited support for vocational and therapeutic services. As of 2013, nearly five million criminalized people in the United States are under community supervision of some type (probation or parole), which is more than *double* the amount of people who are incarcerated.

The carceral expansion of control through the "alternatives to incarceration" track has rightfully received its due media attention, particularly as it relates to privatized probation and privately operated halfway houses. Private probation companies offer their "services" to state courts by collecting court fees from probationers, which has created debtor's jails for those who cannot afford the fees in states like Georgia and Washington. The egregious practices of private community correction companies in Georgia—a $40 million per year industry—are now facing legal suits to the practice of trapping impoverished people into inescapable debts and jail time.[46] While they purport to provide therapy, educational, and vocational services, these agencies expand their profit margin by providing inadequate assistance and poor medical care for their "clients." Community Education Centers, for example, one of the largest private providers of residential rehabilitation care have been historically negligent to the point of severe injury or death among residents.[47] Although we applaud the increased awareness of these issues, the dialogue seems to focus on the privatization of these systems instead of an analysis of the ways in which publicly funded and state-sponsored alternatives to incarceration have been primarily ensnaring impoverished communities and communities of color for decades.

We must ask ourselves how rehabilitation is defined and how rehabilitative logics work to support and maintain both the prison system specifically, and neoliberal structures of inequality broadly. Rehabilitation officially defined, focuses on successfully teaching "offenders" how to lawfully abide by the norms of society and how to learn new ways of being in the world to prevent future criminality. This individually focused project squarely places blame on the deficiencies of criminalized people for *social* failings.[48] The assumption made is that crime results from one's inherent, mental, or cultural inclination toward criminal behavior, instead of understanding street crime as a survival tool or a rational response to the bounded realities of disadvantage. Therefore, modern rehabilitation programming narrowly focuses on human capital rather than concrete vocational or educational opportunities and has thus been transformed into shallow reentry politics.[49]

Most modern reentry programs center their efforts on providing cognitive therapeutic education such as anger-management classes and on the "employability" of ex-offenders, thereby

46. Kent Faulk, "ACLU Files Lawsuit in Georgia Against Private Probation Company, which also Operates in Alabama, for Arresting the Poor," January 29, 2015, available at al.com.

47. Anat Rubin, "A Record of Trouble," April 11, 2015, available at themarshallproject.org.

48. Lynne Haney, *Offending Women: Power, Punishment, and the Regulation of Desire* (Berkeley: University of California Press, 2010).

49. Gottschalk, *Caught*.

attempting to affect individualized, mental change as opposed to social change.[50] Yet this does little in offering a marginalized population concrete vocational training or educational opportunities. Although the Second Chance Act allocated $63 million worth of federal grants toward reentry programs, this pales in comparison to the $60 billion spent on federal and state prisons annually; the dollar amount spent on reentrants per year calculates to less than $100 per person.[51] Moreover, our economy relies more on part-time, temporary, and nonstandard work than ever before; up to 40 percent of the workforce is thus precariously employed.[52] Unemployment has also risen dramatically, and along with it the difficulty of finding a new job as well as the other "consequences of getting laid off or fired."[53] This economy of precarity distributes consequences across a wider but still disproportionately nonwhite strata of unemployed, criminalized, and discouraged people.[54]

Rehabilitation programs largely attempt to teach ex-prisoners how to accommodate themselves to an unjust social order. To graduate from a rehabilitation program has less to do with being changed or rehabilitated and more to do with successfully navigating programmatic norms and developing gestures and performances of remorse, of compliance, of respectability and deservedness that *might* unlock access to the benefits of (lower) middle class life.[55] In a white supremacist capitalist order, advantages are provided to those poor whites and people of color who can successfully disavow vilified categories. As Naomi Murakawa observes, the "formation of the American nation-state relies on oppositional

50. Reuben Jonathan Miller, "Devolving the Carceral State: Race, Prisoner Reentry, and the Micro-Politics of Urban Poverty Management," *Punishment & Society* 16, no. 3 (2014): 305–35.

51. Gottschalk, *Caught*.

52. Charles A. Jeszeck, *Contingent Workforce: Size, Characteristics, Earnings, and Benefits*, U.S. Government Accountability Office, GAO-15-168R (Washington, DC: Government Printing Office, 2015).

53. Charlie Post, "We're All Precarious Now," *Jacobin*, April 20, 2015, available at jacobinmag.com.

54. Aaron Benanav, "Precarity Rising," *Viewpoint Magazine*, June 15, 2015, available at viewpointmag.com.

55. Haney, *Offending Women*.

dualities between white images and black images: law-abiding versus criminal, responsible versus shiftless, industrious versus lazy, moral versus immoral,"[56] and as such, rehabilitation politics do nothing more than to reaffirm and solidify these dualities. In fact, declining labor markets and unstable housing circumstances continuously shut out disadvantaged communities, particularly those who have been marked as "felons" or "ex-felons" and have thus suffered a civil death.[57]

Reentry politics revive the "culture of poverty" thesis by framing the crime issue as one having to do with the problematic *values* of certain raced and classed "others"; according to this logic, if you fix the values of criminals, you fix the crime problem. Considering that just over two-thirds of all prisoners are officially designated as "poor" and most come from racially segregated and under-resourced communities,[58] true rehabilitation necessitates the remedying of social disadvantages and underemployment. But, rehabilitation programs and reentry centers do not have the resources or abilities to address material needs. With little funding, they occupy the fuzzy borderlands between the welfare system and the carceral state, compelled to remedy the injustices of white supremacy, heteropatriarchy, and a capitalist economy while acting as de facto probationers and parole officers, and enforcing the strong arm of the state.[59] We therefore view reentry politics as an arena for abolitionist engagement; the social problems created by the carceral state cannot be solved through shallow efforts and in fact are worsened when control extends into the community vis-à-vis "rehabilitation."

THE TIER SYSTEM

Full decarceration, if ever achieved, will certainly not happen quickly. We therefore think it important to consider the ways in

56. Naomi Murakawa, "Phantom Racism and the Myth of Crime and Punishment," *Studies in Law, Politics, and Society* 59 (2012): 117.

57. Gottschalk, *Caught.*

58. Loïc Wacquant, *Punishing the Poor: The Neoliberal Government of Social Insecurity* (Durham, NC: Duke University Press, 2009).

59. Miller, "Devolving the Carceral State."

which prison administrators are updating their systems of control on the inside. One of the current penal alterations adopted by prisons is known as the "tier system." The tier system is supposedly designed to protect safety, reduce recidivism, and even "give offenders a sense of hope," but it does so by monitoring and sorting prisoners into strict categories.[60] This model was developed within the context of the supermax prison. After isolating and monitoring certain trouble-causing prisoners in a supermax setting, prison administrators began experimenting with expanded behavior modification practices.[61] Brainwashing, sensory deprivation, and misuse of drug therapy are some of the methods used to stress test, harass, and break prisoners. This project necessitates a complex gradation of privilege levels for prisoners to "step down" through. Recently that gradation has grown more sophisticated, often in response to prison rebellions.

Long-term solitary confinement is finally receiving much needed public criticism, including the first-ever congressional hearing on the practice, and some states ending the practice entirely.[62] Meanwhile, the tier system is perpetuating supermax methodologies, behavior modification, and intricate "step down" processes across the entire population of many prison systems. The traditional security level system (typically four or five categories) is breaking into a bewildering array of privilege levels. Privileges such as congregate recreation, property limits, and access to programming or visitation change from each tier and sublevel at the choice of administrators. In this way, every lauded program incentive becomes a privilege to be earned.

Movement from tier to tier is handled by security review and rules infraction boards that often avoid transparency and accountability, thus making it likely for targeted prisoners to receive

60. Gary Mohr, "Reforming A System: An Inside Perspective on How Ohio Achieved a Record-Low Recidivism Rate," March 12, 2012, available at csgjusticecenter.org

61. Eddie Griffin, "Breaking Men's Minds: Behavior Control and Human Experimentation at the Federal Prison in Marion," *Journal of Prisoners on Prison* 4, no. 2 (1993): 1–8; Jason Robb, "Lucasville Amnesty: Behavior Modification," Columbus, OH, June 2012, available at insurgenttheatre.org.

62. C-SPAN, "Solitary Confinement in U.S. Prisons," February 25, 2014, available at c-span.org; Rick Raemisch, "My Night in Solitary," *The New York Times*, February 21, 2014, available at nytimes.com.

harassment. In Georgia, the tier system was adopted after the 2010 work stoppage, and perceived leaders of that movement like Kelvin Stevenson have been held in the uppermost tiers ever since. Supporters of Stevenson and his comrades describe the tier system as "effectively function[ing] as an unaccountable and arbitrary criminal justice system within the prison itself."[63] Many jailhouse lawyers and prisoner advocates have used due process claims to challenge these systems, but often fail. Through years-long relationships with prisoners at Ohio State Penitentiary (OSP) and their outside advocates, one author of this paper has learned of the following arrangement: At OSP, a person sent to level five is never told how long they will stay there, but prisoners and their advocates have observed lengths of time spent on level for various offences and found an almost universally consistent, standardized sentencing structure, though staff and prison officials deny that they are blanket sentences. At the same time, special exceptions can occur without justification. For example, some survivors of the Lucasville Uprising have been on level five since it was created twenty-three years ago, and the Ohio Department of Rehabilitation and Corrections (ODRC) has all but promised they will remain there until they are executed. The rules infraction board is able to operate with unfettered discretion according to the needs of the system.

White supremacy has long colluded with the carceral state to divide, sort, and manage people. Tier systems reinforce white supremacy by managing and controlling relationships between prisoners based on a rigid top-down order. This control takes both targeted and generalized forms. First, the tier system targets prison rebels and organizers. In Georgia and Alabama, the response to historic work stoppages has been to put perceived leaders, like Melvin Ray, Robert Earl Council, or Kelvin Stevenson on the top tier of indefinite isolation. These Black men explicitly organized *as* Black men and were locked down *for* being Black men who organized. Right now we are seeing the process underway in Michigan, Florida, and elsewhere following the September 9th, 2016 work stoppages.[64] This repression also targets other segments of the

---

63. "Anarchist Resistance in Georgia Prisons Continues," April 17, 2015, available at anarchistnews.org.

64. Support Prisoner Resistance, "Repression Continues, Regional Organizing

racialized prison population when they form multiracial coalitions. Prison administrators count on and exacerbate racial tensions as a means to divide and control prisoners. Within such a system, racial grouping can occur in two different ways—one that serves a prison function and one that defies it.[65] Racial grouping as a method of dividing prisoners against each other is embraced and encouraged by administrators, while bottom-up efforts to defy those divisions while also *politicizing* one's racialized identity threatens the control that administrators pursue.

Prison life includes a plurality of distinct and important racial groupings, which may, during moments of struggle, work together not by melting or erasing their difference but by building solidarity across difference. Agreements to end hostilities or statements of unified demands have accompanied every one of the most successful and historically unprecedented prisoner protest movements in recent years.[66] White supremacist institutions such as prisons cannot tolerate this solidarity and punitively lock down prisoners (including the white Aryan affiliated prisoners) in response. They prefer prisoners to remain divided and to blame each other, and hope that by ratcheting up the torture, isolation, and stressful control systems, they will break prisoners' unity and return to a status quo of tension and violence across racial division, rather than coordination. Prison has traditionally had an important role in quelling race-based social movements. Counterinsurgency programs have been dedicated to putting movement leaders and rebellious communities behind bars for decades, and similarly, repressive tier system control tactics are being used to quell prison rebels and organizers.[67]

Second, by enforcing and promoting dehumanizing, degrading, and therefore violent conditions, the tier system exacerbates violent prison culture in general. Long-timers convicted in Georgia,

---

Needed," October 19, 2016, available at supportprisonerresistance.noblogs.org.

65. Anonymous Ohio prisoner, personal communication, January 2016,

66. Todd Ashker et al., "Agreement to End Hostilities," August 12, 2012, available at prisonerhungerstrikesolidarity.wordpress.com; Bruce A. Dixon, "Georgia Prison Inmates Stage 1-Day Peaceful Strike Today," December 9, 2010, available at blackagendareport.com.

67. Berger, "Social Movements and Mass Incarceration."

Alabama, and Ohio have complained about how their living conditions have degraded with the inception of tier systems. A person incarcerated for decades in prison often needs surrogate families, social networks, and affiliations to navigate the deprivation of imprisonment. The tier system multiplies divisions and means to fracture prisoner-created social networks. Administrators claim the tier system reduces violence by isolating dangerous prisoners and separating them from others. Meanwhile, they (perhaps rightly) see prisoner-led organizations as the largest threat to their absolute control of the system, so they label organizers as "gang" leaders or as "violent." Yet long timers, organizers, and sometimes even gang leaders often serve peacekeeping or at least stabilizing roles within the prison community. They educate new prisoners, uphold traditions and norms, and enforce respect for unofficial hierarchies.[68] In this way, the tier system, like prison and police in general, promises safety through isolation and control, but actually creates increased stress, trauma, and danger by removing stabilizing forces. These conditions threaten prisoners in general, as well as staff. In Alabama, the isolation of prisoner organizers has led to increased violence, which the Free Alabama Movement (FAM) believe is being cynically used by the Alabama Department of Corrections to justify a large prison expansion bill.[69] Prison guards at Holman Correctional Facility have also recognized this dynamic and joined FAM's protest by collectively refusing to come to work on certain shifts.[70] The tier system targets gangs, attempting to shut them down and reduce the violence they cause, but aggravating tensions, isolating leadership, and discouraging cooperation or understanding between racialized prison gangs does not shut them down—it exacerbates them.

This culture of manufactured racialized violence is exported to the streets through carceral identities adopted by some prisoners when they return to society. The release of extremist Aryan

---

68. Anonymous Alabama prisoner, personal communication, July 2015,

69. Free Alabama Movement, "The Holman Project," September 17, 2016, available at freealabamamovement.wordpress.com.

70. Amy Goodman, "Alabama Guards Stage Work Strike Months After Prisoner Uprising at Overcrowded Holman Facility," *Democracy Now*, September 28, 2016, available at democracynow.org.

prisoners directly produces white supremacist violence, boosting the ranks of neo-Nazi and white supremacist organizations as well as isolated incidents of racial terror.[71] Patrick Lopez-Aguado argues that in addition to this emboldening of white supremacist terror organizations, the transfer of Latinx racialized prison identities to outside neighborhoods increases police aggression and the recognition of community members as criminal.[72] The tier system increases the prison's role in incubating racialized violence and creating narratives to justify state violence in communities targeted for high incarceration.

CONCLUSION:
THE CARCERAL ARRAY AND ABOLITIONIST LANDSCAPING

Loïc Wacquant predicted that the prison system will become "an appendage to the dark ghetto or supersede it to go it alone and become America's fourth 'peculiar institution.'"[73] Our observations indicate another option, in which carcerality becomes further despatialized and multifaceted. Elite reformers, by prioritizing fiscal responsibility and superficial, exaggerated policy shifts, might succeed in decelerating and decarcerating some of the prison population.

By replacing imprisonment with probation, parole, ankle bracelets, and coercive reentry therapeutics, the elite decarceration movement is creating a wide variety of new carceral forms.[74] These reforms, when combined with excluding geographies, a rehabilitative facade, as well as alterations within the prison system itself, produce increasingly distinct categories of control in a flexible carceral array.

In this essay we have focused on how components of the carceral array serve white supremacist interests and maintain racialized hierarchies. Rather than an inflexible and undeniably evil

71. Anti-Defamation League, "White Supremacist Prison Gangs in the United States: A Preliminary Inventory," 2016. New York; Tyler Dunn, "Exposed: The Northwest's White Supremacy Problem," July 18, 2014, available at koin.com.

72. Lopez-Aguado, "The Collateral Consequences of Prisonization."

73. Loïc Wacquant, "The New 'Peculiar Institution': On the Prison As Surrogate Ghetto," *Theoretical Criminology* 4, no. 3 (2000): 385.

74. Gottschalk, *Caught*.

"one-drop" ideology, the new carceral landscape helps to reproduce an increasingly colorblind form of white supremacy where
even the darkest skin or the thickest accents, "ethnic" fashions,
and gestures are welcomed, so long as the relationship with the
state and social order conforms with expectations established after centuries of white domination on this continent. Those who
fail to conform are sorted into a complex array of stigmatization
and marginalization, which are and have been disproportionately
likely among communities of color. This emerging form of white
supremacist carcerality is entrenched in a complex system of
racialized ordering.

The abolitionist critics of gradual prison reform often point
out that "racism is embedded in the system. . . . Extracting 'bias'
from a particular step [does] not diminish the influence of white
supremacy."[75] White supremacy is not merely an accumulation of
irrational or unconscious racial biases and institutions that exacerbate it; white supremacy is a system that uses coded categori-
zation systems (although sometimes thinly veiled) to sort people
for differentiated treatment. The rejection of personhood and the
imposition of criminalized identities is a project with white supremacist origins, even when it affects impoverished whites. This
"leveling down" threatens populations considered deviant based
on class, ability, gender, and sexuality.[76] The carceral array sorts
marginalized peoples into limited citizenship and access. The
white supremacist origins in the carceral state remain manifest in
the dehumanization of those marked as "other."

Exclusionary geographies, the rehabilitative facade, and the
tier system are just *some* aspects of a white-dominant racial order that continues to control and incapacitate. In centering our
analysis on white-dominance and white racial interests, we hope
to identify the roots of racialized violence that are embedded in
"legitimate" institutions and ideologies. Antiracists, accomplices
to the struggle, and abolitionists must continue these surveys of
the landscape in order to develop effective strategies that work
to dissolve the racial caste system. We must undermine these

---

75. Schenwar, "When Prison Reform Means Expansion."
76. Gottschalk, *Caught.*

emerging systems of carceral white supremacy while we attack, delegitimize, and dismantle the prison state and *all* of its forms.

ACKNOWLEDGEMENTS

Both authors contributed equally to this article. We wish many thanks and solidarity to our incarcerated comrades for the inspiration and motivation to write on this topic. We also wish to thank the anonymous reviewers and the editorial collective for their helpful comments.

REFERENCES

Alexander, Michelle. *The New Jim Crow: Mass Incarceration in the Age of Colorblindness*. New York: The New Press, 2010.

"Anarchist Resistance in Georgia Prisons Continues." April 17, 2015. Available at anarchistnews.org.

Anti-Defamation League. *White Supremacist Prison Gangs in the United States: A Preliminary Inventory*. New York: 2016.

Ashker, Todd, Arturo Castellanos, Sitawa Nantambu Jamaa, and Antonio Guillen. "Agreement to End Hostilities." August 12, 2012. Available at prisonerhungerstrikesolidarity.wordpress.com.

Benanav, Aaron. "Precarity Rising." *Viewpoint Magazine*. June 15, 2015. Available at viewpointmag.com.

Berger, Dan. "Social Movements and Mass Incarceration." *Souls: A Critical Journal of Black Politics, Culture, and Society* 15, nos. 1–2 (2013).

Blackmon, Douglas. *Slavery by Another Name: The Reenslavement of Black Americans From the Civil War to World War II*. New York: Anchor Books, 2009.

Bonds, Anne, and Joshua Inwood. "Beyond White Privilege: Geographies of White Supremacy and Settler Colonialism." *Progress in Human Geography* 40, no. 6 (2015).

Breslow, Jason. "Eric Holder: If Sentencing Reform Dies, 'I'd Be Ashamed.'" *Frontline*. February 23, 2016. Available at pbs.org.

Carter, Terry. "Sweeping Reversal of the War on Drugs Announced by Atty General Holder." *ABA Journal*. August 12, 2013. Available at abajournal.com.

California Department of Corrections and Rehabilitation. "Public Safety Realignment: State and Counties Setting a New Course, Together."

Accessed April 27, 2017. Available at cdcr.ca.gov.

Coates, Ta-Nehisi. "Segregation Forever." *The Atlantic.* April 18, 2014. Available at theatlantic.com.

C-SPAN. "Solitary Confinement in U.S. Prisons." February 25, 2014. Available at cspan.org.

Davis, Angela. *Are Prisons Obsolete?* New York: Seven Stories Press, 2003.

———. *Freedom Is a Constant Struggle: Ferguson, Palestine, and the Formation of a Movement.* Chicago: Haymarket Books, 2016.

De Giorgi, Alessandro. "Reform or Revolution: Thoughts on Liberal and Radical Criminologies." *Social Justice* 40, nos. 1–2 (2014).

Decarcerate PA. "No More Prisons: A Call to Conscience." Accessed April 27, 2017. Available at decarceratepa.info.

Department of Justice. *Investigation of the Baltimore City Police Department, 2016.* Washington, DC: U.S. DOJ, 2016.

Dixon, Bruce A. "Georgia Prison Inmates Stage 1-Day Peaceful Strike Today." December 9, 2010. Available at blackagendareport.com.

Dunn, Tyler. "Exposed: The Northwest's White Supremacy Problem." July 18, 2014. Available at koin.com.

Faulk, Kent. "ACLU Files Lawsuit in Georgia Against Private Probation Company, which also Operates in Alabama, for Arresting the Poor." January 29, 2015. Available at al.com.

Foucault, Michel. *The Birth of the Clinic: An Archaeology of Medical Perception.* New York: Vintage Books, 1994.

———. *Discipline and Punish: The Birth of the Prison.* New York: Vintage Books, 1995.

Frank, Russell. "It's Time to Give Lifers A Chance At Life." October 26, 2016. Available at statecollege.com.

Free Alabama Movement. "The Holman Project." September 17, 2016. Available at freealabamamovement.wordpress.com.

Gilmore, Ruth Wilson. "The Worrying State of the Anti-Prison Movement." *The Social Justice Journal.* February 23, 2015. Available at socialjusticejournal.org.

Goffman, Alice. *On the Run.* Chicago: University of Chicago Press, 2014.

Goodman, Amy. "Alabama Guards Stage Work Strike Months After Prisoner Uprising at Overcrowded Holman Facility." *Democracy Now!* September 28, 2016. Available at democracynow.org.

Gottschalk, Marie. *Caught: The Prison State and the Lockdown of American Politics*. Princeton, NJ: Princeton University Press, 2015.

———. "The Folly of Neoliberal Prison Reform." *Boston Review*. June 8, 2015. Available at bostonreview.net.

Griffin, Eddie. "Breaking Men's Minds: Behavior Control and Human Experimentation at the Federal Prison in Marion." *Journal of Prisoners on Prison* 4, no. 2 (1993).

Haney, Lynne. *Offending Women: Power, Punishment, and the Regulation of Desire*. Berkeley: University of California Press, 2010.

Holder, Eric. Speech before the American Bar Association. San Francisco, CA. August 12, 2013.

Ioanide, Paula. *The Emotional Politics of Racism: How Feelings Trump Facts in an Era of Colorblindness*. Stanford, CA: Stanford University Press, 2015.

It's Going Down. "Prisoners Launch Hunger-Strike Inside Merced's Concrete Hell." IGDCast (podcast). September 15, 2016. Available at itsgoingdown.org.

James, Joy, ed. *The New Abolitionists: (Neo)Slave Narratives and Contemporary Prison Writings*. Albany: State University of New York Press, 2005.

Jeszeck, Charles A. *A Contingent Workforce: Size, Characteristics, Earnings, and Benefits*. Washington, DC: U.S. Government Accountability Office, 2015.

Johnson, Jake. "The Third Way's Last Triumph." *Jacobin*. August 17, 2016. Available at jacobinmag.com.

Kaba, Mariame. "Prison Reform's in Vogue and Other Strange Things..." *Truthout*. March 21, 2014. Available at truthout.org.

Kneebone, Elizabeth and Alan Berube. *Confronting Suburban Poverty in America*. Washington, DC: Brookings Institution Press, 2014.

Lee, Alexander. "Prickly Coalitions: Moving Prison Abolitionism Forward." In *Abolition Now!: Ten Years of Strategy and Struggle against the Prison Industrial Complex*, edited by The CR10 Publications Collective, 109–12. Oakland, CA: AK Press, 2008.

Lipsitz, George. *The Possessive Investment in Whiteness: How White People Profit from Identity Politics*. Philadelphia: Temple University Press, 1998.

Lopez-Aguado, Patrick. "The Collateral Consequences of Prisonization: Racial Sorting, Carceral Identity, and Community Criminalization." *Sociology Compass* 10, no. 1 (2016): 12–23.

Lydon, Jason. "Tearing Down the Walls: Queerness, Anarchism and the Prison Industrial Complex." In *Queering Anarchism: Addressing and Undressing Power and Desire*, edited by C.B. Daring, J. Rogue, Deric Shannon, and Abbey Volcano, 195–206. Oakland, CA: AK Press, 2012.

Massey, Douglas, and Nancy Denton. *American Apartheid: Segregation and the Making of the Underclass*. Cambridge, MA: Harvard University Press, 1993.

McLeod, Allegra. "Prison Abolition and Grounded Justice." *UCLA Law Review* 62 (2015): 1156–1239.

Miller, Reuben Jonathan. "Devolving the Carceral State: Race, Prisoner Reentry, and the Micro-Politics of Urban Poverty Management." *Punishment & Society* 16, no. 3 (2014): 305–35.

Mills, Charles W. "Liberalism and the Racial State." In *State of White Supremacy: Racism, Governance, and the United States*, edited by Moon-Kie Jung, João H. Costa Vargas, and Eduardo Bonilla-Silva, 27–46. Stanford, CA: Stanford University Press, 2011.

Mohr, Gary. "Reforming A System: An Inside Perspective on How Ohio Achieved a Record-Low Recidivism Rate." March 12, 2012. Available at csgjusticecenter.org.

Murakawa, Naomi. "Phantom Racism and the Myth of Crime and Punishment." *Studies in Law, Politics, and Society* 59 (2012): 99–122.

Nastasia, Isabelle. "Live Updates from the National Prisoner Strike." *Mask Magazine*. Accessed April 27, 2016. Available at maskmagazine. com.

Pew Center on the States. *One in 31: The Long Reach of American Corrections*. Washington, DC: The Pew Charitable Trusts, 2009.

Platt, Tony. "Crime and Punishment in the United States: Immediate and Long-Term Reforms from a Marxist Perspective." *Crime and Social Justice*, no. 18 (Winter 1982): 38–45.

Post, Charlie. "We're All Precarious Now." *Jacobin*. April 20, 2015. Available at jacobinmag.com.

Raemisch, Rick. "My Night in Solitary." *The New York Times*. February 21, 2014. Available at nytimes.com.

Rebuild the Dream. "The Bipartisan Summit on Criminal Justice Reform 2015." December 7, 2015. Available at youtube.com.

Rios, Victor. *Punished: Policing the Lives of Black and Latino Boys*. New York: New York University Press, 2011.

Robb, Jason. "Lucasville Amnesty: Behavior Modification." June 2012. Available at lucasvilleamnesty.org.

Roberts, Dorothy. "Constructing a Criminal Justice System Free of Racial Bias: An Abolitionist Framework." *Columbia Human Rights Law Review* 39 (2008): 261–85.

Rose, Nikolas. "The Death of the Social? Re-figuring the Territory of Government." *Economy and Society* 25, no. 3 (1996): 327–56.

Rubin, Anat. "A Record of Trouble." April 11, 2015. Available at themarshallproject.org.

Schenwar, Maya. "When Prison Reform Means Expansion." *Truthout.* April 12, 2016. Available at truthout.org.

Schept, Judah. "Prison Re-Form: The Continuation of the Carceral State." July 15, 2014. Available at tnsocialjustice.wordpress.com.

Support Prisoner Resistance. "Repression Continues, Regional Organizing Needed." October 19, 2016. Available at supportprisoner-resistance.noblogs.org.

Tonry, Michael, and Matthew Melewski. "The Malign Effects of Drug and Crime Control on Black Americans." *Crime and Justice: A Review of Research* 37, no. (2008): 1–44.

Travis, Jeremy, and Bruce Western, eds. *The Growth of Incarceration in the United States: Exploring Causes and Consequences.* Washington, DC: National Academies Press, 2014. Available at nap.edu.

Wacquant, Loïc. "Deadly Symbiosis: When Ghetto and Prison Meet and Mesh." *Punishment & Society* 3, no. 1 (2001): 95–134.

———. "The New 'Peculiar Institution': On the Prison as Surrogate Ghetto." *Theoretical Criminology* 4, no. 3 (2000): 377–89.

———. *Punishing the Poor: The Neoliberal Government of Social Insecurity.* Durham, NC: Duke University Press, 2009.

Wadsworth, Jennifer. "Santa Clara County Sheriff's Deputies Side with Inmates on Fourth Day of Hunger Strike." *San Jose Inside,* October 20, 2016. Available at sanjoseinside.com.

SHADOW BOXING

A CHICANA'S JOURNEY FROM VIGILANTE VIOLENCE TO TRANSFORMATIVE JUSTICE

Lena Palacios

To the victims and survivors of both sexual and state violence, to the many shadowboxers whom I know and love: to those who intimately understand that boxing is war but so is life.

In this video mash-up dedicated to female shadow boxers, I chart my emotional and political journey from wanting revenge against an individual—starting when I was a little girl—to organizing collectively against interlocking forms of interpersonal, structural, and institutional violence—starting as a young woman recently released from juvenile lock-up in the mid-nineties in "Golden Gulag" California. I speak from multiple intersections as a queer Chicana from an urban, working-class background who is a survivor of sexual violence, a feminist anti-violence activist, and a penal abolitionist.

Within our current carceral landscape, transformative justice feminist praxis driven by Indigenous and race-radical girls and women of color is an essential epistemic and organizing tool to achieve such freedom from violence. For those of us who have been victimized by both intimate partner violence and state violence, there is no other choice for us but to continue building community accountability circles and anti-violence movements that guarantee our collective survival. The stakes could not get much higher.

In 2012, I received a SAW Video JumpStart grant aimed at artists producing their first videos. My first video project has been screened at the SAW Gallery (Ottawa, May 2013) for both the "Breaking the Silence—Artists for Justice" a film screening organized by the Criminalization and Punishment Education Project as well as for the annual film festival showcasing the works created through the JumpStart Mentorship Program.

The video is available online at: vimeo.com/87613868

WITH IMMEDIATE CAUSE

INTENSE DREAMING AS WORLD-MAKING

Lena Palacios

We cannot live without our lives.

> —Banner held by Combahee River Collective members protesting the sexual assault and murder of twelve Black women in the Boston area in the first six months of 1979.[1]

THE BODY COUNT OF STIGMATIZED, CRIMINALIZED, INCARCERATED, legally eliminated, socially dead, expendable and disposable, sexually violated, tortured, missing, and murdered Indigenous girls, girls and women of color, queer and trans youth of color continues to climb. The growing murder-suicide rates, statistics of missing and murdered Indigenous and Black women, should no longer surprise or overwhelm us but incite us to urgent action and theorization in line with radical women of color feminist movements mobilizing to end gendered and racialized violence endemic to the carceral state. A feeling of mortal urgency hounds us everywhere, every day, all the time, all at once in white settler societies like ours; it surrounds, envelops, and blankets us, most often lulling us into a deep, depressed, dreamless stupor rendering us hopeless and immobilized. Many of us have already lost the battle. How many Black and Indigenous girls and women have had their lives cut short by interpersonal, intimate, state and state-sponsored violence since the Black socialist lesbian feminist Combahee River Collective first held up that banner boldly declaring "We cannot live without our lives" and initiated a self-help and antiviolence

---

1. Combahee River Collective, "Why Did They Die? A Document of Black Feminism." *Radical America* 13, no. 6 (November/December 1979): 41–50.

community mobilization in the late seventies? At other times, when not killed-off, bought-off, co-opted, or placated by the carceral state and its so-called kinder and gentler politics of recognition and reconciliation and its nonprofit, professionalized social service apparatuses, we channel the pent-up sum of our intergenerational rage into "dreaming big" and "making power" within our families, intimate relations, and communities. The mortal urgency lies in us staying dormant and continuing to patiently over-rely on the carceral state to guarantee the health of our lands and waterways, our human and civil rights, our bodily integrity, our safety and security, our health and well-being, our children's futures rather than aligning ourselves with radical Black feminist, Indigenous de-colonial, and prison abolitionist movements. We fail to listen and actively disengage with these (re)emergent and resurgent movements that resist the liberal and neoliberal state's politics of recognition, visibility, and inclusion at our own peril. Five hundred years after the advent of colonial genocide and chattel slavery, the stakes are as high as ever. As Ntozake Shange declares, "We all have immediate cause."

As Indigenous feminist Paula Gunn Allen put it, so much has been taken away by racialized gendered violence and carceral state violence that "the place we live now is an idea."[2] I am compelled by the kinds of futures that Indigenous feminists and radical women of color feminists envision, and create, outside of Western, non-Indigenous inflections of sovereignty, the nation-state, and a liberal politics of recognition. In order to support these generative and transformative projects and ways of knowing, we need to visualize, speak, and practice toward what we do dream and create.

According to Dian Million, "intense dreaming" is indispensable to the urgent demand made by Indigenous feminist activist-scholars to sidestep the "static taxidermies" of Western epistemologies and to privilege Indigenous non-Western ways of knowing.[3] Million writes,

---

2. Paula Gunn Allen, *The Sacred Hoop: Recovering the Feminine in American Indian Traditions* (Boston: Beacon Press, 1986), 9.

3. Dian Million, "Intense Dreaming: Theories, Narratives, and Our Search for Home," *The American Indian Quarterly* 35, no. 3 (2011): 313–33, 315.

> Dreaming . . . is the effort to make sense of relations in the worlds we live, dreaming and empathizing intensely our relations with past and present and the future without the boundaries of linear time. Dreaming is a communicative sacred activity. Dreaming often allows us to creatively side-step all the neat little boxes that obscure larger relations and syntheses of imagination. . . . Dreaming, theory, narrative, and critical thinking are not exclusive of each other. They form different ways of knowing, and I will ask that we might imagine them as uneasy relations and alliances that may acknowledge inclusion while we call for respecting necessary boundaries.[4]

For me, Million's highly generative "intense dreaming" is founded in radical relational imaginings, the politics of mutual respect and accountability, and transformative justice feminist praxis. Beyond the rational, Western ways of knowing, there are relational ways of knowing that draw from sources we feel, desire, dream, and empathize with rather than from detached positions we rationalize from. The activist scholarship of Indigenous feminist and radical women of color feminists free up our imaginations about what world we really want to live in.

Acknowledging that our minds, hearts, and political imaginations have been captured by the carceral state and white settler imaginaries, I push back throughout my activist-scholarship against a purist politics that mistakenly believes that there is a clearly demarcated and pure "outside" to the current system. As Million reminds us, "we dance in a politically electrified field most of our lives."[5] Indigenous feminist conceptualizations of sovereignty and decolonization as well as Black radical feminist political claims to what Saidiya Hartman would call statelessness, homelessness, and motherless-ness[6] have, however, furnished new ways for breaking the stranglehold of carceral state necro-power as well as provided answers to the questions that have weighed most heavily on my mind throughout this project: To whom do we run for cover from the carceral state? What do these political formations and

4. Ibid., 314–15.
5. Ibid., 316.
6. See Saidiya V. Hartman, *Lose Your Mother: A Journey along the Atlantic Slave Route* (New York: Farrar, Straus and Giroux, 2007).

autonomous spaces that do not rely on the nation-state look and feel like? Can we actually achieve a freedom from interpersonal, sexual, and carceral state violence? The felt theory and activist-scholarship of Indigenous feminist and radical women of color feminist formations, specifically feminist formations like INCITE! Women of Color Against Violence, Young Women's Empowerment Project, Sista II Sista, Project NIA, UBUNTU, the Bay Area Transformative Justice Collective, Families of Sisters in Spirit (FSIS), No More Silence (NMS), and the Native Youth Sexual Health Network (NYSHN), or those found in the Free CeCe Campaign or the Idle No More/Indigenous Nationhood Movement have helped us to denaturalize white settler colonialism, carceral feminisms, and their genealogies. Our present reality no longer has to be assumed.

Driven by a principled sense of mortal urgency, grassroots, volunteer-led, local and transnational groups like FSIS, NMS, and NYSHN, for example, embrace a politics of Indigenous resurgence and are interested in nurturing self-determined and community-led responses to racialized gendered violence targeting Indigenous girls and women rather than relying on the Canadian nation-state and further engaging with and appealing to state institutions and government bodies. In their joint statement, "It Starts With Us," which lays the groundwork to support the resurgence of community-based responses to violence, these three Indigenous-led organizations name specific forms of state violence and identify the harms of going through "the proper channels" of state-led interventions—by way of providing testimonies to British Columbia's Missing Women Commission of Inquiry to making recommendations to the United Nations Committee for the Elimination of Discrimination against Women (CEDAW).[7] For these organizations, heightened calls for a national inquiry into the phenomenon of missing and murdered Indigenous women in the wake of the disappearance and murder of Loretta Saunders, a pregnant young Inuk graduate student who was writing her thesis on the murders of three Nova Scotia Indigenous women, is a waste of time.[8]

7. Families of Sisters in Spirit, No More Silence, and Native Youth Sexual Health Network, "It Starts With Us: Supporting the Resurgence of Community-Based Responses to Violence," *Indigenous Nationhood Movement*, March 14, 2014, available at nationsrising.org.
8. CBC News, "Loretta Saunders Homicide Sparks Call by Native Group for Public

More than a waste of time, however, an inquiry, as Robyn Bourgeois argues, "allows the Canadian state to *appear* that it is doing something about violence against women *without ever having to actually do anything.*"[9] Establishing an inquiry or special committee to examine an issue that has successfully been defined in mainstream media and civic forums as a social problem has historically been a common strategy by the state to silence the voices of opposition. After warning other Indigenous women who are advocating for the inquiry about how the "colonial government can, and will, define, dictate, and decide the purpose, mandate, process, and outcome of that inquiry," Andrea Landry deploys an outlaw discourse that delegitimizes an inquiry "established by a structure meant to murder, rape, and annihilate the Indigenous self."[10] Landry writes, "If the colonial government were to put the dollars in to 'fix' an issue that they continuously create and justify, and if we were to agree to work together, we would be shaking hands with and embodying the oppressor."[11] Landry powerfully equates Indigenous women's falling prey to the "assimilative lure of the statist politics of recognition"[12] in the form of a national inquiry to that of the visceral pain induced by internalized oppression and violent victimization at the hands of the white-settler state. While nothing can be gained from engaging in a liberal politics of recognition, inclusion, and visibility—for Indigenous women, in particular—everything can be lost. Instead of engaging with carceral and settler states, these radical Indigenous feminists are "call[ing] attention back to ourselves; we have the answers and solutions . . . we always have."[13] The solutions in which communities are already actively engaged range from Indigenous resurgence, teach-ins and critical education, media-arts justice,

Inquiry," *CBC News*, February 27, 2014, available at cbc.ca.

9. Robyn Bourgeois, "National Inquiry On Missing, Murdered Women Not Best Answer." *Huffington Post*, December 21, 2012, available at huffingtonpost.ca.

10. Andrea Landry, "Why We Don't Need a Missing and Murdered Indigenous Women's Inquiry." *Last Real Indians*. (blog), 2014, available at lastrealindians.com.

11. Ibid.

12. Glen S. Coulthard, "Subjects of Empire: Indigenous Peoples and the 'Politics of Recognition' in Canada," *Contemporary Political Theory* 6, no. 4 (2007): 437–60, 456.

13. Families of Sisters in Spirit, No More Silence, and Native Youth Sexual Health Network (2014).

community accountability and transformative justice, supporting Indigenous people in the sex trades and street economies, centering Indigenous youth leadership and intergenerational organizing, and Annual February 14th Memorial Marches for Missing and Murdered Women,[14] to the "countless acts of hidden resistance and kitchen table resistance aimed at ensuring their children and grandchildren could live as *Indigenous* Peoples."[15]

It is imperative to provide a historical context and to mine the genealogy of Indigenous, queer woman of color feminist antiviolence activism in order to denaturalize the present; the ability to remember something differently tells us that the carceral state, carceral feminisms, and white settler futurity are not inevitable and can be dismantled. The powerful analytics and politics discussed here have refused to reproduce what Sandy Grande would call the "theory of property holders" perpetuated in "whitestream feminisms."[16] Additionally, as Audra Simpson reminds us—her people—the Mohawks of Kahnawà:ke are "nationals of a precontact Indigenous polity that . . . insist on being and acting as peoples who belong to a nation other than the United States or Canada" and who intimately understand that "there is more than one *political* show in town" beyond the much sought-after and presumed "benevolence" of a multicultural, liberal politics of recognition.[17] While the "place we live now" may seem forlorn, barren, and desolate for Indigenous feminist and radical women of color feminists, there is a historical context and precedent for

---

14. Native Youth Sexual Health Network, "For Each Bead, Moccasin Top & Ceremony for Our Missing and Murdered Indigenous Women and Families: NYSHN Statement of Support & Media Advisory for Walking With Our Sisters," 2013, available at nativeyouthsexualhealth.com; "Responding to the Violence of Ongoing Colonialism on December 17th: International Day to End Violence Against Sex Workers," 2013, available at nativeyouthsexualhealth.com; "February 14th Women's Memorial Marches—Not Forgetting the Legacy and Honoring through Action," 2014, available at nativeyouthsexualhealth.com.

15. Kiera L. Ladner and Leanne Simpson, "This Is an Honour Song," in *This Is an Honour Song: Twenty Years since the Blockades, an Anthology of Writing on the "Oka Crisis,"* edited by Kiera L. Ladner and Leanne Simpson (Winnipeg: Arbeiter Ring Pub, 2010), 8.

16. Sandy Grande, *Red Pedagogy: Native American Social and Political Thought* (Lanham, MD: Rowman & Littlefield Publishers, 2004), 148.

17. Audra Simpson, *Mohawk Interruptus: Political Life Across the Borders of Settler States,* (Durham, NC: Duke University Press, 2014), 2, 11.

antiracist feminist antiviolence coalition- and movement-building by those under siege by white settler colonialism and carceral state violence. While a political formation based in transformative feminist and prison abolitionist praxes may seem incommensurable and (often) impractical in activist circles that privilege short-term legal remedies over long-term political movement-building, it is not—and never has been—an impossible politics. It is both possible and preferred.

To underscore the historical continuity of the imaginative visioning and intense dreaming of Indigenous feminist and radical women of color feminism, I briefly return here to the importance of intergenerational, historical memory. I want to return to a brief discussion of a grassroots, feminist antiviolence movement—active approximately thirty-five years ago—that went beyond discursive resistance and mere survival to engage in transformative feminist praxis and speculate about Black female bodily integrity and Black socialist lesbian feminist sovereignty: the Combahee River Collective.[18]

Black women, "Third World" women of color, and Indigenous activists within the decolonized space of transformative justice feminist organizing, engage in ceremony and the communicative sacred activity of dreaming. Those of us currently working to build a community accountability activist circle driven by criminalized and formerly incarcerated women intimately know another world is possible. At one of our organizing meetings, I would like us to continue to "learn in social action"[19] and study together one of the early transformative justice feminist projects advanced by the Combahee River Collective, a Boston-based Black socialist lesbian feminist organization that began as a chapter of the short-lived National Black Feminist Organization in 1974.[20] The Combahee River Collective's widely circulated, bilingual Spanish-English pamphlet entitled "Black Women: Why Did They Die?" addresses the sexual assault and murder of twelve Black women

18. Combahee River Collective, "Why Did They Die?"

19. Griff Foley, *Learning in Social Action: A Contribution to Understanding Informal Education* (Bonn: Zed, 1999).

20. Alethia Jones and Virginia Eubanks, eds., *Ain't Gonna Let Nobody Turn Me Around: Forty Years of Movement Building with Barbara Smith* (Albany: SUNY Press, 2014), 43.

and one white woman in the Boston area in the first months of 1979.[21] Preceding a list of transformative justice-like measures Black, Puerto Rican, and other "Third World" women could take to protect themselves, participate in radical self-defense classes, and build community safety programs,[22] the pamphlet forwards an intersectional analysis of the murders that goes "beyond 'Don't walk home alone at night.'"[23] Immediately following the analysis is a poem by Ntozake Shange entitled "with no immediate cause," which discusses the state's complicity in racialized gendered violence and Shange's own feelings of impotence to stem the crushing tide of racist, misogynist violence.[24] Noting the devaluation of Black girls' lives by the carceral state, the pamphlet authors write: "The mother of a fifteen-year-old girl, one of the first two victims, says that when she reported the disappearance of her daughter to the police, they hesitated to file a report, claiming that the girl had probably gone off with a pimp."[25] Their analysis investigated the complicity of the racialized carceral state and the mainstream media in these young women's murders, underscoring the difficulties of forging alliances with both white mainstream feminists and hetero-patriarchal Black male leadership. The pamphlet challenged the call for Black men to "protect their women" and called out white feminists' investments in upholding normative white femininity that racializes Black men as well as Black women.[26] The authors noted that "when eleven white women were raped in another part of Boston, all describing their assailant as a Black man, the press and the city officials were quick to recognize their plight and a great deal of attention was drawn to their situation."[27] Through their collective analysis, the Combahee River Collective underscored how a singular focus on race or gender unwittingly reproduced the normative narratives of the carceral state and the normative institutions of middle-class domesticity,

---

21. Combahee River Collective, "Why Did They Die?"
22. Ibid., 47.
23. Jones and Eubanks, *Ain't Gonna Let Nobody Turn Me Around*, 42.
24. Combahee River Collective, "Why Did They Die?," 48–49.
25. Ibid., 41.
26. Ibid., 46.
27. Ibid., 42.

white femininity, and "proper" sexuality. Such a perspective was therefore inadequate to address the interlocking forms of violence targeting Black, Latina, and other "Third World" women of color.

The group CRISIS, with a focus on self-help and anti-violence community mobilization, and the Committee for Women's Safety, a coalition of Black, Latina, and white antiracist feminists working to develop programs for community safety, were formed as a result of Combahee's transformative justice feminist praxis.[28] I would argue that the majority—if not all—of the feminism of color and trans-feminism of color antiviolence movements recognize the Combahee River Collective as one of their direct antecedents. As Robin D. G. Kelley states, "Radical black feminists have never confined their vision to just the emancipation of black women or women in general or all black people for that matter. Rather they are the theorists and proponents of a radical humanism committed to liberating humanity and reconstructing social relations across the board."[29] Demonstrating this radical humanism and one of the most compelling aspects of Combahee's antiviolence organizing work, I have found especially moving a photograph that depicts a banner held by a group of Black and Latina demonstrators at one of the many rallies to protest the murders and lack of police accountability. The banner reads, "3rd World Women: We Cannot Live Without Our Lives."[30] The banner tells us how Black women and other women of color's lives have been marked for legal elimination, social death, and extermination by the carceral state. When the promise of life is not extended universally by the state or when life is premised merely on surviving legacies of interpersonal and state violence, it is rendered meaningless, a "death in life" without ceremony.

Every day that these prison abolitionist and transformative justice collectives meet, break bread together, and model mutual responsibility and accountability in order to interrupt interpersonal, sexual, and state violence against Indigenous and Black girls and women in their families, communities, schools, and workplaces,

---

28. Ibid., 42 and 46; Jones and Eubanks, *Ain't Gonna Let Nobody Turn Me Around*, 71–74.

29. Robin D. G Kelley, *Freedom Dreams: The Black Radical Imagination* (Boston: Beacon Press, 2002), 137.

30. Combahee River Collective, "Why Did They Die?," 43.

they evoke both their ancestors and descendants and partake in ceremony. Every time these collectives of girls and women engage in a politics that calls for collective *self*-recognition and a "turning away" from the carceral state, every time they daydream about the Americas disappearing into a singular landmass and sacred place called Turtle Island, these collectives engage in ceremony. The kinds of futures evoked during these ceremonies are the worlds of which our abolitionist movements dream.

REFERENCES

Allen, Paula Gunn. *The Sacred Hoop: Recovering the Feminine in American Indian Traditions*. Boston: Beacon Press, 1986.

Bourgeois, Robyn. "National Inquiry On Missing, Murdered Women Not Best Answer." *Huffington Post*. December 21, 2012. Available at huffingtonpost.ca.

CBC News. "Loretta Saunders Homicide Sparks Call by Native Group for Public Inquiry." *CBC News*. February 27, 2014. Available at cbc.ca.

Combahee River Collective. "Why Did They Die? A Document of Black Feminism." *Radical America* 13, no. 6 (November/December 1979): 41–50.

Coulthard, Glen S. 2007. "Subjects of Empire: Indigenous Peoples and the 'Politics of Recognition' in Canada." *Contemporary Political Theory* 6, no. 4: 437–60.

Families of Sisters in Spirit, No More Silence, and Native Youth Sexual Health Network. "It Starts With Us: Supporting the Resurgence of Community-Based Responses to Violence." *Indigenous Nationhood Movement*. March 14, 2014. Available at nationsrising.org.

Foley, Griff. *Learning in Social Action: A Contribution to Understanding Informal Education*. Bonn: Zed, 1999.

Grande, Sandy. *Red Pedagogy: Native American Social and Political Thought*. Lanham, MD: Rowman & Littlefield Publishers, 2004.

Hartman, Saidiya V. *Lose Your Mother: A Journey along the Atlantic Slave Route*. New York: Farrar, Straus and Giroux, 2007.

Jones, Alethia, and Virginia Eubanks, eds. *Ain't Gonna Let Nobody Turn Me around: Forty Years of Movement Building with Barbara Smith*. Albany: SUNY Press, 2014.

Kelley, Robin D. G. *Freedom Dreams: The Black Radical Imagination*. Boston: Beacon Press, 2002.

Ladner, Kiera L, and Leanne Simpson. "This Is an Honour Song." In *This Is an Honour Song: Twenty Years since the Blockades, an Anthology of Writing on the "Oka Crisis,"* edited by Kiera L. Ladner and Leanne Simpson. Winnipeg: Arbeiter Ring Pub, 2010.

Landry, Andrea. "Why We Don't Need a Missing and Murdered Indigenous Women's Inquiry." *Last Real Indians* (blog). 2014. Available at lastrealindians.com.

Million, Dian. "Intense Dreaming: Theories, Narratives, and Our Search for Home." *The American Indian Quarterly* 35, no. 3 (2011): 313–33.

Native Youth Sexual Health Network. "For Each Bead, Moccasin Top & Ceremony for Our Missing and Murdered Indigenous Women and Families: NYSHN Statement of Support & Media Advisory for Walking With Our Sisters." Available at nativeyouthsexualhealth.com.

———. "Responding to the Violence of Ongoing Colonialism on December 17th: International Day to End Violence Against Sex Workers." 2013. Available at nativeyouthsexualhealth.com.

———. "February 14th Women's Memorial Marches—Not Forgetting the Legacy and Honoring through Action." 2014. Available at nativeyouthsexualhealth.com.

Simpson, Audra. *Mohawk Interruptus: Political Life Across the Borders of Settler States.* Durham, NC: Duke University Press, 2014.

A MATTER OF NATIONAL SECURITY

Sophia Terazawa

> *I am to be a weapon in the war against black America. Meanwhile, white America can take its seat, comfortable in its liberal principles, surrounded by state-selected Asians, certain that the culpability of black poverty and oppression must be laid at the door of black America. How does it feel to be a solution?*
>
> —Vijay Prashad

My love suggests a ban on my body for the good of this country,
he says, but how do I speak
of ghosts without a body, an eye,

a battlefield?

Kumiko Holtzclaw, mother of a demon.

Our mothers, the mothers of demons.

Now law protects us now. No son, no badge, no liberty.

My love suggests a Watch List to keep the terror out,
but my body is watching go—she weeps, for nothing's left.

A boat, one bag of jasmine leaves, the blood between her hips.

I rise among the tombs.
The tombs will speak no names.

My love, you taste of ash. My love, your touch is death.

My work attempts intimacy with power. In this poem, "A Matter of National Security," my love is the one who claims to know best. He may be white America. He may be a politician. He may even be the one who shares my bed. Poetry forces me to come close to the hand that pulls the trigger. I can see in his violence a desperation for love. But it is a sick kind of love. He conquers. He kills. He touches. He touches everything: Black bodies, colonized bodies, women and children, the poor, and the veiled. We all die under his touch, but he knows nothing else.

Today it is a critical time for Asian Americans. On what side do we stand? This country's hand is on our backs. He says, "My love, if you really care about me, you will honor and obey. In sickness and in health, until death do us part. Amen."

But I write of an allegiance that once demanded a vow the moment our ancestors flew over the Pacific Ocean and arrived with nothing but a thousand tongues. I'm talking to you, Asian America. Do you really want this country's love?

sophiaterazawa.com
facebook.com/sophiaterazawa

THE HORRORS OF WOMANHOOD

Anastazia Schmid

CRAFTING THE PERFECT WOMAN

HOW GYNECOLOGY, OBSTETRICS, AND AMERICAN PRISONS OPERATE TO CONSTRUCT AND CONTROL WOMEN

Anastazia Schmid

I TRY TO TELL MYSELF TO BREATHE. THE GOOD DOCTOR'S IRRITATION radiates through the cold steel he shoves inside me. I am trapped inside my flesh—I am here, but I'm not. The watermarked holes in the ceiling tiles suck me into their blackness.

Voices in this cramped room. The hard wrinkled paper scratches my face. The nurse stares, expressionless. The doctor addresses her as though I am not in the room, ". . . not another one of these . . . complaining about being locked down . . . inventing problems . . . all they want is drugs!" I am angered enough to find my voice; I protest. "I don't do drugs! I'm having problems with my *bladder*! My doctor at home never gave me a pelvic exam for my bladder problem!"

My questioning was unwelcome. He becomes more forceful. I remember why I have refused pap smears for nearly ten years. He jerks instruments out of me jumps up in disgust and snaps off his gloves. Red-faced, he commands the nurse to catheterize me. She reads the instructions on the catheter and tells me without feeling that she's never done this before. There is no preparation and no anesthetic. My genitals burn. Blood and tears do not stop her from finishing the procedure. I am not human in this place.

Still, I am not alone. I exist in a long line, a ruinous tradition. One of my predecessors was a young woman named Mary Jane Schwitzer. One hundred and thirty-five years ago, Mary Jane testified to an Indiana legislative committee about her treatment by a prison gynecologist:

> I was visited by Dr. Parvin. I was very sick, and he was to examine me with instruments. Mrs. Smith on that occasion dragged

me out of my bed and into another room. I told her what I
thought of being treated that way. Dr. Parvin said I was to lie in
bed for several days after the operation.

I envy Mary Jane for one reason. She had the chance to speak
out against her treatment. Over a century later, confined at the
same facility, I want the same chance.

Mary Jane Schwitzer's experiences at the first American wom-
en's prison open a window onto a range of historical phenome-
na with contemporary implications. They highlight the practice
of medical experimentation and torture of female prisoners including medical rape and induced abortion. They show the fear
and obsession with women's bodies and sexuality at the heart of
gynecology. They point to the relationship of gynecology to the
budding field of eugenics, with its profoundly racist implications.
Finally, they remind us of the ways the fields of gynecology and
obstetrics have defined beliefs about women's bodies and the need
for their control in ways that continue to reverberate today.

In 1873, the nation's first state-run women's prison, the Indiana
Reformatory for Women and Girls, opened under the supervision
and operation of Quaker moral reformer, Sarah J. Smith. The institution was managed by a full female staff, with the exception
of a night watchman and one male physician. In the nineteenth
century the actual commission of a crime was an unnecessary ele-
ment to incarcerate a woman. "Illicit" sexual behavior or property
damage was enough to hold women captive, and take control over
body, sexuality, and reproductive function. In the institution's first
five years, "Saint Sarah," as she became known, was lauded for her
reportedly high success rate rehabilitating wayward women. But
things aren't always as they seem.

In 1879, after a few women were released from the reformatory, rumors of scandalous happenings at the prison began to
surface. Margaret Conrad, one of the women who had been incarcerated at the reformatory, hung herself after three days of
solitary confinement. Leaked stories of Conrad's suicide, along
with other rumors, sparked a journalist's interest. Newspaper re-
porters interviewed numerous prison staff members and wom-
en who had been incarcerated in the institution. Two years later,

in 1881, a state legislative committee conducted an investigation into those rumors and allegations of abuse of the women incarcerated at the reformatory. Dark-room isolation, physical and sexual abuse, water torture, food and clothing deprivation, surgical operations, infanticide, and forced abortions were among the charges. Among the perpetrators of the abuse was a certain Dr. Theophilus Parvin. Dr. Parvin was one of the founding fathers of gynecology and obstetrics, the nation's leading expert on female sexual function and disease, and the president of the American Medical Association.

To understand Parvin, we need to step back a moment. This was a time of tremendous transformation for sex, science, and social control. At the intersections of sex, gender ideology, religion, and punishment, orthodox medicine imposed its visions of social control. Historical documents reveal stunning connections among powerful men of science, doctors, politicians, and religious figures—at a moment when aspiring physicians often used the bodies of enslaved and institutionalized people for medical experimentation.

I can't help but note the chilling coincidental timing in this history. Dr. Parvin became the head physician at the newly opened Indiana Reformatory for Women and Girls in 1873, the same year the American Medical Association added an authoritative section on the diseases of women and children, and obstetrics. Still in 1873, in further sexual conquest, Robert Battey published his influential work "inventing" female castration, sparking a gynecological surgical trend. By 1906 roughly 150,000 American women had had their ovaries surgically removed thanks to Battey. Given my experience, I can't help but wonder who those 150,000 sterilized women were, and where they lived. Also 1873: the Comstock Law went into effect, imposing criminal charges, fines and fees for the sale and distribution of any sexually related material including contraception and birth control information (mostly produced by midwives and "sex radicals" who believed in equality in marriage and a woman's right to choose if, when, and with whom she would procreate). Such material was defined as indecent, immoral, lewd, or lascivious, and it was forcefully prosecuted. Only doctors and their medical publications were exempt.

In this profoundly important period for the development of orthodox medicine and its social control functions, Dr. Parvin would spend ten unabated years building his medical legacy in gynecology and obstetrics at the Indiana Reformatory for Women and Girls—my current home—hidden from public scrutiny. Mysteriously, historical accounts of his life and career shroud his work at the prison. In 1886, three years after leaving the prison, Parvin published his magnum opus, a 685-page medical manual, *The Science and Art of Obstetrics*. The tome is replete with graphic illustrations detailing every aspect of female sex organs, as well as illustrations of pregnancy and fetal development at all stages of gestation, labor and delivery. Along with his manual, Parvin developed and released to the medical community an anatomically correct, life-sized, female obstetric manikin, a "pregnant" version with fetuses ranging in gestational phase, complete with life-like genitalia and moveable joints that would permit the figure being placed in any position. Parvin released the manikins as state-of-the-art teaching tools. To me they suggest multiple uses, but that may be because the only illustration of this figure that I've seen, thanks to the archive of the Museum of Obstetrics, was positioned rather suggestively, on all fours, clad in striped stockings and nothing else.

Parvin's in-depth investigation and analysis of women's sex organs, as well as his extensive experience in gynecological and obstetric surgical procedures, would only have been possible through his long-term use of powerless female prisoners as experimental subjects. Captive women were the prime candidates for experimental gynecological surgeries due to their invisibility, and due to the voicelessness of their social position.

Parvin's medical maleficence within the women's prison is clear. His "Notes on Medical Practice at the Indiana Reformatory for Women and Girls," published in an Ohio medical journal, details the medical procedures he conducted on prisoners. One notes his treatment of a sixteen-year-old prostitute known only as "P." Apparently this unidentifiable woman suffered from venereal warts. Parvin snipped off pieces of her genitals with scissors. Noting the mutilation, Parvin scribed, "when those [warts] within the vagina were attacked the hemorrhage was copious and obstinate." No details of the patient's experience—her pain, the outcome, even her survival—were included; nothing more is said. Nor was this, or any other surgical procedure, ever mentioned in his physician's notes within the prison records.

Ironically, Parvin's reports in the prison records omit all gynecology and obstetrics treatment and problems. These were peculiar omissions for this surgical expert in gynecology and obstetrics, working in a prison at a time when prostitution and venereal diseases were considered pandemic and women accused of sex work or suffering from these diseases were overwhelmingly likely to find themselves behind bars. At his death, remembrances of Parvin omitted any reference to his work in or affiliation with the Indiana Reformatory, even while detailing all other aspects of his labors in the Hoosier state.

Parvin claimed to be an expert in all things related to women, as if he had studied them as he would a textbook. He adamantly declared to his colleagues, "[i]f you read women as I do . . . you will agree with me that it is not natural for a woman have a desire for sexual intercourse; it is submitted to as a duty." He also racially described the body of deviant women thusly, "course skin, large lips, black eyes, black hair, dark complexion and . . . contracted and prominent condition of the muscles; there is usually less fat and connective tissue, so that on the whole the body is more angular and less rounded than in the perfect woman." These "less than perfect, unnatural" women would be the targets for his bizarre treatments and bodily control over their reproductive functions. His own clinical lectures about the appropriate treatment of "nymphomania" and masturbation are telling to the part he played in the sinister handling of women and girls at the reformatory. He defined a nymphomaniac as any woman—even married women—who has sexual desire which caused them to "deviously" seek "connection with men and even with dogs," as if women are sex-crazed predators. Expected to take his word for it, Parvin professed his (then widowed) patient claimed to desire sex with her husband "five or six times a week," which purported to make her less than perfect and "unlike other women."

As a theologian as well as a doctor, Parvin supported proscribed gender ideologies. His line of reasoning fell in with the times on "fallen" women (or nymphomaniacs); women believed to have fallen out of the "grace of god," or fallen out of the power and dominion of men and their supporting institutions. Therefore a "fallen" woman is any woman who enacts corporeal claim of her own body, sex, and sexuality as she so chooses, or who wets the appetite of her own desires. Through this line of reasoning, her body itself was seen as an unruly, beastly entity in need of taming. Confinement, water torture, drugs, and bodily mutilations provided the means for forced submission and bodily control over women.

During the years of Parvin's tenure at the reformatory, mistreatment of the prisoners abound. At the forefront of prisoner abuse was forty-five-year-old Mary Jane Schweitzer. In 1877 she was sentenced to two years of incarceration at the reformatory "on suspicion of committing arson." Yet imprisonment was the least of her problems. While in prison, Mary Jane was branded as a thief and deviant then targeted for severe punishment. She would not speak to another person for an extended period of time. Mary Jane was repeatedly subjected to dehumanizing practices, including being locked in solitary confinement after being stripped naked and forced to stand in her cell while being hosed with cold water for nearly half an hour. After which she was given no clean clothes and left alone, chilled and in ill health. Eventually she was left to the devices of the good doctor for her mysterious operation.

Mary's silence was finally broken in 1881. According to the Indianapolis Journal reporting the testimony of her abuse at the reformatory, Mary Jane recalled: "I was punished very frequently. For most of one year, I was not allowed to speak with any other person. Was kept in solitary confinement for one month, fed on bread and water, ducked, and had no clean clothing." Apparently her sanctions included torture to simulate drowning. "Ducking" consisted of repeatedly forcing a person's head under cold water, holding the head under water for several seconds, then pulling it back up just long enough for the victim to gasp for air before being forced back under the water. Mary was one of several women to experience this form of torture, a precursor to modern day waterboarding.

The use of water torture as punishment would be paramount during Parvin's stint of employment at the prison. Sexual deviants became the target for this routine employment of torture and

Parvin's beliefs shaped how the female prisoners were treated. Refuting Mary and other women's claims, Parvin testified that he had not, "prescribed that there should be an application of water upon prisoners for certain diseases." Though despite his testimonial denial, his 1875 Ohio medical journal publication proves otherwise. He notes prescribing cold shower baths to a sixteen-year-old prostitute at the reformatory for urinary incontinence. The "shower bath" was a device resembling a shower stall with a chair inside that strapped its occupant in place by means of wrist and lap restraints. A large spout is positioned over the head that releases forceful, mass quantities of water creating a sense of drowning as the victim gasps for air over the shock and force of cold water rushing the head and face. Like ducking, the process is repeated multiple times, often to the point of unconsciousness, to increase terror and disorientation in the victim. Seemingly, prescribing simulated drowning would cure theft as well as bladder control problems. Furthermore, these forms of water torture were also routinely used as punishment for women who committed the "sin" of "self-abuse."

Women's sexuality was besieged via water torture punishment. Molly Scott, a woman accused of sexual transgressions inside the prison with the night watchman, purported to have been doused with the fire hose, presumably to cool off her heated sexual desires. In addition, a woman who was employed in the reformatory's laundry for five years, Francis Talbutt, reported that the most severe case of punishment she ever witnessed involved the superintendent, Mrs. Sarah Smith, stripping a thirteen-year-old girl naked and holding her in a tub while another prisoner turned on the cold-water tap. The young girl was ducked for twenty minutes, spanked, and sent to bed. That thirteen-year-old girl who was nearly drowned was a purported masturbator. The containment of female sexuality would be circumscribed through these methods of punishment.

There are other references that seem to refer to prisoners as experimental subjects in Parvin's practice, though they are less forthcoming. During a clinical lecture on nymphomania and masturbation, for example, Parvin expressed disappointment at not being able to "bring before his audience" a forty-two-year-old widow complaining of this dual condition. What would have prevented the patient from being present at the lecture, as was common instructional practice? Nonetheless, he goes on in his lecture to explain his methods of clinical diagnosis:

> When I subjected this woman to examination (in the presence of Dr. Morris), I found some peculiar phenomenon. When the finger was introduced into the vagina, as soon as the clitoris was barely touched, there were produced irregular movements of the hips and pelvis. As the finger was advanced the muscles about the vagina were thrown into a state of contraction, which it closed tight on the finger, and this caused a sense of gratification to the woman.

Like many male gynecologists of the time, Parvin raped his female patients (often in the presence of another man) by digitally "examining" them, induced orgasm, and then claimed their bodily response as "proof" of a woman's sexual deviance and disease. In such cases, captive women are utterly defenseless to prevent this type of handling, or what was to be done to them in order to ameliorate their "conditions." During the nineteenth century, experimental medical drug use also came into fashion. Parvin offers a compelling treatment to cure the said nymphomaniac,

> When, in this case, we noted the irritability on the introduction of the finger . . . we applied muriate of cocaine to the clitoris, and I can assure you the effect was wonderful, the vagina at once behaved as well as the most virtuous vagina in the United States.

His patient may have been relieved of her nymphomania and chronic masturbation by perhaps becoming addicted to cocaine instead as he himself may have been. In another medical journal he professed using cocaine on himself to stitch an incision on his arm. There's no way of knowing which came first with Parvin, experimenting with drug treatment, or surgical procedures. During the time Parvin worked at the women's prison (1873-1883) anesthesia was not yet readily used for surgical procedures, and when it was, doctors reserved its use for their affluent clientele. At that time, chances are he used the drug to "treat" disorders, but not as an anesthesia during surgical procedures. Yet it wasn't beyond Parvin to surgically "cure" women who desired sex or masturbated. He defensively stated, "[c]litoridectomy might do good in some cases . . . . [W]hen all other means have failed, we would be justified in resorting to it." Removing a woman's primary source of pleasure would leave her for a solitary sexual function of procreation; a position believed by Parvin to be her sole function in sexual matters.

Drugs and surgery notwithstanding, Parvin's fear over the power of the female body resulted in false medical findings and preposterous treatments upon which the field was founded. Perhaps Parvin's experience with his "nymphomaniac" patient led him to confirm a condition he and his colleagues called "vaginismus" that likened a vagina to a mouth and throat susceptible to a condition similar to laryngitis that would cause the vagina to swell and constrict and thus potentially capture whatever had been inserted inside it. Parvin chronicled in his medical publications of female sexual functions that the vaginal orifice has the power to either, prevent "the introduction of the penis, the speculum, or even a finger . . . [or] may prevent the withdrawal of the penis."

Farcical stories of unnamed, unseen women equated case studies that were used as medical proof of strange phenomenon associated with the prowess of the vagina. Parvin would later solidify this claim by publishing another case study he diagnosed as "penis captivus." He received the fabricated story in the mail as a ruse by a disgruntled colleague who signed it for authenticity using the equally fictitious name and title, "Egerton Y. Davis, Ex. U.S. Army." Any high-ranking male easily passed as an "authority" figure, which automatically asserted their claims as "truth." This farcical story was supposedly an eyewitness account of servants while in the throes of sexual passion had become stuck together during intercourse due to the powerful muscular constriction of the woman's vagina trapping her paramour's penis "captive" inside her, rendering him helpless to escape her bodily clutches. Despite the sheer ridiculousness of the "penis captivus" phenomenon, Parvin's published a case study which the Jefferson Medical College archives claim served as truth within the field for the next hundred years.

In another case study on injuries and diseases of female genitals, Parvin quotes a colleague about the concealment of "foreign bodies" in a woman's vagina, "Levrat says that he has removed a sponge which had been in the vagina twenty-three years, and had only then begun to cause injurious results." Furthermore he cites another ludicrous case titled "double vagina" declaring, "coitus had for some years been practiced through the urethra." These case studies and publications of female 'medical conditions,' despite being far-fetched even for archaic times were nonetheless believed. Are we to assume toxic shock (identified as such or not) ceased to exist and men's engorged penises were small enough to fit inside a urethra in the nineteenth century? Regardless of what we may think reading such farcical statements, the field of gynecology and obstetrics were founded on these beliefs solidified by male physicians.

Those of us who actually have vaginas intrinsically know what utter nonsense this is, but women's words about their lives and bodies (incarcerated or otherwise) are almost completely absent or discredited in early records of female medical science. Perhaps by some strange irony, the primordial fear of women holding men's penises captive provides unconscious justification for a male-dominated criminal justice system that holds women's entire bodies captive. Interestingly, no one seems to question why a counterpart to gynecology as a specialized field of medicine ceases to exist, or the deeper implications as to why it ceases to exist. There is no exclusive medical field limited and dedicated solely to the study, functions, treatment, and diseases of the penis and testicles, particularly not as a profession created and dominated by women. I can't help but note the extreme sardonicism that penology is the study of prisons, not penises, or that prisons became the ideal location to conduct gynecological and obstetrics experimentation.

Interestingly, not all women at the reformatory acted alone in acts of sexual misconduct. The 1881 investigation also reported nefarious happenings involving prisoner pregnancy, abortions, and infanticide. Nancy Clem, another prisoner at the reformatory, reported night watchman, Mr. Barrett as the sexual assailant of Molly Scott and Nancy Evans. While additional allegations of illegitimate pregnancies and abortions were claimed to be performed on the prisoners. In denial and defense against the allegations, Superintendent Sarah Smith protested,

> Seven children have been born in the reformatory and three in prison. In all cases the women were pregnant when they came to the institution . . . . No woman could ever had a miscarriage without our knowing of it. . . .There is not a thread of foundation for any stories of abortion in the institution.

The prison's annual reports fail to document which inmates were pregnant, and whether or not they arrived at the reformatory in that condition. This distinction has only been recorded in a few cases of recidivism with girls returning to the reformatory after a parole violation that returned them to prison. There is at least one such case that Sarah Smith publicly admonished and demanded financial compensation from one of the men she leashed an inmate for work as a domestic servant when she returned to the facility pregnant. No names of mothers or infants, however, are ever listed in cases of childbirths or infant deaths. So what happened to babies that were born or died in the prison? Outsiders notwithstanding, Mrs. Smith was quick to preserve the institution and its staff's credibility while further discrediting Mrs. Clem's allegation insinuating her to be a liar. She then justifiably explained,

> A baby was found in the cesspool, and Dr. Parvin said it was not possible for any woman to have been delivered of that baby. He told the coroner that no woman in the institution could have been its mother. It was a very fine nine-pound baby, and it did not belong to anyone in the institution.

In Parvin's medical manual there are lengthy descriptions and techniques of surgical procedures, including horrifying graphic drawings of embrotomy; a procedure of piercing or crushing a fetus' skull (dead or alive, depending on the obstetrical emergency) to remove it from the womb, and abortive techniques; chock-full of drawings displaying crude instruments of torture he used to perform his procedures.

There was a vested interest in hiding pregnant prisoners at the newly founded women's prison. Prior to the opening of the reformatory, Indiana State Prison South, known as "Jeffersonville," held both men and women in the same building. In 1868, it had been reported by several inmates that the guards had keys to the women's prison and could enter at will to "gratify their lusts." Women who refused to submit were stripped naked and whipped. Those women were easily silenced, often fed whiskey, tobacco, and opium to keep them compliant and quiet. The Jeffersonville warden used the female prisoners as concubines, and prostitutes for other prison officials' open-ended use at the fee of $10 per month. Illegitimate children were born and lived within the prison walls. The discovery of the incarcerated women's sexual exploitation and abuse is what led to the opening of the separate women's prison.

The fact that the campaign to open the reformatory was based on the premise of *ending* sexual violence against female prisoners who had previously been held in men's prisons would be plenty reason to keep such scandals under wraps. Where did the baby come from, found in the cesspool inside the women's prison? Who did the baby belong to if not one of the prisoners? Abortion, embrotomy, and infanticide were all tragic possibilities for women held captive at the reformatory.

Despite these horrors, female prisoners had an even larger grim reality to fear. At least one woman under Parvin's care would die of a female related disease while at the reformatory. Without any details or elaboration of her condition and treatment, he notes in the 9th annual report the uterine cancer death of Kate Linsey. Kate's death would also come into question at an 1881 investigation. In a chilling testimony about Kate being forced to work mopping floors while morbidly ill and her subsequent death, superintendent Sarah Smith, working with Dr. Parvin, justifiably explained that she ordered, "'Now, Katie, let's run up and down the floor' she was in a condition that exercise was necessary. After she took to her bed she never left it again until she died." We are left wondering if Dr. Parvin treated her condition at all, or whether or not he cut into her body (before or after) her death in order to have diagnosed her cancer.

From 1873 to 1884, nine women reportedly died within the institution. Yet there were deaths listed in the annual reports that weren't listed in the registry and vice versa. We have no way of knowing if these were the only deaths that occurred in the prison. However, omissions and discrepancies in recorded deaths would have served multiple purposes. Early news accounts chronicle "resurrectionists" (otherwise known as body snatchers), lucrative business in the trafficking of dead bodies to medical colleges and doctors. "Unclaimed" bodies of prisoners were chronically taken to medical colleges to be used for experimental cadaver research. Dr. Parvin also worked in close affiliation with several medical colleges. Prior to working at the women's prison, he was professor of Materia Medica at the Ohio Medical College for four years, and then professor of obstetrics at the Medical College in Indianapolis. On and off throughout his life, he also worked and taught at the Jefferson Medical College in Philadelphia. He maintained his ties to those academic institutions during his tenure at the prison.

All these practices notwithstanding, gynecology provided the gateway into eugenic social cleansing. The beliefs and medical practices of Parvin and his male colleagues purported that a woman's sex and reproductive organs were to blame for all manners of deviance and social ill. If imprisonment, water torture, packing vaginas full of cocaine, chemical and physical restraint, and chopping off women's most intimate body part failed to cure her sexual proclivities, surely her internal sex organs were to blame. With those body parts intact she may spread her vile deviance onto future generations, which could then infect all of society with her evils. Parvin could kill two birds with one stone through Battey's en vogue surgical "treatment" to sterilize women. This extreme option additionally offered death to the possibility of future procreation thereby eliminating a woman's lineage of DNA. Parvin proselytized ovarectomy as a potential cure for "sexual deviants" (the very type of woman claimed to be held captive in the reformatory) declaring,

> The question of removing the ovaries is to be considered, and we must ask the question whether we can thereby cure the disease. This operation is becoming so extremely fashionable that I imagine that after a time but a small portion of our women will be child-bearing.

Determining *which* women should be child bearing was perhaps the point. Control over reproductive function kept women inferior to white men. In retrospect, sterilization (particularly of institutionalized people) offered a means of state leverage maintaining population and social control. American prisoners and institutionalized people were the initial targets for eugenics. Forced sterilization would become part of the "Indiana Plan" for "social hygiene"—systematic racial, social, intellectual/mental cleansing. By 1907 under the persuasive public policy urging of Amos Butler (Dr. Parvin's brother in law), Indiana became the first place in the world to legalize sterilization. In this case, namely, those ensnared in the carceral state or under other institutions and forms of social control. Indiana's compulsory sterilization law was later deemed unconstitutional, and revised in 1927. Yet the law continued to approve and authorize sterilization of the "insane, feeble-minded, or epileptic persons" in custodial care. This law remained intact until 1974 marking Indiana institutions as the sites for approximately two thousand documented cases of legalized sterilizations. Considering the on-going propensity to omit, hide, and destroy records of institutionalized people this number is most likely inaccurate and grossly deficient.

The violence, sexual abuse, medical experimentation, sterilization and death of a few hundred captive women in the nineteenth century laid the foundation for the field of gynecology to expand into evolving eugenics practices (albeit in more clandestine forms) across time. Our nation's first women's prison housed only seventeen women when it opened in 1873, today there are over 115,000 women incarcerated nationwide. One out of every three women incarcerated in the world is incarcerated in the United States. Numbers fail to illustrate the sobering reality of incarcerated women's lived experience and loss of humanity. The sinister implications of Mary Jane and others' statements only become clear when we examine the evidence with Parvin's publications, what was recorded, as well as what's been omitted. What other "instruments" would a gynecologist be using if not instruments indicative of his field of expertise? And what other "operation" would he have performed if not one of several surgical procedures he proselytized for the "treatment" of female deviants? Perhaps Mary was one of those women relieved of her ability to reproduce.

Eugenic methods of genocide particularly target groups deemed to be society's under-caste. As I further reflect on my own experience of incarceration, I realize that spending over a decade and a half behind bars during the prime years for reproductive functioning, that I too (albeit inadvertently) have been relieved of the possibility of reproducing as well. In this day and age of hyper-incarceration, long-term captivity of women is, in and of itself, a form of eugenic genocide. A woman in her late teens or early twenties sentenced to twenty or more years in prison will lose her years to reproduce right along with her freedom. What does this say of a country that incarcerates women of color at a rate 3.8 times higher than white women?

State violence is enacted on vulnerable populations when reproductive freedom is targeted both chemically and surgically as a tool for social and bodily control. The excessive use of harmful chemical birth control and surgical procedures are routinely used on women leaving jails and prisons, women on federal assistance, women of color, and women with disabilities. Contraceptives like Depo-Provera and Norplant (proven to be harmful, and to potentially cause sterility after experimental testing on Native women) are the most commonly given to these groups. In an analysis of the bodily conquest of Native American women, Andrea Smith reports that up to the late seventies the U.S. Department of Health and Welfare (HEW) paid the majority of the cost to hospitals to perform voluntary sterilizations for Medicaid recipients in violation of federal guidelines by disregarding informed consent procedures for sterilizing women through "elective hysterectomies." Currently, just in case a woman is still able to reproduce, IWP continues to freely offer the Depo-Provera shot to any woman leaving the institution. These clandestine forms of state control over reproductive freedom perpetuate eugenic ideologies against America's most vulnerable women.

It has been reported that in the twenty-first century incarcerated American women are still being subjected to illegal forced sterilization, often unbeknown to them. As recent as 2013, Californian incarcerated women giving birth were routinely subjected to tubal ligations also in violation of state and federal policies. Dr. James Heinrich at the Valley State Prison for Women in California defended the cost of the surgery on at least 148 women stating, "over a ten year period, that isn't a huge amount of money . . . compared to what you save in welfare paying for these unwanted children-as they procreate more." Despite the Freedom of Information Act, the records of Heinrich and other institutional or prison doctor's reprehensible practice are nearly impossible to obtain for public access. In nearly all such cases, hospital, governmental agencies and prison records chronically omit pertinent information from patient charts or fail to report these practices, making them unreliable sources for retrieving accurate statistical data on these practices and procedures. For this reason the actual number of sterilized American women is nearly impossible to pinpoint. Without the testimonies of victimized women, these practices persist and remain hidden. All of these forms of silence aid in the genocidal conquest of targeted populations via gynecological and obstetrical practices, working in conjunction with state control.

Institutionalized women however aren't the sole conquest of ob/gyn doctors. Dr. Parvin has left us with a legacy medicalizing *all* women's bodies by using vulnerable imprisoned women as the targeted population for his experimental practice. Female medical science has expanded into a multi-billion dollar a year business. This remains glaringly apparent in obstetrics medicine. U.S. physicians have an annual childbirth customer market of four million women. Approximately 99 percent of American women give birth in a hospital and one-third of those women give birth via major abdominal surgery. Cesarean sections and hysterectomies are comparatively the most commonly performed major surgeries in this country. The historical continuum of the medicalization of women's bodies is alive and well far beyond prison walls.

Gynecology and obstetrics has normalized women's acquiescence to routine graphic displays and probing of their most intimate body parts by (predominantly) nonintimate "professional" men. This field of medicine seems to have caused a collective amnesia to the fact that prior to the advent of gynecology and obstetrics women had given birth naturally without the least bit of male intervention since the dawn of humanity. There is not a "free" vagina or womb in the world today due to the silencing of America's most vulnerable women and the experimentation on captive women's vaginas and wombs in the nineteenth century.

Yet vulnerable populations (particularly women of color and women in prison) remain the least likely to benefit from female medical care. Deliberate indifference to a prisoner's precarious health conditions and forced labor would lead to Kate Linsey's demise. This too is nothing out of the ordinary in women's prisons. In 2015 six more women would die while incarcerated at the Indiana Women's Prison: Glenda Robinette, Tina Burton, LaTonya Robinson, Princola Shields, Tonya Moore, and Yolanda Currie. Under the care of privatized healthcare prison physicians these women's treatment (or lack thereof) was questionable at best, sparking modern inquiries of investigation against prison medical practitioners. Ironically, Princola Shield's experience is mimetic of Margaret Conrad's as she also committed suicide while in solitary confinement within this institution. How different is American incarceration for women in the twenty-first century compared to the nineteenth century?

For every nineteenth century woman's story I have highlighted, a modern version exists. We are the living incarnates of nearly two centuries worth of captive American women who have lost the rights to our own bodies and progenies. Our losses have resulted in corporeal captivity for women far and wide. It is imperative to recognize the interconnection between science, medicine, prisons, and state control and how these interconnected power structures affect the lives of women and society as a whole. Are gynecology and obstetrics solely "good medicine" due to the advent of this historically seedy medical field and its connection to state-sanctioned institutions of social control? I speak out on the untold horrors of myself and my late historical incarcerated sisters to release our voices and break the shackles on our bodies. I seek to leave my readers pondering how their own gender and sexuality have been shaped, and how much freedom they truly have over their bodies and lives.

PHOTO OF THE AUTHOR

GUARD TOWER

Leslie Gray

As an American woman artist of Japanese descent, I am sensitive to the waves of political rhetoric that vibrate occasionally calling for the incarceration of certain types of people based on race, religion or some other labeling. My mother, an American citizen born in California, was forcibly moved as an eleven-year-old with her family to an American concentration camp in Colorado during World War II because fear of "the other" destroyed "reason." Can such a family history cause anything but reluctance to condone blanket policies against any group? Can there be equity, justice, kindness at least? I take my mission as a creative human being and my task as an artist to present thought provoking work very seriously. My art, whether figurative or abstract, seeks to highlight moments for decision, meetings in the road and incidents that drive us to search for where we keep our soul.

"Guard Tower" is from my illustrated book about the Japanese American Internment called *The Pink Dress*.

laprintmaking.com/site/user_gallery/uid/132
tri-pi.org

"PRISON TREATED ME WAY BETTER THAN YOU"

REENTRY, PERPLEXITY, AND THE NATURALIZATION OF MASS IMPRISONMENT

Renée M. Byrd

INTRODUCTION

During the last ten years, a critique of mass imprisonment has become significantly more mainstream in the United States. In 2015 we witnessed the U.S. president visiting a federal prison, new legislation to reduce drug sentences, and more widespread media coverage of the racial disparities of the criminal punishment system. For many in the mainstream media and in academia, these developments signal a profound shift in our longstanding punitive orientation toward crime.[1] The shifting discourses surrounding crime and punishment in the contemporary moment, however, signal both opportunity and danger. It is vital to move beyond reformist reforms[2] and unpack the constitutive imaginings that rendered mass imprisonment a legible project from the outset.[3] Seemingly progressive trends such as sentencing reforms and prisoner reentry initiatives will simply bolster racialized state violence in the absence of a critique of the root causes of mass imprisonment. Grappling with questions of representation and

---

1. Joan Petersilia, "Beyond the prison bubble." *Federal Probation* 75, no.1: 26–31.

2. André Gorz defines the difference between reformist and nonreformist reform in this way: "A reformist reform is one which subordinates its objectives to the criteria of rationality and practicability of a given system and policy. Reformism rejects those objectives and demands—however deep the need for them—which are incompatible with the preservation of the system. On the other hand, a not necessarily reformist reform is one which is conceived not in terms of what is possible within the framework of a given system of administration, but in view of what should be made possible in terms of human needs and demands. . . . A non-reformist reform is determined not in terms of what can be, but what should be." André Gorz, *Strategy for Labor: A Radical Proposal* (Boston: Beacon, 1967), 7–8.

3. Renée M. Byrd, "'Punishment's Twin': Theorizing Prisoner Reentry for a Politics of Abolition," *Social Justice* 43, no. 1 (2016): 1–22.

power, this essay details how the disposability of imprisoned people is reproduced and renaturalized through carceral practices. Specifically looking to the interplay between a women's prison and people's narratives upon release, I show how these programs appear progressive on the surface while expanding the prison industrial complex through perplexing logics that make it harder for people to navigate toward freedom. Using the notion of perplexity as a rubric for understanding penal logics and subjectivities as they emerged in my interviews with people recently released from Minnesota's only women's prison, I analyze how carceral logics reproduce the vulnerability of people leaving prison. The gender-responsive façade of this unique prison and the surveillance orientation of reentry programs naturalized imprisonment as a solution to social problems in deeply problematic ways.

"WHAT IS NARRATED IS NO LONGER WHAT HAPPENED"

In 2011 and 2012, I interviewed twenty women who had been imprisoned at Minnesota Correctional Facility-Shakopee (MCF-Shakopee) and released within the previous six months. I originally met women through a legal clinic that focused on reentry and from there used a snowball sample. Formerly imprisoned people heard of the study from legal clinic staff, staff from other reentry programs, formerly imprisoned people, and probation/parole officers. Interviews were semi-structured, lasting between one and two hours. After some initial questions to establish rapport, I largely allowed participants to direct the dialogue and tell their stories of incarceration and reentry with their own framing.

Any account of this research is necessarily a representation of formerly imprisoned women. It is also a representation of the punishment system within which they are often caught. The interview is a coconstituted site, an act of representation, where researcher and participant make meaning and represent themselves to the other. As David Valentine writes in *Imagining Transgender: An Ethnography of a Category*, "everything can be narrated, but what is narrated is no longer what happened."[4] The interview, itself—as

---

4. David Valentine, *Imagining Transgender: An Ethnography of a Category* (Durham, NC: Duke University Press, 2007), 210.

well as the transcript of what was said—are never simply accurate portrayals. In the act of representation, "what happened" is narrated, remembered, forgotten, interpreted, and transformed. The act of representation is an act steeped in power relations. In a way, prisoner reentry itself was produced as a discursive formation within the interview encounters making up this study. Together, participants and I collectively gained a picture of the "reentry experience" as we negotiated power, subjectivity, and representation. The participant is an agent of representation, constructing a narrative that is a meaningful version of their individual realities. The power dynamics of who I was, how we were brought together (whether by another formerly imprisoned person or a parole officer), shaped what we said and how we negotiated making ourselves intelligible to one another. In writing up this research, I reinterpret, rework, and rerepresent prisoner reentry as it emerged in the interview encounter.

My aim is to be attentive to power within the representation that will necessarily emerge from these narratives, and to see what the interview encounter tells us about the punishment system. Formerly imprisoned people have the right to what Avery Gordon calls "complex personhood."[5] Gordon reminds us, "even those living in the most dire circumstances possess a complex and oftentimes contradictory humanity and subjectivity that is never covered by viewing them as victims, or as superhuman agents."[6] In this essay, I aim to honor the complex personhood of the folks who shared their stories with me, even as I unpack the dehumanization of state violence and logics of disposability in their lives.

---

5. "Complex personhood means that all people, albeit in specific forms, are beset by contradiction, remember and forget, and recognize and misrecognize themselves and others. Complex personhood means that people suffer graciously and selfishly too, get stuck in what symptomizes their troubles and also transform themselves. Complex personhood means that even those society names 'other' are never that. Complex personhood means that even those who haunt the dominant society are haunted too by things they sometimes have names for and sometimes do not. Complex personhood means that the stories people tell about themselves, about their problems, about their society and about their society's problems are entangled and weave between what's immediately available as a story and what their imaginations are reaching toward." Avery Gordon, *Keeping Good Time: Reflections on Knowledge, Power, and People* (St. Paul, MN: Paradigm, 2004), 100.

6. Ibid.

"MINED AS RICH SOURCES"

Over the course of two years, I interviewed people recently released from prison in an effort to develop an analysis of prisoner
reentry with an eye toward the workings of race and gender. Along
the way, I began to wonder whether another study of people in
women's prisons was desirable or useful.[7] We have to ask, what
work do these stories do in the world? How has academic knowledge representing prisoners been central to the development of
mass imprisonment and the naturalization of carceral logics? The
punishment system has been exceedingly skilled at making use of
knowledge of prisoners in order to more effectively govern marginalized populations. Despite the liberatory intentions of many
researchers, more often than not, academic knowledge is co-opted
by the state to reproduce the palatability of state violence.

The following is an excerpt from my writing as I initially began to process my interview data:

> Housing instability was a major concern for the women that I
> interviewed. Many articulated that losing stable housing began a
> domino effect where their lives unraveled. Rita, a thirty-year-old
> Native American woman, argued that her imprisonment began
> with losing her public housing. She was evicted after allegations
> of marijuana use in her apartment. As Rita explained, "everything
> began to unravel from there." Rita became involved with child
> protective services after she lost her housing. She and the chil-
> dren moved around constantly, making it difficult to comply with
> CPS. Eventually, her children were removed from her home. She
> was allowed visitation, but the court moved forward on terminat-
> ing her parental rights. Her tribe worked to prevent termination
> and was successful. However, after this her children remained
> in foster care and the state no longer allowed visitation. Rita at-
> tempted suicide and began using drugs more heavily. After years
> of substance abuse and prostitution, Rita was imprisoned in
> Shakopee on drug charges. She articulated that what began as oc-
> casional use of marijuana had a domino effect that led to her im-
> prisonment. The loss of her children was devastating. Discussing

---

7. Julia Sudbury, "From Women Prisoners to People in Women's Prisons:
Challenging the Gender Binary in Antiprison Work." In *Razor Wire Women: Prisoners,
Activists, Scholars, And Artists* (Albany: SUNY Press, 2011), 169–83.

her recovery, Rita stated, "I work hard for my kids. I just want to be ready if I ever get to see my kids again." Housing instability made accessing social services and staying sober difficult for Rita. Moving constantly between the homes of friends and living in cars, she frequently lost important paperwork and struggled to keep track of the many components needed to access social services. Additionally, Rita articulated difficulty remaining sober given her housing situation. At the time of our interview she had been sober for 18 months. However, she stated that she felt unable to control her environment because of her unstable housing, "if I need somewhere to stay, I have to take what I can get. But I don't like it. I don't want to be around pot or ice or booze. I do my best to stay to myself, leave it alone. But, it gets stressful being on the street. Sometimes I think using will make it all go away."

The narrative account of Rita's life articulated above is one way of telling her story. It conforms to a common formula of incarceration and reentry as told in scholarly and journalistic work on women in prison. Researchers, policy makers, advocates, and imprisoned folks themselves often dutifully reiterate the focus on drug use, prostitution, housing instability, and trauma. The question is not whether it is accurate per se. We must also ask about the ideological work done by narratives of this sort. The question we may need to ask is not whether these narratives are the truth of imprisoned people but what are the truth effects of this particular way of framing the issue of mass imprisonment? What does this story do in the world?

The use of personal narratives by liberal feminist criminologists has tended to contribute to representing people in women's prisons in individualizing ways.[8] There is an intense amount of focus oriented toward people in women's prisons. Even as there are occasional attempts within the literature to represent people in women's prisons as resisting or complex, one is still often left with a voyeuristic and pathologizing examination. We must move beyond an individual level account of prisoner reentry. Research on "women in prison" has often disproportionately focused on their histories of trauma and abuse. Their experiences are:

---

8. Julia Sudbury, ed., *Global Lockdown: Race, Gender and the Prison-Industrial Complex* (London: Routledge, 2005).

mined as rich sources for understanding this aberrant behavior, and childhood abuse, domestic violence, or familial dysfunction [is] presented as the root cause. Presenting women's experiences of abuse as the cause of incarceration individualizes and personalizes their treatment at the hands of the criminal justice system. It obscures the broader social disorder signified by mass incarceration, and it sidesteps the question of why the state responds to abused women with punishment. . . . While the spotlight is turned on the personal failings of poor women and women of color, the political and economic interests that drive prison expansion remain in the shadows.[9]

A focus on lost paperwork, difficulties remaining sober, and histories of abuse and prostitution often confines our analysis to the individual psychology of imprisoned people as opposed to the discourses, logics, and violences that render some things possible and other potentialities effectively foreclosed. This approach fails to question the conditions of mass imprisonment's emergence.

How can we move beyond pathologizing representations of people in women's prisons? We must shift our attention from the inner lives of prisoners themselves back onto the punishment system and the emerging discourses and strategies of governance within prisoner reentry policy and programming. At the same time, formerly imprisoned people must be centered in prison abolitionist movement-building and abolitionist reentry work. Is it possible to bring these two potentially contradictory aims into productive tension? With this essay, I hope to keep formerly imprisoned women's voices centered, while disrupting the often pathologizing gaze in the scholarship on people in women's prisons. Scholars, policymakers, and activists as well as formerly imprisoned women themselves must begin to read penal narratives differently.

PERPLEXING LOGICS

Priti Ramamurthy uses the concept of "subjects-in-perplexity" to elaborate a transnational feminist perspective on Indian women's consumption within a global economy:

Perplexity is a conceptual platform to think about the experiential contradictions of globalization as a series of processes that often overwhelm subjects. As an analytic with multiple subtexts, perplexity is a way of marking the tension between overlapping, opposing, and asymmetric forces or fields of power. Perplexity indexes the puzzlement of people as they experience the joys and aches of the global everyday, often simultaneously. Individually experienced feelings of confusion, of loss, and of desire are not separate.[10]

This notion of subjects-in-perplexity offers a useful rubric for thinking about the complex subjectivities and penal logics narrated in the interview encounters for this study. The perplexity of formerly imprisoned people disrupts the notion of experience as a direct window onto reality or truth. As Wendy Brown writes,

> dispensing with the unified subject does not mean ceasing to be able to speak about our experiences as women, only that our words cannot be legitimately deployed or construed as larger or longer than the moments of the lives they speak from; they cannot be anointed as "authentic" or "true" since the experience they announce is linguistically contained, socially constructed, discursively meditated and never just individually "had."[11]

This allows us to highlight the social construction of contemporary penal subjectivities and to disrupt the way that analyses of former prisoners' lives stay on an individual scale. Additionally, it opens up a lens through which to view the seemingly contradictory rationalities circulating within penal policies in Minnesota.

For Tiffany, a forty-three-year-old African American woman, the clearest way that she could see to disentangle herself from the punishment system was to go to prison. By "executing her sentence," Tiffany went to prison for a year instead of doing fifteen years on probation. She stated, "I took my freedom from myself by turning myself in. I couldn't see doing fifteen years probation. I

---

10. Priti Ramamurthy, "Material Consumers, Fabricating Subjects: Perplexity, Global Connectivity Discourses, and Transnational Feminist Research," *Cultural Anthropology* 18, no. 4 (2003): 525.

11. Wendy Brown, *States of Injury: Power and Freedom in Late Modernity* (Princeton, NJ: Princeton University Press, 1995), 40–41.

turned myself over because it was the best way for me to get away from this system. But, giving up your freedom [pauses] sometimes it's your choice, sometimes it's not." This passage from Tiffany's interview highlights the complex and contradictory ways that formerly imprisoned people negotiate rationalities of choice and individual responsibility. Many participants framed their narratives in terms of choice and accountability.

Kyala, a thirty-two-year-old African American woman stated, "I chose to hurt people, smoke pot, party before 'cause I was messed up, I was hurtin.' Now, I keep my calendar on track. I am more responsible. I want my life to be better for my daughter. She really missed me when I was gone and I know I gotta get off paper [get off parole] and stay off, so I stay home and take care of my business so I can never go back to prison." The women interviewed for this research often framed their narratives in terms of choices they had made. How might we read these ways of framing their lives? To a degree this demonstrates a kind of internalization of neoliberal rationalities of individual responsibility, but I came to see this as necessary in order to maintain dignity and humanity while attempting to extricate oneself from the punishment system. Neoliberal discourses of individual responsibility often offered the only vocabulary for making one's humanity and dignity intelligible within these systems. Additionally, these narratives were crucial to marking oneself as deserving of a second chance and of help with immediate survival needs. Given that participants were often referred to the study by service providers, their decision to articulate their lives in those terms when talking with me makes sense. By marking their former selves as "unfree" and themselves as subjects in the process of becoming free, participants simultaneously marked themselves as deserving and motivated to succeed, as well as more than their status as felons allows.[12] As Jasmine stated, "I understand that we are felons and we have made bad choices. But, sometimes it's just our felony makes us look suspicious all the time and they don't look at you

---

12. Freedom does particular kinds of work in this context. "Getting free" was framed as disentangling oneself from the system, getting off parole, getting one's children back and staying out of prison. The "unfree subjects" upon which this notion of freedom was predicated was often themselves or the women they had been.

like a human being. You're just a felon. It's a lot of pressure. You need to understand that even though we've made mistakes that [pauses] you know [pauses], we are changing. Understand that we are starting over."

Formerly imprisoned people are not simply duped by neoliberal discourses within the punishment system. Additionally, they are not unified and coherent subjects of resistance to penal power. The narratives of formerly imprisoned people produced within these research encounters reveal the perplexing nature of subject formation within late modern regimes of punishment. Formerly imprisoned folks simultaneously framed themselves as responsible, choice-making subjects and as vulnerable to abuse and exploitation because of a lack of options that resulted from their status as felons. Their narratives are "entangled and weaved between what's immediately available as a story and what their imaginations are reaching toward."[13]

To be *perplexed* is to be full of uncertainty, puzzled, or full of difficulty. Perplexity, as a noun, refers to the state of being perplexed, but also to being entangled. This certainly seems a fitting description of the narratives of women being released from prison. I do not use this term to portray participants as incapable of understanding their situations. They had nuanced theories about how they became caught, as it were, in the punishment system. But the meaning of perplexity as entangled allows us to see both the ways that formerly imprisoned folks represented themselves as ensnared by various systems and also how they attempted to make sense of the contradictory and bewildering logics of the system. These perplexing logics demanded that people take on contradictory framings of themselves in turn. Perplexity helps describe the way that seemingly contradictory discourses operate simultaneously within the punishment system. Formerly imprisoned women are expected to simultaneously be rational, entrepreneurial subjects and deserving victims in need of intervention. The convergence of these two expectations is mirrored at a broader level in the reentry discourses that circulate in Minnesota. In Minnesota, neoliberal and more welfarist rationalities come together. That

---

13. Gordon, *Keeping Good Time*. 100–101.

convergence can also be seen in the way that formerly imprisoned women narrated their lives. Negotiating the dual expectation to be rational, entrepreneurial subjects and deserving (properly gendered) victims requires a delicate and complex maneuvering.

The way that Tiffany had to go to prison to "get free" is perplexing and it was clear in talking to her that she was perplexed by the fact that "choosing prison" was the most effective way to disentangle herself from the punishment system. Tiffany stated, "When I got out and went to my parole officer, I thought well 'maybe it would be easier for me to stay in prison.' But then that's more confinement." Tiffany's perplexity asks prison activist scholars to take a more complex approach to subjectivity.

The "empowering prison" model of MCF-Shakopee was perplexing for me as a prison abolitionist researcher. Prisons are contradictory and perplexing institutions. MCF-Shakopee is particularly perplexing because of its unique empowerment focus as compared with the majority of U.S. prisons. Increasingly, as mainstream criminologists lament the obvious failure of the mass imprisonment binge, the palatability of imprisonment is shored up by bringing the rehabilitative ideal back in and framing the prison as a potential site of liberation.[14] In working through this research, I found myself entangled, caught, and perplexed by the ways in which relations of power are reinscribed through the research process. How do we interrupt the ease with which penal logics contain and constrain the potential of activist scholarship? In "Material Consumers, Fabricating Subjects," Ramamurthy encourages "the scholar-critic to recognize herself also as a subject-in-perplexity," entangled in the very material and discursive structures as her research participants. This means that activist scholars must disrupt the unified, modernist subject both in how imprisoned people are represented as well as in the ways that we, as authors, come into the writing ourselves. Through this redefinition, of ourselves as also "subjects-in-perplexity," we might ally ourselves with other subjects-in-perplexity to "open up the possibility for democratic conversations about what it is we desire for each other and ourselves"[15]

---

14. Byrd, "Punishment's Twin."

15. Ramamurthy, "Material Consumers, Fabricating Subjects," 543.

I found that participants simultaneously framed themselves as responsible, choice-making subjects, and as vulnerable to abuse and exploitation because of a lack of options resulting from their gendered status as felons. Subjectivities are not fixed or singular. Formerly imprisoned women "exceed always their singular inter-pellation" within discourses of punishment.[16] Their subjectivities exceed the bounds of penal discourses, neoliberal rationalities, and representations of prisoners as always resisting in particular, convenient ways. Former prisoners take up and add on to penal discourses in contradictory ways in order to navigate bureaucracies and maintain their personhood. Sometimes the most potent method of resistance is to insist on one's humanity within the vocabularies within which that humanity can be intelligible.

(RE)PRODUCING DISPOSABILITY

Another significant finding of this study is that the barriers attached to felony status often (re)produce the very vulnerability expected in accounts of imprisoned women's lives. The barriers facing returning prisoners often produce or at least increase their vulnerability to exploitation and abuse by others in the community. In the academic literature on women in prison, these vulnerabilities are often located within the individual, as opposed to the system as a whole.[17]

Difficulty in finding work is one facet of this increased vulnerability. Nadine, a twenty-nine-year-old African American woman, discussed experiencing sexual harassment and abuse while working in telemarketing. Nadine related that the abuse was a continuation of a longer history of trauma. Her father, who had introduced her to crack cocaine, attempted to abuse her while high. Nadine related the story about her father as one where she had some agency, saying, "I was a fighter. I fought him off. It was still traumatic though." In relating this to the harassment and abuse she faced in the workplace, Nadine's narrative shows a much greater feeling of powerlessness. Nadine stated that she "had to stay." Despite wanting to leave the telemarketing job, she stayed because of the conditions

16. Ibid., 543.
17. Sudbury, *Global Lockdown*.

of her parole: "I couldn't change jobs. I didn't think I was gonna get a new job quick enough if I left. They said I had to keep a job if I was gonna stay outside [of prison]."

Tracy, a Native American woman in her thirties, related a similar situation. Tracy's boss refused to pay her unless she had sex with him. In her interview, Tracy said that she had doubts about whether her boss really had the power to stop her payroll check from being dispersed. However, the centrality of employment to demonstrating successful reintegration and the difficulty finding work with a criminal background made formerly imprisoned people more likely to remain in situations where their safety was threatened.

Employment discrimination is one of the most cited barriers facing formerly imprisoned people. In almost every state, private employers can legally deny jobs to people on the basis of a criminal conviction. Additionally, most states allow employers to discriminate on the basis of a past arrest even if a person was never convicted.[18] In recent years, a "ban the box" movement has gained more attention. Referring to the box on applications that asks whether one has been arrested and/or convicted of a crime, prison activist Susan Burton says, "It's not only [on] job [applications] . . . . It's on housing. It's on a school application. It's on welfare applications. It's everywhere you turn."[19] Former prisoners are often denied professional licenses, even if their conviction is unrelated to their professional obligations. Globalization and the accompanying process of deindustrialization in the United States have eliminated many of the jobs that former prisoners would be most likely to obtain, such as manufacturing jobs. Former prisoners are much less likely to be hired for retail positions, which represent a large number of low-skilled jobs, because they require continual contact with the public and often access to cash registers, etc.

Participants suggested that employers viewed them as easy targets. As Nadine articulated, "he thought he could treat me any way he wanted because I am a felon. He [her supervisor] used to say 'where else you gonna work? This is a good deal.'" Racialized

---

18. Michelle Alexander, *The New Jim Crow: Mass Incarceration in the Age of Colorblindness,* revised edition (New York: The New Press, 2012).

19. Gene Johnson, "'Ban The Box' Movement Gains Steam," *Wave Newspapers,* August 15, 2006.

and gendered relations of ruling produce the view of former prisoners as disposable.[20] The ascription of criminality onto the bodies of people of color has been central to racial formation throughout U.S. history.[21] Prisons are race-making institutions and white supremacy is central to how mass imprisonment and the supposed disposability of prisoners are rendered palatable.[22] As Angela Davis writes, "Ideologies of sexuality—and particularly the intersection of race and sexuality—have had a profound effect on the representations of and treatment received by women of color within and outside of prison."[23] There is nothing natural about the idea that formerly imprisoned people are disposable. The barriers attached to felony status enable this idea and (re)produce the exploitation and abuse faced by formerly imprisoned women. What I want to suggest is that the women's vulnerability here is produced and reproduced, in part, by discriminatory policies that exclude them from full citizenship, but also importantly by the representation of them as vulnerable. The idea that the women are disposable structures their exclusion from employment, housing, and social services. But it also reproduces more vulnerability whether from a predatory employer or someone else in the community. When Nadine's boss says, "Where else you gonna work," he is reiterating a broader idea that she is disposable as a formerly imprisoned woman of color and using it to further her disposability. The pathologizing representations of people in women's prisons produces the very vulnerability we expect based on the representation.

20. Dorothy E. Smith, *The Everyday World As Problematic: A Feminist Sociology* (Boston: Northeastern University Press, 1989).

21. Mass imprisonment in the United States cannot be explained without reference to racial formation and gendered rationalities. Mass imprisonment is *a racial project*, "simultaneously an interpretation, representation, or explanation of racial dynamics, and an effort to reorganize and redistribute resources along particular racial lines." Michael Omi and Howard Winant, *Racial Formation in the United States: From the 1960s to the 1990s* (London: Routledge, 1994), 56. Michael Omi and Howard Winant theorize the concept of racial projects to think through the smaller building blocks of the more general process of *racial formation*, which they define as "the sociohistorical process by which racial categories are created, inhabited, transformed, and destroyed"; ibid., 55. Despite the prominence of color-blind ideology, race remains a salient category of analysis.

22. Loïc Wacquant, "From Slavery to Mass Incarceration: Rethinking the 'Race Question' in the US," *New Left Review* 13 (January–February 2002): 41–60.

23. Angela Y. Davis, *Are Prisons Obsolete?* (New York: Seven Stories Press, 2003), 79.

In addition to being more vulnerable to employers, the vulnerability of participants was increased because of the barriers they faced in obtaining housing. Participants articulated living with family and friends, despite abuse, drugs, and other problems, because they felt that they had nowhere else to go. Housing discrimination is a particularly devastating barrier for formerly imprisoned people. One of the first questions a released prisoner must face is where she will stay. Housing within the private housing market can be difficult for someone with a felony conviction. Background checks are a routine part of the rental application process. Unless a former prisoner has substantial financial resources, so as to reassure a private landlord, it can be difficult to find housing. Additionally, public housing can present many barriers. Federal law bars many people with felony convictions from eligibility for public housing, Section 8 voucher lists, and project-based Section 8, particularly former prisoners with drug convictions, histories of violence, or who are registered sex offenders.[24] While in recent years, reentry reformers at the federal level have sought to "educate" former prisoners about their eligibility for subsidized housing, the degree to which former prisoners are screened out of housing programs is underestimated and rarely acknowledged.[25] People with felony convictions who are technically *eligible* for public housing are still often screened out of project-based Section 8 sites that are run by private housing developers and HUD-funded programs that want to "keep their numbers up" by choosing only the most likely to be successful.[26] The families of former prisoners are often reluctant to allow a returning prisoner to stay with them for fear that they will be evicted and lose their HUD-funded housing.[27]

---

24. Jeremy Travis, Amy L. Solomon, and Michelle Waul, "From Prison to Home: The Dimensions and Consequences of Prisoner Reentry," Washington, DC: Urban Institute, 2001.

25. Federal Interagency Reentry Council, *Reentry Myth Buster: On Public Housing* (New York: National Reentry Resource Center, 2011), available at nationalreentryresourcecenter.org.

26. This claim is based on my experience as a housing advocate in a HUD-funded program, as well as my interviews with former prisoners. Additionally, in my fieldwork, Department of Corrections officials also recognized and articulated this problem of "creaming the crop."

27. Travis, Solomon, and Waul, "From Prison to Home."

Sandra, a Native American woman who was imprisoned for four years in MCF-Shakopee, reported experiencing constant housing instability. She stated,

> While I was there [in the sober living house], the owner foreclosed on the house. That was another shock. I was like "Wow I'm homeless again." I ended up back at the shelter. I was worried and I was scared. I didn't want to sleep outside. [With] the shelter, you have to call every night to get a bed. The doors open at 6 pm, but you never know whether you'll get a bed. That was scary. There was a time when I had to sleep in like a stairwell. That was embarrassing. You wake up feeling dirty and have to wonder "where am I going to wash up, where am I going to clean." You sleep with one eye open when you're sleeping in stairwells or under stairs. It's a struggle when you don't have housing.

This housing instability resulted in increased vulnerability on a number of fronts. At the time of our interview, Sandra was primarily staying with a cousin. She reported, "I'm living with a cousin. That's not working out well. I gave her three months' rent. My phone bill is $50 a month. So, I'm left with about $30 a month. Something's gotta change. Something's gotta give." She went on to say, "It's scary. I have no one to turn to, nowhere to go. My mom, my sister. There's no one left. I wish she was here, my mom, I could use somewhere to sleep. It's really hard being homeless. Everyone else is dead or in prison, so I'm out here alone." Sandra described her cousin's house as a problematic environment because it triggered her posttraumatic stress disorder (PTSD), and was a challenge in maintaining her sobriety:

> I'm always doing what I can to keep myself safe. I'm always looking ahead, looking around. There was a lot of abuse in my childhood. My mother. She was an alcoholic. There was a lot of verbal abuse, psychological abuse. There were attempts on me [attempts at sexual abuse] by uncles and strangers. Because mom was an alcoholic, there were parties, people around. It's kind of like the house I'm livin' in now. People everywhere. You got strange men coming in here. I'm not happy with the environment that I'm in.

Sandra was clear about not wanting to remain in her current living situation. She reported constant drugs and alcohol in the house, which made sobriety difficult. Additionally, the number of people, particularly strangers, triggered her PTSD. However, without somewhere else to go, she decided to stay. In order to maintain her sobriety and her housing, Sandra stayed to herself, "I just stay in my room. That's how I stay sober."

Our analysis of housing insecurity must be moved out of an individualizing frame and situated within the context of post-WWII shifts in housing. During the Second World War, transient populations became increasingly less common. Home ownership emerged as an important emphasis for middle-class families and "prosperity's discontents" became largely confined to "Skid Rows," living in single room occupancy dwellings (SROs).[28] During the sixties and seventies, urban redevelopment schemes and the idea of "revitalizing" neighborhoods facilitated the demolition of skid row districts and the SROs began to decrease in number.[29] The elimination "of this form of housing had both immediate and long-term effects—immediate in the displacement of residents and long-term in the erosion of a form of private housing on which future populations in need of low-cost shelter could no longer depend."[30] Individual experiences of housing insecurity must be understood within this wider context of political, social, and economic shifts. Deindustrialization, the withdrawal of the social safety net, and neoliberal political rationalities produce homelessness and housing insecurity.

Sandra also reported being more vulnerable to sexual assault because of her housing instability. She decided to store her most important possessions (her social security card, birth certificate, and a new pair of shoes) with a friend because he had the most stable housing of anyone she knew. On occasion, she went to his

---

28. Kim Hopper, "Homelessness Old and New: The Matter of Definition," *Housing Policy Debate* 2, no. 3 (1991): 755–813; Craig Willse, "Neo-Liberal Biopolitics and the Invention of Chronic Homelessness," *Economy and Society* 39, no. 2 (2010): 155–84.

29. James D. Wright and Beth A. Rubin, "Is Homelessness a Housing Problem?" *Housing Policy Debate* 2, no. 3 (1991): 937–56.

30. Willse, "Neo-Liberal Biopolitics," 161–62.

house when her cousin's home became unbearable or when she was staying in a shelter. Regarding this friend, she said,

> You know you do get tired when you're out there. They kick you out of the shelter at seven in the morning and you know, where are you going to go at that time in the morning? Maybe I can sneak a blanket out and go lay in the park. But you've got to find the right park. It's rough. Men think that if you're in their house, they are entitled to touch you. I haven't come across a respectful man yet. And its really hard you know. I try not to exchange sex for, you know, a room or whatever. That's not me. I'm just not interested in men, period. He was trying to fondle me. He knows I have nowhere to stay.

Sandra felt that she had no options for housing. She repeatedly applied for public housing and was denied because of her criminal background. She described her life as constantly "bouncing around" between the shelter, her cousin's house, and this male friend's house. However, she remained hopeful that she would turn things around, stating, "I'm strong. I'm very strong. I haven't allowed this stuff to break me." She attempted to keep her days filled with Alcoholics Anonymous meetings, outpatient drug treatment, therapy, and other appointments in order to avoid being imprisoned again or experiencing abuse and exploitation. While participants described their lives as difficult prior to imprisonment, the barriers attached to felony status exacerbated and increased their vulnerability to abuse and exploitation.

In order to understand Sandra's story, an analysis of settler colonialism in Minnesota is necessary.[31] For Native communities, housing insecurity, addiction, and violence are part of the everyday life of being a colonized people.[32] As one participant in the

---

31. Minnesota is home to seven Ojibwe and four Dakota reservations. As a result of relocation policies and the poverty on reservations, Minneapolis has a large Native American population. John Poupart et al., *Searching for Justice: American Indian Perspectives on Disparities in Minnesota Criminal Justice System* (St. Paul, MN: American Indian Policy Center, 2005). In some neighborhoods in the Twin Cities (for example, the Phillips area, where the Little Earth housing project is located), over fifty percent of the population is Native American or American Indian.

32. It is also important to note Minnesota's long and vibrant history of Native American activism. The American Indian Movement (AIM) began in Minnesota

American Indian Policy Center's *Searching for Justice: American Indian Perspectives on Disparities in Minnesota Criminal Justice System* study asserts,

> Why do Indians go to jail? And that's basically from, that stems from almost three hundred years ago, from the culture. Think, what happened to our forefathers was a really bad thing, and through the generations have been traumas and traumas and traumas that have been carried over and carried over. And then multiplied by the shockwaves that came after that, which hit us bad in the boarding school days. I was from a boarding school myself—we're just now getting hit by that, let alone learning how to float through it, and get past it and deal with it—you know, how are we going to deal with this? What happened to our forefathers and what carried over all the way from them— about 275 years ago to now, and what's happened to us, that's the multiple factor and how are we gonna deal with that?[33]

Sandra's stories must be understood within this wider, collective context of colonial rule and the violence of wave after wave of U.S. policies through removal and termination to relocation. Additionally, the political and economic formation of settler colonialism is constituted by gender and sexual relations of ruling.[34] Sexual violence is not only a central feature of colonialism. Colonialism is "itself structured by the logic of sexual violence."[35] The sexual violence as well as the violence of housing instability faced by Sandra is part of a larger genocidal project. The supposed disposability of Sandra is connected to the theft of Native lands and natural resources.

How might we open up space for complex personhood even as we detail the ways that state violence operates through these

---

in the summer of 1968. Calls for revolution by AIM leaders drew the attention and violence of the FBI and CIA. The suppression of the movement, including the criminalization and imprisonment of important leaders, is still very much a part of the everyday life of the Native American community in the Twin Cities.

33. Poupart et al., *Searching for Justice.* 30

34. Scott L. Morgensen, "Theorising Gender, Sexuality and Settler Colonialism: An Introduction," *Settler Colonial Studies* 2, no. 2 (2012): 2–22.

35. Andrea Smith, "Not an Indian Tradition: The Sexual Colonization of Native Peoples," *Hypatia: A Journal of Feminist Philosophy* 18, no. 2 (2003): 70–85.

logics of disposability? State violence and its concomitant logics attempt to foreclose prisoner's humanity and justify their premature death.[36] An analysis of representation in this context is vital because it is central to the production of that disposability.

WORSE THAN PRISON

Field note (November 2010)—*My first visit to MCF-Shakopee was like nothing I could have anticipated. Yesterday, I received a call from the lawyer, Nancy, who took me to speak to the transitions class today. The transitions class is a course for women within three months of their release date. She told me that I could talk about housing services in the Twin Cities. I was prepared. I had collected applications for public housing, information on transitional housing programs, and emergency shelters. What I was unclear about was what to wear.*

When Nancy called me, I asked, "what can I wear?" She paused, silent on the phone. "What do you mean? Wear whatever you want." I persisted, "What can I not wear?" I thought maybe changing the phrasing would make my question clearer. She persisted, "Wear whatever you want." Looking back she must have thought I was pretty strange. Well, today I learned why. This morning, I drove to MCF-Shakopee, fully prepared to be turned away for wearing blue or an underwire bra, as one would be in a California prison. But, that's not what happened. I met Nancy in the parking lot and we entered the prison. It looked more like a middle school than any prison I had ever seen. When we entered the front door, I was instructed to put my purse in a locker and was given a visitor ID. Then I was led through a metal detector that the airport puts to shame. As we walked through another set of doors, I looked around confused. When were we going to go through security? My guide turned to me, "You just did."

We walked out into a courtyard, where women walked about in a large circle. There was no fence to keep them from escaping. Later a guard would turn to me and say, "we've only had a couple walk off the grounds in the last few decades, but they always come back."

---

36. Ruth Wilson Gilmore defines racism as "the state-sanctioned or extralegal production and exploitation of group-differentiated vulnerability to premature death." Ruth Wilson Gilmore, *Golden Gulag: Prisons, Surplus, Crisis, and Opposition in Globalizing California* (Berkeley: University of California Press, 2007), 28.

Participants in this study continually expressed that their reentry programs and facilities felt more like prison than did the actual prison, MCF-Shakopee. Shakopee is, as one Department of Corrections official told me, focused on "empowerment." During my fieldwork, this official told me, "At Shakopee, we are really all about empowering the women and giving them services."

Again and again in interviews, formerly imprisoned women articulated perplexity and confusion over their feelings upon release. Gwen, a thirty-three-year-old African American woman, stated, "I thought when I got out, I would feel free. But, they [reentry program staff] are worse than the guards. It feels like I won't ever get out. But I try to keep a positive attitude. They can say I'm lying even if I'm not, or nit-pick on the rules." Gwen felt like there were more programs and services within the prison than in her reentry program. Additionally, she articulated feeling like the prison staff had been more committed to her transformation than reentry program staff. Of the reentry program staff Gwen said, "They will be sleeping at the job when they should have been working . . . . The other lady caseworker, she lost my paperwork. I have to keep her on top of my paperwork. They don't care."

Betsy, a forty-six-year-old Native American woman, articulated this view of the reentry program, where she was living: "When I got there [transitional living house], it seemed a little bit too much like prison to me. It really feels like prison. We can't come out of our rooms. So, it is too much like prison." A number of participants characterized reentry facilities as "worse than prison." Shanice, a thirty-eight-year-old African American woman, described her time in a residential reentry facility:

> It was the worst place in the world. They treated us like crap. They promised they had groups [support and other life-skills groups] for us. I got out and they told me first that I could not hug my mom. I was like "are you serious?" I hadn't seen my mom in years. It was just a rule. You can't hug. Even in prison they let us hug. They had promised they had groups for us. I had really wanted a program with groups. So, I started doing the groups myself. I started group facilitating because if we weren't in group, we had to be in our rooms. And I thought, "this is worse than prison."

This participant eventually decided to leave this particular reentry facility and return to prison to finish her sentence. Shanice recalled, "I said 'I tell you what, I want to go back to prison.' I said 'prison treated me way better than you' and I chose to go back to prison than to be there. So, I went back to prison. They treated us like we was garbage." Shanice chose to serve the remainder of her sentence in prison, instead of remaining in this reentry program.

Tiana, a forty-three-year-old African American woman, said of a reentry facility in which she had lived,

> They just made you feel like trash. I felt like that's not what I'm here for . . . for you to humiliate me, or belittle me. I'm here to get myself better. I want to get the help I need. I already had negative feelings about myself. I didn't need another person making me feel bad. Getting out, I was already stayin' away from negative people that I used to deal with. I didn't need negative people running that place [the reentry facility]. I needed support. I didn't need them to keep kicking me. But they kept kicking me, you know? And I kept saying, "I'm going to end up using if I stay here."

Participants articulated feeling disrespected within many reentry facilities. They characterized reentry program staff as not genuine in their desire to help former prisoners. Participants continually expressed frustration with sitting in their rooms or being idle in reentry programs, which was different than their time in prison. Tiffany stated, "To lose your freedom, to be locked up in Shakopee. I was scared. But when I got there, it didn't look like a prison. At least there you can go to the library. Here, you just sit there. I don't praise prison. But, I did more positive things there. I learned how to work on a computer."

Of the six reentry facilities discussed with participants, the programming and policies of all facilities were overwhelmingly characterized by a focus on control and monitoring rather than rehabilitation. This reveals some interesting questions. What does it mean if reentry facilities felt more like prison than the actual prison? What sort of work is this assertion by the participants doing? The women interviewed for this research consistently articulated a desire to "get free," but where that vision could be realized was complicated by the way that the prison was shaped around a notion of empowerment, while reentry services were more focused on control, surveillance, and monitoring. There is something here about confronting the way that they are treated as disposable. Prison time was most often articulated as an event, which if they simply endured it, they would eventually get out. It was a fixed part of life that one simply had to choose to get through. It was being marked as a prisoner on the outside that produced perplexity.

The framing of MCF-Shakopee as an "empowering prison" produced the articulation of contradictory feelings and a sense of bewilderment within women's narratives. The dissonance between Shakopee's institutional framework as an "empowering prison" and disciplinary reentry programs produced confusion about where freedom could be obtained. The idea of an "empowering prison" is particularly insidious. It naturalizes prison as the proper place where women can get help because that support either does not exist or does not feel genuine on the outside. The development of surveillance-focused reentry programs, coupled with the prison's gender-responsive empowerment façade, shores up the palatability of state violence, masking the way that families and communities are torn apart. This highlights one instance of a larger shift in penal logics, whereby the prison is rebranded as a space of potential rehabilitation and empowerment.

CONCLUSION
"YOU REALLY CAN'T JUST KEEP SURFACING US"

In this essay, I have attempted to do justice to the conversations I had with formerly imprisoned women during my fieldwork: to negotiate the perplexity of representation, power, and subjectivity in the research encounter, while still saying something about the context of prisoner reentry as it is constituted in the Midwest. MCF-Shakopee is a unique penal institution in its seemingly benign focus on empowerment. It has no fence and nothing resembling the security of more punitive prisons. However, this is precisely why such an institution is vital to abolitionist intellectual and political work. This kind of reformist prison renaturalizes incarceration as a solution to social problems and fails to genuinely transform the logics of disposability at the heart of the prison industrial complex. Participants in this research still missed the funerals of loved ones, the milestones in their children's upbringing, and genuine opportunities for giving their gifts to the world. Surveillance-focused reentry programs provide a counter to this empowering prison model and this produces a dynamic where we are only left with the criminal punishment system's current imagination.

As a researcher and a prison activist most familiar with California's state prisons, Shakopee left me perplexed. I came to understand this perplexity as insidious and useful in shoring up the palatability of the prison. In a time where prison reform is going mainstream, abolitionist intellectuals must be cautious of the ways in which we are encouraged to accept seemingly empowering models such as this. We have to ask whether these are reforms that genuinely transform the logics that made mass imprisonment a legible project from the outset. The concept of subjects-in-perplexity, along with Avery Gordon's notion of complex personhood, point abolitionist intellectuals toward a more nuanced view of penal politics. This research points toward a politics of abolition where imprisoned and formerly imprisoned people are centered in the conversation, without requiring them to perform as unified, Cartesian subjects always resisting penal power in the ways that fit our analysis easily. Perhaps by sitting with the messiness of imprisoned people's and our own perplexity, we will develop the capacity for experimentation and ambiguity necessary for building a world without prisons.

The participants in this research allowed me to come into their lives and shared intimate aspects of their experience with me. It is possible that "doing justice" is foreclosed in a context where formerly imprisoned people are expected to be both victims and superhuman agents; rational subjects and the other in contradictory ways. Power is inherently exercised in the production of knowledge. Still, the voices of formerly imprisoned people must come to the center of critical work on prisoner reentry. As one participant, Tiana, stated, "The thing about women in prison is that there's things that go much deeper. You really can't just keep surfacing us and wondering why we keep committing crimes and stuff. You gotta do some deep sea diving."

REFERENCES

Alexander, Michelle. *The New Jim Crow: Mass Incarceration in the Age of Colorblindness.* Revised Edition. New York: The New Press, 2012.

Brown, Wendy. *States of Injury: Power and Freedom in Late Modernity.* Princeton, NJ: Princeton University Press, 1995.

Byrd, Renée. "'Punishment's Twin': Theorizing Prisoner Reentry for a Politics of Abolition." *Social Justice* 43, no. 1 (2016): 1–22.

Davis, Angela Y. *Are Prisons Obsolete?* New York: Seven Stories Press, 2003.

Federal Interagency Reentry Council. *Reentry Myth Buster: On Public Housing.* New York: National Reentry Resource Center, 2011. Available at nationalreentryresourcecenter.org.

Gilmore, Ruth Wilson. *Golden Gulag: Prisons, Surplus, Crisis, and Opposition in Globalizing California.* Berkeley: University of California Press, 2007.

Gordon, Avery. *Keeping Good Time: Reflections on Knowledge, Power, and People.* St. Paul, MN: Paradigm, 2004.

Gorz, André. *Strategy for Labor: A Radical Proposal.* Boston: Beacon, 1967.

Hopper, Kim. "Homelessness Old and New: The Matter of Definition." *Housing Policy Debate* 2, no. 3 (1991): 755–813.

Johnson, Gene. "'Ban The Box' Movement Gains Steam." *Wave Newspapers*, August 15, 2006. Available at news.newamericamedia.org.

Morgensen, Scott L. "Theorising Gender, Sexuality and Settler Colonialism: An Introduction." *Settler Colonial Studies* 2, no. 2 (2012): 2–22.

Omi, Michael, and Howard Winant. *Racial Formation in the United States: From the 1960s to the 1990s.* London: Routledge, 1994.

Petersilia, Joan. "Beyond the Prison Bubble." *Federal Probation* 75, no. 1 (2011): 26–31.

Poupart, John, John Redhorse, Melanie Peterson-Hickey, and Mary Martin. *Searching for Justice: American Indian Perspectives on Disparities in Minnesota Criminal Justice System.* St. Paul, MN: American Indian Policy Center, 2005. Available at prisonpolicy.org.

Ramamurthy, Priti. "Material Consumers, Fabricating Subjects: Perplexity, Global Connectivity Discourses, and Transnational Feminist Research." *Cultural Anthropology* 18, no. 4 (2003): 524–50.

Smith, Andrea. "Not an Indian Tradition: The Sexual Colonization of Native Peoples." *Hypatia: A Journal of Feminist Philosophy* 18, no. 2 (2003): 70–85.

Smith, Dorothy E. *The Everyday World As Problematic: A Feminist Sociology.* Boston: Northeastern University Press, 1989.

Sudbury, Julia, "From Women Prisoners to People in Women's Prisons: Challenging the Gender Binary in Antiprison Work." In *Razor Wire Women: Prisoners, Activists, Scholars, and Artists,* edited by Jodie Michelle Lawston and Ashley E. Lucas, 169–83. Albany: SUNY Press, 2011.

————, ed. *Global Lockdown: Race, Gender and the Prison-Industrial Complex.* London: Routledge, 2005.

Travis, Jeremy, Amy L. Solomon, and Michelle Waul. *From Prison to Home: The Dimensions and Consequences of Prisoner Reentry.* Washington, DC: Urban Institute, 2001. Available at urban.org.

Valentine, David. *Imagining Transgender: An Ethnography of a Category.* Durham, NC: Duke University Press Books, 2007.

Wacquant, Loïc. "From Slavery to Mass Incarceration: Rethinking the 'Race Question' in the US." *New Left Review* 13 (January–February 2002): 41–60.

Willse, Craig. "Neo-Liberal Biopolitics and the Invention of Chronic Homelessness." *Economy and Society* 39, no. 2 (2010): 155–84.

Wright, James D., and Beth A. Rubin. "Is Homelessness a Housing Problem?" *Housing Policy Debate* 2, no. 3 (1991): 937–56.

MASS INCARCERATION IS RELIGIOUS (AND SO IS ABOLITION)

A PROVOCATION

Joshua Dubler and Vincent Lloyd

THE UNITED STATES IS NOT JUST A NATION WITH AN ENORMOUS number of prisons. It is a prison nation. Carceral logics and effects pervade U.S. culture, including in the arguments we make and in the fear and fury we feel. Not all Americans are equally implicated, but none of us is untouched. Just as Clifford Geertz once read from a cockfight a set of collectively shared secrets endemic to and constitutive of Balinese culture, so too in the United States today, careful observers can witness the knot of pathologies rooted in our prisons, pathologies that are also endemic to the politics and culture outside the walls. Mass incarceration contributes to this culture and politics, and it depends on it. A cursory list of our carceral maladies would include racial inequities, brutal class conflict, the violence of rigid gender norms, broken health-care system, hollow rhetoric of rights, the management of bare life, and much more. For our nation the prison is an apt synecdoche, and there's no way to disentangle the part from the whole. For readers of *Abolition*, in asserting the preceding we are surely breaking little new ground.

Where we might stir you to surprise or resistance pertains to the issue of religion. Coastal elites and the media they control generally portray a country governed by fundamentally secular ideals, but the majority of our fellow citizens and noncitizens know better. We say this not to trot out statistics showing how many of us believe in God, or to venerate the vantage point of the marginalized millions who do. It is to make a more substantive claim about the ideals and values that motivate Americans to collective action. Namely, the spirit of religion fills to roughly the same degree even those of us who would never be caught dead in a church, so much so that we are subjects of this great and grotesque nation. American culture is soaked through with religious languages, practices, and themes: redemption, hope, love of neighbor, hate of other neighbor, beloved community, holy crusade. These and other religious tropes are woven into the national cultural fabric, and they furnish the tools by which Americans fashion selves and collectivities. This is true of those who comprise the ruling order, and it is equally if not *especially* true of those of us who struggle to dismantle that order. Considered in this way, religion then becomes a promise and a problem. In public, private, and in mass mediated spaces, elites frequently repress or carefully manage religion—just as they repress or carefully manage race, gender, sexuality, disability, immigration, and labor, so as to smoothly and seamlessly integrate these sites of potential disruption into the workings of power and flows of capital. To understand the United States as a prison nation—and to cure the maladies that afflict us—it is imperative that we understand the United States as a *religious* prison nation, and more specifically, as a *Christian* prison nation.

How to best approach the religiosity of our prison nation? One route would be to start at the beginning with the familiar story about the religious origins of the prison, the "penitentiary": a place for penance, a place for reform, a place for redemption. These themes endure, but in this brief intervention, we'd rather start with the present. What role does religion play in sustaining mass incarceration today? What role has religion played in underwriting the explosive growth of prisons over the last four decades? And most crucially, what role does religion have to play in destroying mass incarceration?

Three explanations currently circulate for the rise of mass incarceration, none of which accounts for religion in the least. Let's call these the race account, the politics account, and the economics account. First, and most seismically, is the framing of mass incarceration as perpetuating a racial caste system. It has been the pull of this political frame, as embodied most influentially in *The New Jim Crow* phenomenon, that has made "ending mass incarceration" a point of public conversation. Second, mass incarceration is sometimes framed as a political problem, a bipartisan project rooted in ill-conceived ideals and baked through with cynicism and expediency—a grand public works project collectively executed to the catastrophic detriment of the disenfranchised. At the national level, Nixon developed this game, Reagan and Bush perfected it, and after Michael Dukakis's shellacking, the Clintons went all in. In the third rendering, mass incarceration is a cunning adaptation to post-industrialization, a corporate and civic profit center and a method for managing an urban underclass. Correctional officers and private prison profiteers are the most obvious examples, but in countless ways the subjugated bodies of incarcerated people have become necessary fuel for keeping the wheels of the economy turning. These three explanations, sometimes in isolation, sometimes braided together, are the stories we tell about why mass incarceration happened and what mass incarceration is essentially about.

The critic Kenneth Burke writes of *terministic compulsion,* the power of compelling explanatory devices to cause those who avow them to stick to their guns, even to their own detriment. So it sometimes seems with the above comprehensive diagnoses. When ossified into ideologies, these blanket diagnoses have the tendency to stifle mass mobilization with their righteous defeatism. When we lash ourselves to the mast of an apocalyptic vision, in which good must confront evil without mercy, ameliorative measures like educating those who are incarcerated, improving prison conditions, restricting solitary confinement, or leveraging austerity politics to shutter a prison or two often seem woefully inadequate. Rather, it is said, we must deal with the depths of the problem: intransigent racism, the stranglehold of neoliberalism, a broken democracy. If these problems are not addressed, prison culture will remain undiminished; indeed, for every marginal "improvement," some as yet unimagined and more invidious mutation is sure to arise.

Needless to say, we are not unconcerned with systemic injustice on all fronts, including the racial, the economic, and the political. But for combatting prison culture in particular we propose an alternative approach. Yes, prison culture is tied to vexing, deep-seated problems, to original sins and systems of sacrifice. But where the primary mode of political engagement is ideology critique—of diagnosing the "real cause" of the problem—the possibility for large-scale movement building is limited. Moreover, as we can't resist but point out, this kind of ideological orientation is animated by a religious spirit, made plausible by background theological concepts of discernment and redemption. If only we can pierce the illusions and identify the right social evils, then we can exorcise the demon. Our souls (and bodies) might then live in peace, our collective soul might be redeemed.

We are suspicious of redemption narratives. We propose, rather, to actively and openly engage with that which—for worse and for better—is inextricable from American life: religious traditions, practices, affects, and communities. By bringing such engagement to analysis of and organizing against American prison culture, we might tap a reservoir of revolutionary resources, and in the process, radically expand our coalition. If it could be shown that religion was intimately involved in enabling exponential prison growth, then we might also imagine how religious languages, practices, and communities may be mobilized to abolish prisons. In this vision, religious communities need not be relegated to one coalition partner in a pragmatic, secular movement for prison reform (one that too often results in Pyrrhic victories). Rather, to the extent that religious dissent represents an essential component of the national cultural fabric, by "getting religion," contemporary abolitionism unleashes the potential to jar our prison nation. Just as religiously fueled abolitionists transformed the national conversation about slavery in the nineteenth century, so too today an abolitionism doused in religion may be able to revolutionize the public conversation about prisons, and energize the mass movement necessary for eviscerating America's prison culture.

What might a religious explanation for mass incarceration look like? Here's a gloss: At the same time the prison populations were beginning to explode a half century ago, American religious culture was also undergoing a dramatic transformation. Membership in liberal Protestant denominations began to nosedive; evangelical and agnostic affiliations shot up. More important than membership numbers was a shift in public discourse: henceforth, liberal Protestantism no longer formed the assumed backdrop of American political culture. Now, religion came to mean an individual's choice to believe—in a personal God or in no God at all. Before, religiosity pervaded American culture and God was thought to work through history. To do the collective work of God, to pursue divine justice, meant to make worldly laws more just—that was the political theology famously expounded not only by Martin Luther King, Jr. but also, for the first half of the twentieth century, by mainstream politicians of all stripes. Now, however, with the focus on personal conviction, divine justice no longer has a place in American politics. Religion's only place (to the extent that religion has a place) is in the individual's heart. If on the right, neoliberal economics and neoconservative foreign policy remained constitutive of an alleged divine plan (with pastors rallying the laity to vote accordingly), for liberals God absconded, and to complementarily malignant effect. For the precise duration of mass incarceration, progressive politics has been pursued on a purely secularist plane. For far too long, liberals have been tackling problems rather than pursuing higher ideals. What ideals remained have been hollowed out into thin slogans like Obama's "hope." Policy rules, and wonks and administrators are the only ones left at the table. To focus on ideals, and not policies, has become the purview of children and cranks. In such an impoverished landscape, justice as an abstract ideal ceded its existence to the criminal justice *system*. This system is now everything. Justice has come to mean little more than the proper functioning of the law. This being so, officers of the law—the police, most notably—come to be seen as gods on earth. The cult of law enforcement isn't merely pernicious; it is, in our view, downright idolatrous.

In short, America doesn't only have a prison problem, it has a religion problem. While prison culture is inadequately described without sufficient attention to economics, politics, and race, explanations that ignore religion are similarly incomplete. This knot of many strands is what "prison culture" signifies. On which string should we pull? The economic, the racial, and the political all have their promise, but so too, we argue, does the religious. As well, all four also have their perils.

American history is steeped in resources for thinking about divine justice and for interrogating worldly practices that run afoul of God's law. These religious resources have been essential to American culture, and they remain salient today even as loud professions of personal faith or personal disbelief drown them out. Even communities seemingly animated by evangelical or secularist commitments are formed by deep, old, rich currents of American religion with strong collectivist potential. It is these currents, these lower frequencies of American religious life to which we must attune ourselves today. The justice we want, the justice we need, is larger than ourselves. Now we must own it, testify to it, and enact it here on earth.

These are the frequencies of abolitionism: as it fought slavery, as it fought segregation, as it has fought patriarchy and homophobia, and as today it is beginning to fight not merely *mass* incarceration but incarceration as such. Like our abolitionist forbearers declared in the Prophet Isaiah's name: "to loose the chains of injustice and untie the cords of the yoke, to set the oppressed free and break every yoke"—this is what we will.

As Angela Davis has so persuasively argued, abolition is much more than the singular act of eliminating prisons. Just as America has a prison culture, America also has an abolition culture. Just as American prison culture is religious, American abolition culture is also religious. The spirit of abolition catalyzes social movements. It builds institutions for social democracy. It challenges and reshapes the ways of the world. It addresses concrete injustices but its vision exceeds the pragmatic. It is the spirit of John Brown and Nat Turner, Harriet Tubman and Frederick Douglass. To date, it has not sufficiently been the spirit of prison abolitionism. But herein lies the opportunity that we preach. We honor the Black Nationalists, Marxists, and other hard left thinkers and organizers who have made us who we are, and who have kept the abolitionist fire burning throughout this dark era of acute national disgrace. But it's time for a religious turn.

Today, we invite our comrades on the secular left to provincialize their secularism, just as we invite our religious sisters and brothers to transcend their reformism. We are not calling for abolition theology—whether you believe in God or don't believe in God isn't to us the important thing. We are calling for, rather, religion. In an expansive, critical, and practical sense, religion must be woven into the growing prison abolition movement. In righteous struggle, as spiritual revival, let us conjure together the spirit of abolitionism, and let us tumble the prison walls down.

REFERENCES

Anidjar, Gil. *Blood: A Critique of Christianity*. New York: Columbia University Press, 2014.

Dorrien, Gary. *The New Abolition: W.E.B. Du Bois and the Black Social Gospel*. New Haven, CT: Yale University Press, 2015.

Douglas, Kelly Brown. *Stand Your Ground: Black Bodies and the Justice of God*. Maryknoll, NY: Orbis, 2015.

Kahn, Jonathon, and Vincent Lloyd, eds., *Race and Secularism in America*. New York: Columbia University Press, 2016.

Ruggiero, Vincenzo. *Penal Abolitionism*. New York: Oxford University Press, 2010.

Sinha, Manisha. *The Slave's Cause: A History of Abolition*. New Haven, CT: Yale University Press, 2016.

Smith, Ted A. *Weird John Brown: Divine Violence and the Limits of Ethics*. Stanford, CA: Stanford University Press, 2014.

Taylor, Keeanga-Yamahtta. *From #BlackLivesMatter to Black Liberation*. New York: Haymarket Books, 2016.

Taylor, Mark Lewis. *The Executed God: The Way of the Cross in Lockdown America*. Minneapolis, MN: Augsburg Fortress, 2015.

OPIATE OF THE MASSES

Dan Tague

The many nuances associated with the dollar bill serve as an unrelenting source of inspiration for me as I fold the monetary engravings obsessively to reveal messages. These manipulated promissory notes take on new meanings as the messages are realized in the ready-made light of the U.S. currency. At the very core of this fiscal narrative is the tug-of-war between politics and the pursuit of happiness. This photo series offers a moment of reflection to further consider the good, bad, and the ugly in these portraits of a monetary centric world.

WE DON'T NEED NO EDUCATION

DESCHOOLING AS AN ABOLITIONIST PRACTICE

Sujani K. Reddy

THIS ESSAY COMES FROM THE GUT, ABOUT A SET OF CONCERNS THAT have both guided me and been a perpetual source of *dis*-ease as I continue to make my way to and through school. I am not here with answers, but instead am pursued by burning questions. The intensity of their flames might make it seem that everything I write actually ends with an exclamation point, when it is in fact also always shadowed by a question mark, the proper punctuation for the perennial question: "What is to be done?" What is to be done in the face of the contemporary crises engendered by neo-liberal capitalist imperialism as it manifests through the United States, an imperial nation that continues to form itself through modes of conquest, colonization, and white supremacy—both "at home" and abroad?

Opening with this question is not a way to obscure the fact that many are at work to oppose existing forms of oppression and exploitation. I write here in and through those efforts, with a particular eye to how dominant interests continue to shape current crises to their advantage.[1] I believe we need to keep a fluid account of what they are up to in order to mount effective opposition and build meaningful alternatives. The "we" in this case refers most specifically to those of us working at the nexus of scholarship and activism. Not all of us who do this are located within

---

1. To put it in overly simple terms: it is my understanding that "the crisis" that was once the aspiration of many leftists, with the belief that it would propel a resolution to the fundamental contradictions of capitalism, will not arrive. Instead, capital has turned perpetual crisis into its own raison d'être. I am here following interpretations of *this* crisis as they are found in works such as *To Our Friends*, released by the Invisible Committee in 2014. Invisible Committee, *To Our Friends*, trans. Robert Hurely (Boston: MIT Press, 2015).

the educational system, but my comments are geared primarily to those of us who are because I have found it inevitable, across the different kinds of projects that I have engaged in, that I butt my head up against the limits of this system as a means for liberation. By "this system" I mean obligatory education, consisting of kindergarten through twelfth grade as mandated by U.S. law, as well as higher education, particularly at the community college and undergraduate levels.

My analysis of obligatory education takes its cue from Ivan Illich's *Deschooling Society*, a book that I first stumbled upon while researching in the Brooklyn Public Library. The title was in their catalog but not in their stacks, kept instead in the basement along with other books that they deemed no longer useful enough to be in circulation but not worthless enough to actually throw away. In this manifesto, Illich outlines how the educational system in capitalist societies such as the United States (and indeed *especially* in the United States) is one that confuses process with product; conflating schooling with the acquisition of knowledge, and mistaking the acquisition of skills with their just, equitable, and even emancipatory utilization. He points out how, instead, the educational system in a capitalist society is geared toward class stratification and the maintenance of class privilege through capitalist exploitation. Illich wrote at a time when the school system divided pupils into those destined for vocational training and those on the path through liberal arts education to, possibly, professional graduate degrees. His divisions can account for the range of higher education, which spans community colleges to research-one universities, but it is actually kindergarten and the obligatory education of K–12 where his point is most clearly made that school is a, if not the, primary site for the reproduction of oppression and inequality. Of particular concern to Illich, writing at the dawn of the seventies, was how school became the first in a series of institutions that train individuals to become clients rather than autonomous agents. It was thus a primary gateway to an institutional web where "Medical treatment is mistaken for health care, social work for the improvement of community life, police protection for safety, military poise for national security, the rat race for productive work."[2] Of particular concern to me, here, is also how among these institutionalizations, school remains the primary place where the myth of meritocracy as a means for upward mobility remains lodged. *For most, schooling still represents the means of liberation within a system that nevertheless attempts to institutionalize us and our ambitions.*

In spite of the persistence of this promise, if we return our focus to the current conjuncture, what we find is an educational system that is clearly in crisis. Everything from the mass closing of public schools in major U.S. cities like Philadelphia and Chicago to the battles over standardized testing and the rise of corporatized charter schools and for-profit colleges indicates how this crisis provides an opportunity for the restructuring of education to fit the agenda of neoliberal capital. When it comes to college education we must also now account for the majority of students who are graduating with disastrous amounts of debt. The burden is so untenable that some have begun to publicly resist repayment.[3] I have also been in conversation with colleagues who feel that it is no longer ethical to support a structure that channels students into what scholar-activists such as Andrew Ross and Silvia Federici have identified as a new kind of indentured servitude.[4] To expand upon that concept we might also turn to the increasingly unstable workforce at colleges and universities, which has trickled upward (so to speak) to include teaching faculties made up more and more of part-time, temporary, and casual workers whose plight is being brought home to all of us through the brave organizing of adjuncts across the nation. The precarious position of both students and employees increases the likelihood of stress-related illnesses and the inability to access resources for adequate and timely healthcare. This is thus a matter not only of life and debt, but also of life and death. Indeed, it is a case of if not one, then probably the other.

---

2. Ivan Illich, *Deschooling Society* (London: Marion Boyers, 2002), 1. This is a reissue of the original 1971 edition.

3. James Cersonsky, "5 Ways Student Debt Resistance is Taking Off," *AlterNet*, October 25, 2013, available at alternet.org.

4. Andrew Ross, "NYU Professor: Are Student Loans Immoral?" *Daily Beast*, September 27, 2012, available at thedailybeast.com; Silvia Federici, "From Commoning to Debt: Financialization, Microcredit, and the Changing Architecture of Capital Accumulation," *South Atlantic Quarterly* 11, no. 2 (2014): 231–44.

Here I can turn to my own experience working at an elite private liberal arts college that guaranteed that its students did not have to take out loans. This was part of a long overdue push to diversify their student body, and the result has been a larger number of students of color and/or low-wealth students on campus who were not getting a degree in debt so much as a lesson in indebtedness. The latter formed a kind of backdrop for the backroom drama that was a regular occurrence in my office: streams of students of color (and most often women of color) depressed, contemplating dropping out, or on the verge of a nervous breakdown. Mental health, physical health, and social health were all at stake. The combination of dis-ease was such a regular occurrence that after years of mentoring students through such moments I actually found myself saying, repeatedly, "Well, at least you get to leave after four years. I'll still be here." The weight of their cumulative pain, as well as the kinds of marginalization that I also experienced institutionally, had led me to that utterance. The sentiment was not unattached to physical symptoms, either, as I had suddenly found myself developing new auto-immune issues.

Lest these symptoms be read as an idiosyncratic or individualized response, let us remember the studies that have appeared, periodically, pointing to the disproportionate rates of cancer and disease among women, women of color, and particularly Black women in the academy.[5] While there are many ways to explain this, what I want us to consider is the relationship between stress, the internalization of different forms of marginalization, and chronic or malignant (or both) physical manifestations.[6] My own recognition of this reality has led me to consider how debt and premature death structure higher education and how historically underrepresented communities—people of color, women, LGBTQ+ folk, and undocumented immigrants—bear a disproportionate share of both. What is more, these trends have taken root over precisely the same decades when colleges and universities have been

5. For more on this see, for example, the articles collected under the Feminist Wire Forum, "Take Care: Notes on the Black (Academic) Women's Health Forum," available at thefeministwire.com.
6. Gabor Maté, *When the Body Says No: Exploring the Stress-Disease Connection* (Hoboken, NJ: John Wiley, 2011).

opening their doors more widely, if incompletely, to historically underrepresented and underserved communities. This, then, is a picture of what we could term education in the post-civil rights United States.

And yet, the diversity that exists has also been the outcome of our insistent, persistent demands, even as these demands meet the dominant imperative to create and manage a multiracial middle class. We want more faculty and students from oppressed and marginalized groups because we are still woefully underrepresented. We want our histories, cultures, and ways of knowing included in the curriculum and supported so that we don't have to continuously fight for their upkeep. In this sense, ours is a demand for inclusion. But, for me, it also simultaneously raises the question of inclusion into what? As I have just outlined above, inclusion is killing us—literally. So, what are the alternatives? I used to believe that Black Studies, Asian/Pacific American Studies, Latinx Studies, and Native and Indigenous Studies (often lumped together under "Ethnic Studies") were the answer. Indeed, discovering Ethnic Studies, as a practice, is what kept me from dropping out of graduate school. For here were areas of study with storied roots in student-led social movements centered on a critique of the relationship between power and knowledge, and calling for a dialectical relationship between thought and action. What is the possibility for this kind of a demand to complicate inclusion as I have analyzed it? Is it sufficient to retain a critical edge as we collaborate to maintain our often precarious status as Ethnic Studies scholars and students in underfunded and almost always on the verge of dissolution programs and departments? I don't think so.

In fact, after many years of toeing something akin to that critical line (as I am even now doing to some extent), I have come around to the wise warnings issued by Fred Moten and Stefano Harney in *The Undercommons: Fugitive Planning and Black Study*, and by Robin D.G. Kelley in his introduction to "Black Study, Black Struggle" (written during another wave of student-led protests that hit college campuses across the nation over the past couple of years).[7] Part of their point is quite basic, actually. Critics

---

7. Stefano Harney and Fred Moten, *The Undercommons: Fugitive Planning & Black*

whose critique demands more of the institution than it currently gives continue to justify that institution's existence, and implicitly if not explicitly empower it as the necessary site of redress. *The system of higher education needs us to believe in it, and there is a way in which our protests can profess—willy-nilly—a kind of belief. In this sense critique leads to complicity.*

Consider this: I have built a career based on teaching Ethnic Studies courses that open up windows onto an interrogation of society and its structures and that explore, in thought and action, possibilities for social justice. Rarely has a semester passed when I haven't gotten a handful of students coming to me and asking their own version of the question, "What is to be done—and how can I do it?" In doling out advice I usually stress that each student work to fulfill their true talents, whatever they may be, and keep themselves connected to struggles for social justice. Liberation needs everyone to show up in all of our variety. During these conversations I am also very careful, because I am wary of producing a cadre of college-educated organizers who feed the nonprofit industrial complex that continues to corral social movements in the United States.[8] The point at which underrepresented college students return to work in their communities as part of this complex is also a point where the neoliberal privatization of social services meets the myth of meritocracy embedded in the U.S. educational system.

Let me approach this from another institutional angle, given the ways in which mass criminalization has become a hallmark of the post-civil rights United States. A key feature of this development has been a cradle-to-prison pipeline that systematically denies whole segments of society access to school. Confronted with this reality, toward the end of graduate school, I began to cross the lines between prisons, jails, and schools. I have since worked on developing curricula with men serving life sentences in a maximum security prison in Pennsylvania, taught a college course for credit at a local county jail that is also an Immigration

---

Study (New York: Minor Compositions, 2013), available at minorcompositions.info; Robin D.G. Kelley, "Black Study, Black Struggle: Opening the Debate," *Boston Review*, March 7, 2016, available at bostonreview.net.

8. INCITE! Women of Color Against Violence, ed., *The Revolution Will Not Be Funded: Beyond the Non-Profit Industrial Complex* (Cambridge, MA: South End Press, 2007).

and Customs Enforcement (ICE) detention center, and worked as an educator with the formerly incarcerated and individuals in alternatives to incarceration. In the last case, students came to the classroom either voluntarily (ex-prisoners) or because of a court mandate (alternatives to incarceration) in order to prepare for the high school Graduate Equivalency Diploma (GED). I don't wish to deny the very real sense of accomplishment (especially among ex-prisoners) or punishment (especially for those with court mandates) that people felt as they worked in this setting. Many of us, however, labored under the knowledge that the GED is, in some sense, a failing proposition. It does not get its holder that much more than life without it would. Its promise lies in the possibility that it *might* become a stepping stone into a system that is, ultimately, set up to fail the majority of individuals and communities who have become wards of the state through the prison-industrial complex. So, in the face of all of this, I have found myself calling not only for us to abolish the prison-industrial complex but also to de-school society.

Now, am I being too harsh? If so, it is on purpose and as a means to be provocative. As someone who has been in the school system for longer than it should perhaps be legal, I am hardly in a position to tell anyone not to pursue their GED, attend community college, or get a college degree if that is what they have the desire and means to do. Nor am I here to deny that even in the face of debt and death, a college education might be able to provide access to needed resources. But it should be clear from the structure of our society as it stands that at best this will bring up an individual or an individual family, and leave whole communities behind. In fact, acculturation within the system of education is often a means for students to become estranged from their communities of origin. This was, in effect, the lesson that was underscored for me at the aforementioned liberal arts college. At the root of so many a student's dilemma was the simultaneous weight of collective responsibility and the cultural separation engendered by a college education. Lest we attribute this malaise too exclusively to the post–civil rights making of a multiracial middle class, we would be wise to remember the role that Indian boarding schools have had in cultural genocide and the breaking apart of indigenous families and communities. *Naming the relationship between education and settler colonization is critical, particularly given the way in which school curricula promotes a national culture characterized by an amnesia that enables the continuous reproduction of settler colonialism and its social, political, economic, cultural, biological, and spiritual brutality.*

My essay has, in some sense, now reached a point of no return. Centering indigenous sovereignty undoes the project of capitalist imperialism as it has taken shape through the white settler colonial nation-state. And yet it is at this very point that the project of undoing this unholy alliance begins to unravel in my mind. This unraveling has less to do with acquiescence to a system whose goal is to debt us to death, and more to do with being tired of focusing on already existing forms of dominant power in a way that reinforces them. This is again me butting my head up against a wall where critique can be a form of complicity. Lest this lead down a road of despair, I want to first recognize that for me, what we call Ethnic Studies did not actually start with the student led social movements at the dawn of what I have been calling the post–civil rights United States. To start there is to center educational institutions as the beginning and end of our horizon. *Instead, I want to remember that inasmuch as Ethnic Studies bears a relationship to the long histories of our communities, our cultures, and our ways of knowing, it has its roots in practices that were and are antithetical to the institutions of capitalist imperialism. It is in the ongoing struggle to maintain indigenous epistemologies and cosmologies; it is with the enslaved who taught themselves to read against the master's will; it is with the immigrants who were excluded and detained and who carved their voices into the walls of their holding cells; it is with the imprisoned whose quest for knowledge is self-led and oriented toward collective liberation; it is with the movements for migrant rights that work to link their struggle to ones for indigenous sovereignty.* This list is obviously not exhaustive, but just a beginning, a way to think about who we understand as having knowledge, and how we come to learn not simply skills that will lead to resources within a capitalist system but also ways of knowing that are inherently oppositional to that system. The question of ways of knowing is critical. Following the insights of Leanne Betasamosake Simpson, while specific to the context of Nishnaabeg intelligence, also allows me to see how the unraveling of my mind is perhaps also a way out of having been schooled in this system, and into new epistemologies.[9] This, then, is an attempt to reframe what we can understand as resources, and re-vision ourselves as having access to an abundance. It is also to recognize that efforts to de-school, while not always going under this particular moniker, are and have been ongoing.

But what about those of us who remain, in some way or other, working within the system as such? Here I want to turn to our capacity to practice small acts of marronage. In keeping with the proposition itself, I will proceed by being more suggestive than comprehensive or proscriptive as I reflect on how the practice of Ethnic Studies evolved for me and a small group of students at my last job. These were young people whom I had worked with over multiple semesters and years, both inside the classroom and outside as an advisor and fellow activist in local struggles around migrant justice and against mass criminalization. We were in a setting where institutional resources were available for "service learning." The college encouraged collaboration between faculty, students, and underserved communities who were not, until now, under its purview. It is important to recognize how this is a neoliberal manifestation of noblesse oblige for the ways in which it privatizes the distribution of resources and services that were once part of the purview of the state. Given this context, my student collaborators and I slowly but surely came to understand that the most meaningful forms of action for us came to be the ones that went under the radar—the ones that were sideways and slanted and drew upon the undercommons as so powerfully articulated by Harney and Moten. *We found ways to be in the institution but not of it, to not subordinate ourselves to its forms of recognition but instead to employ its resources in ways that were not legible or reducible to its designs or demands. We were not poster children; we were poachers.* Thus, I have already said too much and must leave the rest purposefully vague because publicity is precisely not the point. The question of whether or not we de-schooled Ethnic Studies is open. So too is the question of how

---

9. Leanne Betasamosake Simpson, "Land as Pedagogy: Nishnaabeg Intelligence and Rebellious Transformation." *Decolonization: Indigeneity, Education and Society* 3, no. 3: 1–25.

the undercommons relates to visions of abolition. What I want to leave you with, at this juncture, is simply a practice of diversity that is not a demand for inclusion so much as it is a call to diversity our tactics—as a strategy for survival.

REFERENCES

Cersonsky, James. "5 Ways Student Debt Resistance is Taking Off." *AlterNet*, October 25, 2013. Available at alternet.org.

Federici, Silvia. "From Commoning to Debt: Financialization, Microcredit, and the Changing Architecture of Capital Accumulation." *South Atlantic Quarterly* 11, no. 2 (2014): 231–44.

Feminist Wire Forum. "Take Care: Notes on the Black (Academic) Women's Health Forum." Accessed January 29, 2016. Available at thefeministwire.com.

Harney, Stefano, and Fred Moten. *The Undercommons: Fugitive Planning & Black Study*. New York: Minor Compositions, 2013. Accessed January 29, 2016. Available at minorcompositions.info.

Illich, Ivan. *Deschooling Society*. New York: Harper & Row, 1971.

INCITE! Women of Color Against Violence, ed. *The Revolution Will Not Be Funded: Beyond the Non-Profit Industrial Complex*. Cambridge, MA: South End Press, 2007.

Kelley, Robin, D.G. "Black Study, Black Struggle: Opening the Debate." *Boston Review*, March 7, 2016. Available at bostonreview.net.

Maté, Gabor. *When the Body Says No: Exploring the Stress-Disease Connection*. Hoboken, NJ: John Wiley, 2011. Originally published 2003.

Ross, Andrew. "NYU Professor: Are Student Loans Immoral?" *Daily Beast*. September 27, 2012. Available at thedailybeast.com.

Simpson, Leanne Betasamosake. "Land as Pedagogy: Nishnaabeg Intelligence and Rebellious Transformation." *Decolonization: Indigeneity, Education and Society* 3, no.3: 1–25.

The Invisible Committee. *To Our Friends*. Translated by Robert Hurely. Boston: MIT Press, 2015.

IF YOU WANT YOU CAN HAVE

Maya Weeks

I am interested in disrupting the status quo through everyday means. I use primarily found and salvaged materials to synthesize issues of pollution, climate change, gendered violence (e.g. how plastic pollution transmitted via water disproportionately affects women and girls), ocean acidification, and transnational police states in photographs, installations, and collage. As I work on relationships between humans and the environment with a focus on waste, some of my major preoccupations include water, ecosystems, and borders. I am currently working on a project about the gendered violence of marine debris considering both how the Great Pacific Garbage Patch exists in the cultural imagination and the material realities of marine pollution as byproduct of global capitalism.

anaturalhistoryofcolours.tumblr.com.

SOUTH AFRICAN
STUDENTS' QUESTION

REMAKE THE UNIVERSITY,
OR RESTRUCTURE SOCIETY?

Alexandre Publia (pseudonym)

FROM SOUTH AFRICA TO INDIA,[1] HONG KONG TO CHILE,[2] CANADA to the United Kingdom,[3] and California to Missouri and beyond,[4] student protests worldwide are at a crossroads. In October 2015, South African students led the "Fees Must Fall" protests, which culminated in a weeks-long national shutdown that halted approximately 10 percent tuition increases.[5] These were the largest protests since the 1976 Soweto Student Uprisings.[6] University students led thousands in a march on the national capitol.[7] In the Western Cape, students took over flagship universities, such as University of Cape Town (UCT) and Stellenbosch

---

1. Basani Baloyi and Gllad Isaacs, "South Africa's 'Fees Must Fall' Protests Are About More Than Tuition Costs," *CNN*, October 28, 2015, available at cnn.com; David Matthews, "Student Protests Trigger U-Turn in India over Scholarships," October 27, 2015, available at timeshighereducation.com.

2. Chleu Luu and Vivian Kam, "Hong Kong Student Leaders Spared Jail for Pro-Democracy Street Protests," *CNN*, August 15, 2016, available at cnn.com; Eva Vergara, "Chile Students Protest Corruption, Demand Education Reform," April 16, 2015, available at salon.com.

3. Rachel Lau, "Montreal Students March Against Austerity," November 5, 2015, available at globalnews.ca; Laura Hughes and Nicola Harley, "Students Clash with Police During Protest in Central London over University Fees," *The Telegraph*, November 4, 2015, available at telegraph.co.uk.

4. Sam Sanders, "California College Students Walk Out of Class to Protest Tuition Hikes," November 24, 2014, available at npr.org; Alia Wong and Adrienne Green, "Campus Politics: A Cheat Sheet," April 4, 2016, *The Atlantic*, available at theatlantic.com.

5. Normitsu Onishi, "South Africa Freezes Tuition Fees After Student Protests," *The New York Times*, October 23, 2015, available at nytimes.com.

6. "The June 16 Soweto Youth Uprising," May 21, 2013, available at sahistory.org.za.

7. Bogani Nkosi, "#FeesMustFall Takes Fight to Union Buildings," *Mail & Guardian*, October 23, 2015, available at mg.co.za.

A WOMAN HOLDS UP A PROTEST SIGN READING "1976?"
DURING SOUTH AFRICA'S 2015 OCTOBER FEES MUST FALL PROTESTS.
MEDIA CREDIT: IMRAAN CHRISTIAN AND RHODES MUST FALL.

University (SU).[8] They even attempted to shut down Cape Town International airport.[9]

Nearly a year later, students continue to protest and demand more than free education.[10] They endure despite widespread suppression of protests, through expulsions and trumped-up charges.[11] Assaults and property damage occurred from confrontations with security forces.[12] Many security personnel were private contractors.[13] South Africa's university students have asked the critical question that underlies all student-led and education-focused protests, and that Californians and students across the United States must also ask ourselves: How far must we go? Must we focus on the more achievable, shorter-term project of transforming our schools? Or, must we focus on the more ambitious, longer-term project of remaking our societies?

---

8. Babalwa Quma, "UCT Students Occupy Bremner Building," October 19, 2015, available at livemag.co.za; Nicolette Dirk, "Activists Removed as Protest Spreads to CPUT," October 21, 2015, available at iol.co.za.

9. Zenzile Khoisan, "UWC Students, Cops Clash Near Airport," October 24, 2015, available at iol.co.za.

10. Ahmed Essop, "Decolonisation Debate Is a Chance to Rethink the Role of Universities," August 16, 2016, available at theconversation.com.

11. Jane Duncan, "#FeesMustFall: A Question of Human Rights Violations," *Mail & Guardian*, November 9, 2015, available at mg.co.za.

12. Geoffrey York, "South African Tuition Protests Turn Violent as Police Use Stun Grenades on Students," *The Globe and Mail*, October 21, 2015, available at theglobeandmail.com.

13. Masa Kekana and Ziyanda Ngcobo, "HRC Asked to Investigate Brutality by UJ Security Guards," *Eyewitness News*, November 9, 2015, available at ewn.co.za.

Universities

- University of the Witwatersrand
- University of Cape Town
- Rhodes University
- Stellenbosch University
- University of Fort Hare , Alice Campus
- University of the Free State
- Cape Peninsula University of Technology
- University of Pretoria
- University Of Johannesburg
- University Of Western Cape
- University of Limpopo
- University Of KwaZulu Natal
- North West University Library

MAP SHOWING CITIES ACROSS SOUTH AFRICA WHERE UNIVERSITIES WERE ENTIRELY SHUT DOWN BY FEES MUST FALL PROTESTS
(MEDIA CREDIT: P. KIM BUI)

The Rhodes Must Fall collective (RMF), which is overwhelmingly led by marginalized, Black university students, has demanded more than institutional "transformation." Instead, they have consistently demanded total "decolonization": a radical abolition and reimagination of entire social structures. RMF has refused shallow reforms to fundamentally colonial, Eurocentric, and anti-Black institutions. They have repeatedly called out universities' corporate lip service and empty promises over twenty years of negligible change.[14] They have highlighted the connections of universities to military-industrial complexes, and attacked the way that universities and Global North firms remain dependent upon the exploitation of Black labor. RMF's radical demands and their strategy of aiming beyond academia has led the way in raising consciousness about South Africa's and other postcolonies' negligible social and economic transformations. By addressing neoliberalization and corporatization of universities in a frame of colonial violence against Black and LGBTQ+ bodies, students have raised larger questions of neoliberal governance by white-owned, global capital.

RMF has consistently alleged that, in the current neocolonial/neoliberal system, wealthy, elected, multiracial elites have simply replaced the former, unelected, all-white, apartheid-era

---

14. Karen MacGregor, "Higher Education in the 20th Year of Democracy," April 27, 2014, available at universityworldnews.com.

elites. Both pre- and post-apartheid governments are beholden to white-owned, global capital. Because of, and not in spite of, such radical, ambitious claims, RMF inspired South African students to demand more, protest longer, include more stakeholders, and ultimately achieve more of their goals. In doing so, they have highlighted the global predicament of neoliberalism and so-called postcolonialism, and they have significantly changed the conversations around not only education but also around public services, racism, democracy, and social movements. Other university students, like those in California and across the United States, have much to learn from RMF.

FROM "RHODES MUST FALL" TO "FEES MUST FALL" TO "THE DEATH OF A DREAM"

How, and how much, has RMF succeeded? While students have indisputably changed the conversation and won short-term victories, more than a year of direct actions, demonstrations, and occupations have endured increasing suppression. By the time of October's Fees Must Fall, most of South Africa's universities had been primed by RMF for larger protests that would move beyond the confines of the universities and into the communities and towns around them. By 2015, South African students were exasperated by slow and exploitative university bureaucracies, as well as by elected but unresponsive Student Representative Councils (SRCs).

RMF formed in March 2015 when marginalized students led protests with a clear, immediate demand: removal of a statue to Cecil Rhodes from the center of UCT's campus.[15] RMF's success with the statue, and their proudly radical and transgressive tactics, inspired and directly contributed to a renewal of other student protest groups.[16] In April, Open Stellenbosch (OS) emerged.[17] OS was led by students at the even more unequal and segregated Stellenbosch University (SU), located near Cape Town in Stellenbosch—the

---

15. "UCT Rhodes Must Fall Mission Statement," March 22, 2015, available at uncensoredvoice.blogspot.com.

16. Ra'eesa Pather, "Rhodes Must Fall: The Movement after the Statue," *The Daily Vox*, April 21, 2015, available at thedailyvox.co.za.

17. Open Stellenbosch. "Statement Following Demonstration Who Belongs Here?"

historic "cradle of apartheid."[18] OS demanded major reforms to actually address endemic institutional racism, beginning with all classes being available in English, not Afrikaans.[19]

In July, the Marikana Commission Report exonerated all government officials, exacerbating national tensions.[20] In August, as the school year resumed, RMF seized the moment and escalated dramatically through evocative demonstrations about persistent anti-Blackness, evidenced by the Marikana Massacre.[21] RMF highlighted negligible gains for Black students and South Africans with a transgressive campaign of graffiti- and performance art-based demonstrations that demanded students, administrators, and community members all "Remember Marikana," largely by comparing it to the 1960 Sharpeville Massacre.[22] Furthermore, RMF highlighted universities' involvement, through board seats and investments, with Global North firms that remain dependent upon overwhelmingly Black labor for dangerous, underpaid, and degrading forms of labor—like mining.

Backlash increased against students who supposedly should have been satisfied by the removal of UCT's Rhodes Statue, and whose protests were increasingly disrupting business as usual. As graffiti and other forms of transgression increased, outspoken faculty began dismissing as "ideological essentialising" RMF's "attacks on liberalism."[23] Many white faculty and students refused to consider how or why students were becoming increasingly transgressive when faced with increasing oppression. RMF's unashamedly pro-Black attacks on UCT's anti-Blackness transgressed

April 15, 2015, accessed September 10, 2016, available at facebook.com.

18. "The Ivory Tower Is Too White," *The Economist*, December 5, 2015, available at economist.com.

19. Open Stellenbosch Collective, "Op-Ed: Open Stellenbosch—Tackling Language and Exclusion at Stellenbosch University," *Daily Maverick*, April 28, 2015, available at dailymaverick.co.za.

20. "Main Findings and Recommendations from the Marikana Inquiry," July 1, 2015, available at actsa.org.

21. On August 16, 2012 police opened fire on striking miners in Marikana, North West Province, killing thirty-four and seriously injuring seventy-eight people.

22. Rhodes Must Fall, "#RhodesMustFall—Media Statement—Marikana Campaign," August 18, 2015, accessed September 10, 2016, available at facebook.com.

23. Rebecca Hodes, "Op-Ed: How Rhodes Must Fall Squandered Public Sympathy," *Daily Maverick*, August 20, 2015, available at dailymaverick.co.za.

RMF PROTESTERS BLOCK A UCT ENTRANCE WITH A BANNER FEATURING AN IMAGE
OF A MURDERED MARIKANA MINER WITH STRIKE LEADER MGCINENI "MAMBUSH" NOKI."
(MEDIA CREDIT: EYEWITNESS NEWS AND RHODES MUST FALL)

established norms of respectable, slow, and ineffective bureaucracy-based change, which the most marginalized students were no longer accepting.

Between August and October, drawing on the success and controversy of RMF and OS, many other universities and students increased their protests. Because of RMF, critiques increasingly became about anti-Blackness, white supremacy, Eurocentrism, abolition, decolonization, and radical change, instead of past acceptance of incremental change espoused by political parties.

With RMF and OS leading the way, university students educated the public on social systems of exploitation and oppression, both online through widely circulated documentaries and opinions, as well as in the streets.[24] Performative, transgressive, and ostensibly radical tactics blazed a trail by aggressively denouncing the persistent Eurocentrism and anti-Blackness at ostensibly democratic and meritocratic institutions, like universities.

The targets of their protests included, but were not limited to:

- Increasing privatization and exclusivity of universities, especially the wealth and power of elite populations within academia;

---

24. Greg Nicolson, "Luister: The Viral Film Exposing South Africa's Ongoing Racism Problem," *The Guardian*, September 7, 2015, available at theguardian.com.

- White supremacy and cultural hegemony, manifested through universities' Eurocentric epistemologies, methodologies, monuments, language policies, and hiring practices;
- Outsourcing of service jobs, disproportionately impacting Black and women laborers;
- White-owned, global capitalist hegemony dependent upon connections between universities and Global North extractive, security, and financial firms;
- The marginalization of intersectionality, Black Feminism, and LGBTQ+-identified people and women within universities and historical social movements.

By October 2015, when many universities announced tuition increases of approximately 10 percent, the kindling for a wildfire of social movements had been laid by RMF; the exorbitant increase was the spark for the fire. Over two weeks of massive, militant, occupation- and demonstration-based protests forced President Zuma and Higher Education Minister Nzimande to cancel planned increases.[25] Despite some premature claims that "Fees Have Fallen," RMF students and laborers continued to be demand free and decolonized education, as well as to "End Outsourcing."[26] From November through December, South African students and laborers continued demonstrating, despite heavy police violence. After weeks of ongoing disruptions, including major property damage and clashes with police, UCT finally announced intentions to insource laborers, with negotiations beginning in November.[27] SU also announced intentions for all-English language policies.[28]

Students at UCT and SU maintained pressure to demand deeper changes, while elsewhere students, laborers, families, politicians, and the media began to reflect on the protests. The temporary tuition freeze was achieved largely thanks to RMF's

25. Normitsu Onishi, "South Africa Freezes Tuition Fees After Student Protests."

26. Rhodes Must Fall, "Oct6: 'We Demand Insourcing for All University Workers," October 5, 2015, accessed September 10, 2016, available at facebook.com.

27. "South Africa: UCT Signs Historic Agreement to Insource Services," October 29, 2015, available at allafrica.com.

28. "Academics Back New Maties Policy," November 18, 2015, available at iol.co.za.

ambitious, abolitionist "must fall" rhetoric, which helped mobilize far more people than only university students. Both students and the authorities recognized the success of these tactics as a pivotal moment. Unfortunately, as of mid-2016 things look grim. Impressive short-term victories may never become permanent, deep, structural changes.

While negotiations regarding insourcing continued from November onward, OS pointed out that "the question naturally arises of what areas of the budget will be affected in making the books balance" following the tuition freeze.[29] OS and RMF continued to demand that universities lead society in ambitious resistance capitalism, rather than giving into privatization. In February 2016, RMF held the Shackville protest to highlight housing insecurity and the ongoing shanties in which many South Africans still live.[30] Unfortunately, police and private security destroyed Shackville, and in the tumult, a university truck was set ablaze.[31]

Subsequently, UCT de facto expelled suspected students who were critical members of RMF, by charging them and putting them on trial. They were found guilty, and ordered to pay legal and other fees to the university.[32] Simultaneously, conflict arose within RMF between its more intersectional/Black Feminist members, and its more masculinist, heteronormative members. One key RMF man assaulted an LGBTQ+ protester, which led to breakdowns of the collective's effectiveness.[33] The final, most visible protest of the 2015–16 academic year was titled "The Death of a Dream," where students broadcast UCT's expulsion of student protest leaders and delays on insourcing.[34] The

---

29. Open Stellenbosch, "Open Stellenbosch Statement of 31 October: Corruption at Stellenbosch University," October 31, 2015, accessed September 10, 2016, available at facebook.com.

30. Annzra Denita, "#SHACKVILLE: UCT Protests Flare Up Again," February 17, 2016, available at capetownetc.com.

31. Ashleigh Furlong, "GroundUp Report: Rhodes Must Fall Protesters Burn UCT Art," *Daily Maverick*, February 17, 2016, available at dailymaverick.co.za.

32. Andrea Teagle and Sumeya Gasa, "'UCT Is Winning': Judgment with Costs Leaves RMF Protesters Demoralised," *Daily Maverick*, May 13, 2016, available at dailymaverick.co.za.

33. Lisa Isaacs, "Maxwele under Fire from #FeesMustFall Feminists," April 6, 2016, available at iol.co.za.

34. Rhodes Must Fall. "Death of a Dream." May 12, 2015, accessed September 10,

HIGHLY VISIBLE GRAFFITI AT THE UCT SPORTS FIELD

students' message remains clear and brutal: UCT is anti-Black, a site of colonization, and somewhere that students seeking liberation should avoid.

HOW DID SOUTH AFRICA'S UNIVERSITY STUDENTS GO SO FAR?

They knew they needed to go beyond academia and to focus on more than only curricula, enrollment, tuition, or other education-specific institutional processes. One critical RMF member, who spoke to me in August 2015 during the Remember Marikana campaign, argued the following: "If you don't frame the struggle overall as first and foremost total decolonization, you're just setting yourself up for another battle after whatever you fight in the university alone."

One of the most effective strategies of RMF has been their connection of the simultaneous anti-Blackness of the UK-based extractive firm Lonmin and the Marikana Massacre;[35] Global North firms' connections with universities and political elites[36]; and neoliberalism's ubiquitous outsourcing of impoverished

2016, available at facebook.com.

35. Rhodes Must Fall, "#RhodesMustFall—Media Statement—Marikana Campaign."

36. "Zuma, Ramaphosa Have Blood on Their Hands: UCT Students," August 18, 2015, available at enca.com.

laborers.[37] RMF connected with students, their families, and the overwhelmingly Black, nonacademic laborers at UCT—while clashing with the overwhelmingly white and/or European-educated professors, who insisted their demands were too radical. Their approach to coalition-building generated broad and consistent sympathy outside of universities, as well as pressure within universities. By refusing further engagement with consistently ineffective bureaucracies,[38] and by circumventing questionable labor unions now beholden to white-owned, global capital,[39] RMF's university students created an environment more conducive to a coalition against a common threat of neoliberalism's ubiquitous and inevitable anti-Blackness. Without RMF's consistent, transgressive, and highly visible rejections of UCT's empty promises, Fees Must Fall may have never occurred.

Analyzing RMF's demands for "decolonization" versus OS's initial demands for "transformation" reveals an ideological and discursive split between the two groups, which yielded different strategies and tactics, and reflected the different needs of students at different universities. UCT is situated within a major metropolitan center, entirely surrounded by majority Black townships.[40]

Compared to SU, UCT has a much more diverse student population, and a very different historical relationship to apartheid. SU is more geographically isolated, an hour east of Cape Town, and surrounded by rolling hills and wineries, not townships. Historically, Stellenbosch and SU served as the intellectual home

37. Rhodes Must Fall. "Oct6: We Demand Insourcing for All University Workers," October 5, 2015, available at facebook.com.

38. Brian Ihirwe Kamanzi and Rhodes Must Fall, "Written by Brian Ihirwe Kamanzi, Fuck the UCT SRC and Others Like It—A Response to the Emergency Mass Meeting Set by UCT SRC Due for Thursday," July 28, 2016, accessed September 10, 2016, available at facebook.com.

39. David Smith, "Lonmin Emails Paint ANC Elder as a Born-Again Robber Baron," *The Guardian*, October 24, 2012, available at theguardian.com; "Marikana Report: NUM, AMCU and Lonmin Could Have Done More," June 25, 2015, available at enca.com; Alex Smith, "Union Leadership under Fire in South African Labor Dispute," June 29, 2013, available at adn.com; Jared Sacks, "Marikana Prequel: NUM and the Murders That Started It All," *Daily Maverick*, October 12, 2012, available at dailymaverick.co.za; Paul Trewhela, "A Corrupt Elite Is Fighting for Its Life," May 27, 2013, available at politicsweb.co.za.

40. Oliver Wainwright, "Apartheid Ended 20 Years Ago, So Why Is Cape Town Still 'A Paradise for the Few'?" *The Guardian*, April 30, 2014, available at theguardian.com.

of apartheid and right-wing Afrikaner white supremacy.[41] No less than four white supremacist prime ministers (Hertzog, Malan, Verwoerd, and Vorster) and other top apartheid officials attended SU. SU students of color face disturbing levels of intimidation. Entirely surrounded by histories, structures, and armed forces of Afrikanerdom, students who dare to speak up at SU are at a much greater risk of retaliation. In the early days of OS, at least one OS leader was directly threatened by SU faculty.[42] Threats against "disrespectful" and "ungrateful" students leading OS increased proportional to the group's activities, even though OS's tactics tended to be much more subdued and respectable, compared to RMF.

OS and RMF could be put into an oppositional binary, such as "transformation v. decolonization," "university v. society," or "evolution v. revolution," respectively. Indeed, there were initial tensions between the groups regarding radicalism and understanding of the extensiveness of neocolonialism and neoliberalism. OS maintained a hierarchical organization, with leaders, spokespeople, and white students allowed. RMF remained as structureless and leaderless a network as possible, and deliberately excluded white students from leadership circles, similar to Biko's South African Student Organization (SASO) under apartheid. However, both movements' short-term demands were more alike than not. Even though OS focused on a more achievable, specific goal of English language instruction, it did so while maintaining a critique of the persistence of apartheid culture and Eurocentrism. In fact, South African university students' ability to find common ground and work together, while critiquing their radical goals and identity politics, is what makes South Africa's university student-led protests so significant.

After months of RMF serving as the most transgressive voice, every student movement, beyond just those in the Western Cape, were demanding higher-quality, more accessible education, humane labor practices, and university populations that were representative of, and responsive to, the rest of society. Despite longer-term ideological and strategic differences between RMF, OS, and

41. "The Ivory Tower Is Too White."
42. Masa Kekana, "Verbal Threats Follow Racist SMS at Stellenbosch University," *Eyewitness News*, August 5, 2015, available at ewn.co.za.

other key student groups, massive fee increases provided an opportunity for disparate groups to form a coherent short-term coalition. Armed with the abolitionist rhetoric of "must fall," students nationwide were primed to lead protests with a clear short-term goal and a specific militant tactic: abolish fees by occupying and shutting down cities and universities. Months later, fees remain prohibitively high, and several students have been expelled. It has been argued by disillusioned protesters that "UCT is winning."[43] Universities continue to expend vast sums on private security to quell students who they now perceive as dangerously powerful, when organized.

SOUTH AFRICA, CA, AND THE UNITED STATES ARE MORE ALIKE THAN NOT, DESPITE DIFFERENCES

The question facing South Africa could be easily asked in California: Where do we go from here? How far must we go? It seems obvious that backing down in either context will not stop further neoliberalization. Some may insist we cannot compare "the other" of South Africa to the United States and California. There remain significant disparities between states, cultures, and histories of colonialism. However, despite the Great Recession, the failures of austerity, and the United States' role in economic catastrophe, nearly all universities now conform to U.S.-created neoliberal models. The hegemony of the United States, including the educational systems' privatization, has a global impact.

Most established universities now exploit as much labor as possible, while increasing tuition, and selectively reward tiny, elite populations.[44] Management of profitability now takes priority over teaching, learning, and empowerment of students. Any past dreams of high-quality, low-cost, public education have

---

43. Andrea Teagle and Sumeya Gasa, "'UCT Is Winning': Judgment with Costs Leaves RMF Protesters Demoralised."

44. "Runaway Equality at the University of California: How Students, Workers, and Taxpayers Fund UC's Executive Excess," ASFCME-3299, January 2014, 1–12, accessed September 10, 2016, available at afscme3299.org; "Working in the Shadows: How Outsourcing at the University of California Adds to the Ranks of California's Working Poor," ASFCME-3299, July 2015, 1–12, accessed September 10, 2016, available at afscme3299.org,

been replaced by nightmares of neoliberalized, highly stratified, for-profit, corporate models. California and the United States were both sites of historical colonization, but were also states that came to drive colonialism. They arguably continue to drive neocolonialism. Like South Africa, we do not only face "corruption" of our politics but face a system operating on the same foundation as its colonial predecessor: oppression and exploitation of the many for the profit of the few. "The many" still tend to be darker-skinned, while "the few" tend to be lighter-skinned or in service to white-owned, global capital (or both).

Across South Africa, most of the population still lives in colonial-style townships. Rates of poverty, unemployment, inequality, and access to basic services, as well as racial disparities for these indicators, are roughly the same as pre-1994. In the postcolony, even a robust university does little to create a middle class. It is true that on average, in California and the United States, most students' expected and lived material experiences are less bleak than in historically colonized regions of the globe. However, ideologically and operationally, the system in the United States differs only by a matter of degree, and shares the same foundations as that of South Africa. In the United States, even an expansive network of universities and increasing rates of educational achievement fail to guarantee a certain quality of life for people of different racial, sexual/gender, and class identities.

Our policymakers remain overwhelmingly men who embrace neoliberal capitalism, and do not reflect the demographics of the larger society. The military-industrial complex necessary for state security and surveillance apparatuses remains supported by universities' physics, robotics, and engineering departments. Our legally color blind New Jim Crow frighteningly parallels the neocolonialism of post-apartheid South Africa.[45] Here and there, anti-Blackness remains a fundamental part of society, and yet is simultaneously declared to be impossible.[46]

The disparities between white and nonwhite residents and university students in both the United States and in South Africa

---

45. Michelle Alexander, *The New Jim Crow* (New York: The New Press, 2010).
46. Veli Mbele, "South Africa: The Fall of Cecil John Rhodes and the Rise of Black Power," April 2, 2015, available at allafrica.com.

today is nearly as bad as in the past. The persistent racism of the United States is further evidenced in negligibly changed white v. Black rates in all of the following: poverty[47]; income[48]; housing access[49]; home ownership; health issues[50]; general homicide rates[51]; homicide by police[52]; general police brutality[53]; incarceration[54]; legislative representation[55]; judicial appointments[56]; (un)employment[57]; youth unemployment[58]; tertiary degree attainment[59]; and student loan debt.[60]

The most illustrative similarities between both states are their similar historical systems of apartheid: state-sanctioned, violently

47. "Poverty in the United States Frequently Asked Questions," Gerald R. Ford School of Public Policy National Poverty Center, 2015, accessed September 10, 2016, available at npc.umich.edu.

48. Eileen Patten, "Racial, Gender Wage Gap Persist in U.S. Despite Some Progress," Pew Research Center, July 1, 2016, accessed September 10, 2016, available at pewresearch.org.

49. The Leadership Conference Education Fund, "Despite the Promise of the Fair Housing Act, the Rate of Housing Discrimination Remains High," December 2008, accessed September 10, 2016, available at civilrights.org.

50. Jeff Guo, "The Racial Gap in Health Has Been Shrinking for Decades—But It Still Hasn't Closed," *Washington Post*, December 29, 2014, available at washingtonpost.com.

51. U.S. Department of Justice, Federal Bureau of Investigation, "Crime in the United States 2013, Expanded Homicide Data Table 6," 2014, accessed September 10, 2016, available at ucr.fbi.gov.

52. "The Counted," *The Guardian*, 2016, available at theguardian.com.

53. Ryan Gabrielson, Ryann Grochowski Jones, and Eric Sagar, "Deadly Force, in Black and White," October 10, 2014, available at propublica.org.

54. Leah Sakala, "Breaking Down Mass Incarceration in the 2010 Census: State-by-State Incarceration Rates by Race/Ethnicity," May 28, 2014, available at prisonpolicy.org.

55. Philip Bump, "The New Congress Is 80 Percent White, 80 Percent Male and 92 Percent Christian," *Washington Post*, January 5, 2015, available at washingtonpost.com.

56. Andrew Cohen, "Why Aren't There More Black Federal Judges in Alabama, Florida, and Georgia?" *The Atlantic*, November 12, 2013, available at theatlantic.com.

57. Valerie Wilson, "State Unemployment Rates by Race and Ethnicity at the End of 2015 Show a Plodding Recovery," February 11, 2016, available at epi.org.

58. U.S. Department of Labor, Bureau of Labor Statistics, "Employment and Unemployment Among Youth Summary," Bureau of Labor Statistics Economic News Release, August 17, 2016, available at bls.gov.

59. Ben Casselman, "Race Gap Narrows in College Enrollment, But Not in Graduation," April 30, 2014, available at fivethirtyeight.com.

60. Andrew Dugan and Scott Vanderbilt, "Black College Grads More Likely to Graduate With Debt," September 18, 2014, accessed September 10, 2016, available at gallup.com.

enforced, anti-Black segregation.[61] Both states also share histories of police militarization, alongside condoning widespread use of lethal force by police and by private gun owners. Consequently, both states effectively perpetuate disparities between white and nonwhite peoples' experience of state and nonstate violence, even years after ostensibly liberating political change. For one example, in South Africa, an RMF student's car was set on fire immediately after the climax of Fees Must Fall.[62] In the United States, two prominent anti–police brutality activists in Missouri— Deandre Joshua in 2014[63] and Darren Seals in 2016[64]—were both murdered by being shot and placed inside a burning vehicle. In the United States, the protests by Black Lives Matter groups face heightened surveillance and visibly militarized police responses.[65] In South Africa, increasing reliance on private security has resulted not only in property damage for universities but also in hospitalizations for students, alongside allegations of police sexually assaulting student protesters.[66] In both cases, protesters are terrorized by both state and nonstate actors, whose violence against protesters is considered acceptable.

On one hand, the United States' disproportionately high levels of homicides of people of color, both by police and otherwise, far exceed that of South Africa. On the other hand, the slow violence[67] of absolute poverty in South Africa all but guarantees a

---

61. Douglass Masey and Nancy Denton, *"The Missing Link." American Apartheid: Segregation and the Making of the Underclass* (Cambridge, MA: Harvard University Press, 1998), 1–16. Accessed September 10, 2016, available at socrates.berkeley.edu.

62. Rhodes Must Fall. "Last Night One of Our Comrade's Cars Was Set on Fire Outside Azania House. Moves Are Being Made to Silence Us." October 26, 2015, accessed September 10, 2016, available at twitter.com.

63. Jon Swaine, "Homicide Investigation Under Way in Ferguson after Body Found Following Night of Protest," *The Guardian*, November 25, 2014, available at theguardian.com.

64. Lois Beckett, "Ferguson Protest Leader Darren Seals Shot and Found Dead in a Burning Car," *The Guardian*, September 8, 2016, available at theguardian.com.

65. George Joseph, "Exclusive: Feds Regularly Monitored Black Lives Matter Since Ferguson," *The Intercept*, July 24, 2015, available at theintercept.com; see also Robert Mackey, "Images of Militarized Police in Baton Rouge Draw Global Attention," *The Intercept*, July 11, 2016, available at theintercept.com.

66. Daneesha Pillay, "Parliament Committee Demands 'Full Report' on Alleged Rape of Teen at Montague Police Station," September 6, 2016, available at timeslive.co.za.

67. Rob Nixon, *Slow Violence and the Environmentalism of the Poor* (Cambridge, MA: Harvard University Press, 2011).

lifetime of third-class citizenship, subordination to the power of white-owned, global capital, and disproportionately high levels of overall crime.[68] In both cases, darker-skinned people face an omnipresent threat of violence and crime of various forms, while remaining second or third-class citizens in a "color blind" state.

In another lens, the 2012 Marikana Massacre saw police "armed only with automatic weapons and loaded with sharp ammunition" shoot and then hunt down and further slaughter fleeing wildcat strikers.[69] Most South Africans immediately recognized Marikana's similarity to the apartheid-era, 1960 Sharpeville Massacre. In the United States, however, many remain reluctant to recognize some persistent similarities between police brutality now and in the past. However, there has been no recent massacre of unarmed students or protesters in the United States, analogous to Kent State or Jackson State. Ultimately, in both South Africa and the United States, the darker one's skin is, the more painful and violent one's existence will likely be. This is especially true for those who protest. This is because, in both states, the system has been founded on anti-Blackness, which the state continues to fail to address.

In tertiary education, similar white and nonwhite disparities are undeniable, evidenced by persistent enrollment, retention, and graduation gaps.[70] Students from historically colonized communities suffer especially as tuition increases exclude more and more people. Precarious "financial aid" schemes only tentatively allow lower-income students to study, often with unforgivable debt.[71] White men still account for most senior staff, academic, and faculty positions in the University of California

---

68. Gavin Silber and Nathan Geffen, "On Race and Crime in SA," January 11, 2010, available at politicsweb.co.za.

69. Peter Alexander, "Marikana, Turning Point in South African History," *Review of African Political Economy* 40, no. 138 (December 17, 2013): 605–19. Accessed September 10, 2016, available at tandfonline.com.

70. Ben Casselman, "Race Gap Narrows in College Enrollment, But Not in Graduation."

71. Andrew Dugan and Scott Vanderbilt, "Black College Grads More Likely to Graduate With Debt."

(UC) system.[72] This is true across the United States.[73] It is also true in South Africa.[74] These racial disparities exist alongside universities' increasing reliance on "contingent" instructors.[75] Contingent faculty are paid poverty wages, further degrading quality of instruction.[76] Simultaneously, the laborers who keep universities running are overwhelmingly people of color, and are often outsourced to disreputable firms with histories of severe labor abuses.[77]

CAN CALIFORNIA'S UNIVERSITY STUDENTS DEMAND SUCH AMBITIOUS ABOLITION?

Because of so many similarities in both universities and societies, university students protesting in California or elsewhere in the United States could learn from the successes and obstacles of protesters in South Africa, who have achieved greater success through demands that, because of their radicalism, have created broader coalitions capable of more militant protests.

Like South Africa, California's protests also won short-term results, but did not roll back fees, transform the university, or restructure society. In 2013–14, UC student-led protests against five years of 5 percent-per-year tuition increases partly contributed to a two-year partial tuition freeze, followed by promises of "predictable" tuition increases.[78] There was no freeze for UC's "system-wide

---

72. University of California, Office of the President, "Chapter 7: Diversity," Accountability Report, 2015, Section 7.3, accessed September 10, 2016, available at accountability.universityofcalifornia.edu.

73. Frank Tuitt, Michelle Hannah, Lisa M. Martinez, Maria del Carmen Salazar, and Rachel Griffin, "Teaching in the Line of Fire: Faculty of Color in the Academy." *NEA Higher Education Journal* (Fall 2009): 65–74. Accessed September 10, 2016, available at nea.org

74. Karen MacGregor, "Higher Education in the 20th Year of Democracy."

75. "Background Facts on Contingent Faculty." Accessed September 10, 2016, available at aaup.org.

76. Caroline Fredrickson, "There Is No Excuse for How Universities Treat Adjuncts." September 15, 2015, Laura McKenna, "The Cost of an Adjunct," *The Atlantic*, May 26, 2015, available at the atlantic.com.

77. Miranda Dietz, "Temporary Workers in California are Twice as Likely as Non-Temps to Live in Poverty: Problems with Temporary and Subcontracted Work in California," UC Berkeley Labor Center, August 2012, accessed September 10, 2016, available at laborcenter.berkeley.edu.

78. Nanette Asimov and Melody Gutierrez, "UC President, Governor Agree to Freeze

student services fee" and "Professional Degree Supplemental Tuition" (PDST), whose increases would be 20 percent to 30 percent over the course of five years.[79]

However, unlike South Africa, or Chile, India, Hong Kong, and elsewhere, there have been relatively few recent, widespread, student-led, militant occupations here in California. In March 2015 at UC Santa Cruz, six students blocked the main highway between San Francisco and Santa Cruz, resulting in their incarceration and effective expulsion.[80] In May 2015, around fifty students—a group that was overwhelmingly made up of women of color—occupied the UC Santa Barbara chancellor's office to demand immediate sexual violence reforms.[81] The Million Student March in November 2016 marked widespread demonstrations and clear student demands for a living wage, cancellation of student debt, and free higher education, with significant turnout at UC campuses.[82] However, the demonstration explicitly avoided any militant action, even though the students had the numbers for it.

In November 2015, at an annual Students of Color Conference, students protested UC outsourcing and labor exploitation.[83] Throughout 2015–16 at UC Berkeley, the Student Labor Committee led protests against outsourcing, including the transgressive "Dirks is a Racist" allegations against Berkeley's then-chancellor. A brief fossil fuel divestment sit-in occurred at UC Berkeley, too.[84] At UC Davis in early 2016, there occurred

---

Tuition for 2 Years," May 14, 2015, available at sfgate.com.

79. Janet Napolitano, "President Napolitano's Letter to UC Community on Gov. Brown's Revised Budget Proposal." May 14, 2015, accessed September 10, 2016, available at ucanr.edu.

80. Alexa Lomberg, "Five of 'Highway 17 Six' Students Sentenced to 30 Days in Jail, Eligible for House Arrest." June 29, 2015, available at cityonahillpress.com.

81. Alexandra Skovos, "How Activists Improved the Handling of Campus Sexual Assault This Year," *Huffington Post*, June 2, 2015, available at huffingtonpost.com.

82. Kaitlin Mulhere, "The Million Student March Protesters Say They're Just Getting Started," *Time*, November 13, 2015, available at time.com.

83. Andrea Platten, "UC Students Rallying for Worker Rights March to Dirks' Residence, Hop Gate," *The Daily Californian*, November 8, 2015, available at.dailycal.org.

84. Kristy Drutman, "Fossil Free UC Berkeley Are Currently Staging a Sit-In in the UC Investments Office," May 4, 2016, available at thetab.com.

UC BERKELEY PROTESTERS MARCH
HOLDING A SIGN THAT READS: JUSTICE4UCWORKERS"
MEDIA CREDIT: JONATAN GARIBAY

antiracist Black Under Attack protests.[85] Soon after, students occupied administrators' offices to demand the university "Fire Katehi."[86] These at least partly contributed to that chancellor's resignation.[87] Berkeley's chancellor, too, has now recently announced their resignation.[88]

The "Must Fall" demand has spread beyond South Africa, at least to Oxford and Harvard.[89] In November 2015, University of Missouri President Wolfe fell.[90] This followed antiracist protests with extra power through student coalitions with student athletes of color.[91] UC Chancellors Katehi and Dirks have fallen,

---

85. Gabrielle Karol, "Black Student Group Releases List of Demands at UC Davis," February 22, 2016, available at abc10.com.

86. Sangeetha Ramamurthy, "Fifth Floor of Mrak Hall Closes to Public after Fire Katehi Sit-In," May 31, 2016, available at theaggie.org.

87. Cassandra Vogel, "Linda Katehi Resigns as Chancellor of UC Davis," *The Daily Californian*, August 9, 2016, available at dailycal.org.

88. Phil Matier and Andy Ross, "UC Berkeley Chancellor Nicholas Dirks Announces Resignation," August 16, 2016, available at sfgate.com.

89. Sheena Louise Roetman, "Royall Has Fallen: Harvard Law to Remove Slavery-Based Crest," March 15, 2016, available at indiancountrytodaymedianetwork.com.

90. John Eligon and Richard Perez-Pena, "University of Missouri Protests Spur a Day of Change," *The New York Times*, November 9, 2015, available at nytimes.com.

91. Marc Tracy and Ashley Southall, "Black Football Players Lend Heft to Protests at Missouri," *The New York Times*, November 8, 2015, available at nytimes.com.

albeit with different terminology employed in demanding their removal. However, demands to abolish specific chancellors are only effective in the short term, if not accompanied by demands for long-term restructuring of the systems. Any chancellor, even one vetted by students, will become compromised the moment they assume a position so prone to corruption, and so beholden to the forces of global capital. Unlike South Africa, abolitionist rhetorics like "decolonization," or ambitious demands to totally overhaul educational governance, have been largely invisible in California. Instead, the trend has been toward more respectable, institutionally sanctioned approaches: demonstrations without occupations, or relying on elected student government to pursue incremental reforms.

Besides the few occupations noted above, there has been little statewide coordination of widespread student militancy, nor has there been a single campus that has inspired protests across and beyond academia. Demands for free education or tuition abolition have largely failed to address larger political, economic, and cultural systems, or to address the United States' widespread resistance to public services. Even a demand as concise as "Education, not Incarceration" will be ignored when made to a corrupt government without significant support of people in the streets.[92]

Despite this, the official, elected, statewide UC Student Association (UCSA) has run nonstructural campaigns year after year to highlight serious issues with the UC. Their well-intentioned work has somewhat increased awareness of the worst parts of the UC's privatization but has only slightly slowed it. UCSA, and other elected student governments, have rarely organized effective, widespread demonstrations. There is no statewide, militant, direct-action coordinating body for Californian students. The vast majority of student militancy to date has been conducted by marginalized students, who act outside of official university groups, receive minimal support, and usually face significant backlash. Only recently have attacks on specific top-level officials,

---

92. Amy Larson, "UC Santa Cruz Campus Entrances Blocked by Protesters," March 5, 2015, available at ksbw.com.

or for abolishing certain processes, gained wider support and yielded success for students.

There are currently three separate divestment campaigns occurring at the UC, with no common strategy among them. The most infamous, the pro-Palestinian BDS movement, faces intense opposition on most campuses.[93] Fossil fuel divestment, which forced the UC to sell its coal and oil sands investments in mid-2015, has no connection with BDS divestment movements.[94] Neither does the Black Student Union (BSU)/Afrikan Black Coalition (ABC) campaign that forced the UC to divest from private prisons shares in late 2015.[95]

ABC now seeks UC divestment from $425 million in Wells Fargo holdings.[96] Fossil Free UC continues building statewide support for divestment from all fossil fuels. BDS continues fighting the staggering power of the United States' pro-Israel, anti-Arab military-industrial complex. All three groups have made significant progress on their own in raising awareness of racist, capitalist violence. Despite a common tactic, and significant overlap in their goals of justice and liberation for those oppressed by white-owned, global capital, these three groups remain disconnected from one another. What could they accomplish if they coordinated a common, mass divestment, sustainable investment campaign to totally restructure the UC's finances? .

There is much more that can and must be done to stop a totally privatized University of California.

There is growing awareness of the failure of a college degree to secure an acceptable quality of life in the United States for graduates—especially graduates of color. There is growing awareness of structural, institutional, financial, and sexual violence against both

93. Bill Simonds, "Posters Linking Muslim Students and BDS Activists to Terrorism Appear on College Campuses in California and Washington, DC," *Mondoweiss*, November 19, 2015, accessed September 10, 2016, available at mondoweiss.net.

94. Larry Gordon, "UC Sells Off $200 Million in Coal and Oil Sands Investments." *Los Angeles Times*, September 9, 2015, available at latimes.com.

95. Anthony Williams, "Afrikan Black Coalition Accomplishes UC Prison Divestment!" December 18, 2015, available at afrikanblackcoalition.org.

96. Amelia Mineiro, "Afrikan Black Coalition Petitions for Wells Fargo to End Association with Private Prison Industry," *The Daily Californian*, January 22, 2016, available at dailycal.org.

students and laborers. Much like how apparently dissimilar groups coalesced together under a common cause in South Africa, the same can, and indeed must, happen in California. The UC relies on hundreds of thousands of laborers, many of whom are subcontracted to brutally exploitative private firms. Alliances between students and laborers seem an as-yet-unrealized necessary component.

WHAT "MUST FALL" IN CALIFORNIA?

Tuition and student loan debt remain at unprecedented levels, and increase annually.[97] Worldwide, neoliberal populists are threatening even more aggressive forms of capitalism, nationalism, sexism, and racism. In deciding next steps, we must consider what those in power, who have much to lose, may now be asking out of fear: What "Must Fall" here? There are seeds of discontentment and conscientization in California now, which students could cultivate together into widespread, coalition-based protests and movements for system-wide restructuring. There have been significant escalations throughout 2014–16, and 2016 is a significant anniversary of many past protests.

In South Africa, it has been four years since Marikana and forty years since Soweto. Given the prevalence of mass incarceration and state-sanctioned violence in the United States, the 45th anniversary of the Attica Prison Uprising seems relevant. It has been thirty years since the UC's 1986 Shantytown Protests. It has been eight years since California began its most recent massive tuition increases, and since ineffective protests began at the UC. It marks only the third year of former DHS Secretary Napolitano's tenure as president of the UC. Now seems as good a time as any to demand that Napolitano must fall.

Must we topple tuition and student fees that perpetuate an exclusive, classist, racist university that fails to create an educated labor force or a middle class, or to meaningfully move society forward? Should we go further, and abolish politicians and government bodies forcing universities to privatize? In California, should we demand "Tuition Must Fall" or "Racism Must Fall"?

---

97. Derek Thompson, "The Scariest Student Loan Number," *The Atlantic*, July 19, 2016, available at theatlantic.com.

Should we demand "Fire Napolitano," or that the "UC Regents Must Fall"? Why not demand that capitalism or imperialism must fall, so long as we can communicate that in a way that brings together many different stakeholders and achieves at least short-term successes?

Students must assert an abolitionist demand that sounds and seems impossible. Aiming for anything less will likely only yield more disconnected protests that at best only slow the privatization of education. At the same time, students must issue demands in a way that can rally as many marginalized people as possible together. Students must not unite by erasing important differences, a la Professor Ananya Roy's contentious 2011 claim that "We are all students of color now."[98] If abolition frameworks can become central to California's students, they must come from the most marginalized university populations. As evidenced by incredibly robust and comprehensive policy proposals recently released by Black Lives Matter and the Movement for Black Lives, those who are the most oppressed are those who are most knowledgeable about the systemic violence that must be abolished.

Much like how students at UCT and SU faced different levels of intimidation and had different resources available, students at CSU Long Beach, UC Davis, and San Francisco City College represent diverse needs within the overall frame of neoliberal exploitation. As in South Africa, where the most marginalized students were those able to effectively imagine alternatives and to facilitate protests, California's marginalized students' demands must be supported by other students. Students of greater relative privilege must not assume that they may override the demands and needs of those suffering even more. As in South Africa and elsewhere, leadership by the marginalized is likely the best hope for all to resist the terrors of neoliberalism.

---

98. Chris Chen, "'We Have All Become Students of Color Now': The California Student Movement and the Rhetoric of Privilege," *South Atlantic Quarterly* 110, no. 2 (2011): 559–64. Accessed September 10, 2016, ; Ananya Roy, "'We Are All Students of Color Now,'" *Representations* 116, no. 1 (Fall 2011): 177–88.

REFERENCES

"Academics Back New Maties Policy," November 18, 2015. Available at iol.co.za.

ASFCME-3299. *Runaway Equality at the University of California: How Students, Workers, and Taxpayers Fund UC's Executive Excess.* Oakland: 2014. Accessed September 10, 2016. Available at afscme3299.org.

ASFCME-3299. *Working in the Shadows: How Outsourcing at the University of California Adds to the Ranks of California's Working Poor.* Oakland: 2015. Accessed September 10, 2016. Available at afscme3299.org.

Alexander, Michelle. *The New Jim Crow.* New York: The New Press, 2010.

Alexander, Peter. "Marikana, Turning Point in South African History." *Review of African Political Economy* 40, no. 138 (December 2013): 605–19. Available at tandfonline.com.

American Association of University Professors. "Background Facts on Contingent Faculty." 2015. Accessed September 10, 2016. Available at aaup.org.

Asimov, Nanette and Melody Gutierrez. "UC President, Governor Agree to Freeze Tuition for 2 Years." May 14, 2015. Available at sfgate.com.

Baloyi, Basani and Gllad Isaacs. "South Africa's 'Fees Must Fall' Protests Are About More Than Tuition Costs." *CNN.* October 28, 2015. Available at cnn.com.

Beckett, Lois. "Ferguson Protest Leader Darren Seals Shot and Found Dead in a Burning Car." *The Guardian.* September 8, 2016. Available at theguardian.com.

Bump, Philip. "The New Congress Is 80 Percent White, 80 Percent Male and 92 Percent Christian." *Washington Post.* January 5, 2015. Available at washingtonpost.com.

Casselman, Ben. "Race Gap Narrows in College Enrollment, But Not in Graduation." April 30, 2014. Available at fivethirtyeight.com.

Chen, Chris. "'We Have All Become Students of Color Now': The California Student Movement and the Rhetoric of Privilege." *South Atlantic Quarterly* 110, no. 2 (2011): 559–64. Available at dukepress.edu.

Cohen, Andrew. "Why Aren't There More Black Federal Judges in Alabama, Florida, and Georgia?" *The Atlantic.* November 12, 2013. Available at theatlantic.com.

Denita, Annzra. "#SHACKVILLE: UCT Protests Flare Up Again." February 17, 2016. Available at capetownetc.com.

Dietz, Miranda. *Temporary Workers in California are Twice as Likely as Non-Temps to Live in Poverty: Problems with Temporary and Subcontracted Work in California.* Berkeley: UC Berkeley Labor Center, 2012. Accessed September 10, 2016. Available at laborcenter.berkeley.edu.

Dirk, Nicolette. "Activists Removed as Protest Spreads to CPUT." October 21, 2015. Available at iol.co.za.

Drutman, Kristy. "Fossil Free UC Berkeley Are Currently Staging a Sit-In in the UC Investments Office." May 4, 2016. Available at thetab.com.

Dugan, Andrew and Scott Vanderbilt. "Black College Grads More Likely to Graduate With Debt." September 18, 2014, accessed September 10, 2016. Available at gallup.com.

Duncan, Jane. "#FeesMustFall: A Question of Human Rights Violations." *Mail & Guardian.* November 9, 2015. Available at mg.co.za.

Eligon, John and Richard Perez-Pena. "University of Missouri Protests Spur a Day of Change." *The New York Times.* November 9, 2015. Available at nytimes.com.

Essop, Ahmed. "Decolonisation Debate Is a Chance to Rethink the Role of Universities." August 16, 2016. Available at theconversation.com.

Fredrickson, Caroline. "There Is No Excuse for How Universities Treat Adjuncts." *The Atlantic.* September 15, 2015. Available at theatlantic.com

Furlong, Ashleigh. "GroundUp Report: Rhodes Must Fall Protesters Burn UCT Art." *Daily Maverick.* February 17, 2016. Available at dailymaverick.co.za.

Gabrielson, Ryan, Ryann Grochowski Jones, and Eric Sagar. "Deadly Force, in Black and White." October 10, 2014. Available at propublica.org.

Gordon, Larry. "UC Sells Off $200 Million in Coal and Oil Sands Investments." *Los Angeles Times.* September 9, 2015. Available at latimes.com.

Guo, Jeff. "The Racial Gap in Health Has Been Shrinking for Decades—But It Still Hasn't Closed." *Washington Post.* December 29, 2014. Available at washingtonpost.com.

Hodes, Rebecca. "Op-Ed: How Rhodes Must Fall Squandered Public Sympathy." *Daily Maverick.* August 20, 2015. Available at dailymaverick.co.za.

Hughes, Laura and Nicola Harley. "Students Clash with Police During Protest in Central London over University Fees." *The Telegraph.* November 4, 2015. Available at telegraph.co.uk.

Isaacs, Lisa. "Maxwele under Fire from #FeesMustFall Feminists," April 6, 2016. Available at iol.co.za.

Joseph, George. "Exclusive: Feds Regularly Monitored Black Lives Matter Since Ferguson." *The Intercept.* July 24, 2015. Available at theintercept.com.

Karol, Gabrielle. "Black Student Group Releases List of Demands at UC Davis." February 22, 2016. Available at abc10.com.

Kekana, Masa. "Verbal Threats Follow Racist SMS at Stellenbosch University." *Eyewitness News.* August 5, 2015. Available at ewn.co.za. Available at ewn.co.za.

Kekana, Masa and Ziyanda Ngcobo. "HRC Asked to Investigate Brutality by UJ Security Guards." *Eyewitness News.* November 9, 2015. Available at ewn.co.za.

Khoisan, Zenzile. "UWC Students, Cops Clash Near Airport," October 24, 2015. Available at iol.co.za.

Larson, Amy. "UC Santa Cruz Campus Entrances Blocked by Protesters." March 5, 2015. Available at ksbw.com.

Lau, Rachel. "Montreal Students March Against Austerity." *Global News.* November 5, 2015. Available at globalnews.ca.

Lomberg, Alexa. "Five of 'Highway 17 Six' Students Sentenced to 30 Days in Jail, Eligible for House Arrest." June 29, 2015. Available at cityonahillpress.com.

Luu, Chleu and Vivian Kam. "Hong Kong Student Leaders Spared Jail for Pro-Democracy Street Protests." *CNN.* August 15, 2016. Available at cnn.com.

MacGregor, Karen. "Higher Education in the 20th Year of Democracy." April 27, 2014. Available at universityworldnews.com.

"Main Findings and Recommendations from the Marikana Inquiry," July 1, 2015. Available at actsa.org.

"Marikana Report: NUM, AMCU and Lonmin Could Have Done More," June 25, 2015. Available at enca.com.

Massey, Douglass, and Nancy Denton. *American Apartheid: Segregation and the Making of the Underclass.* Cambridge, MA: Harvard University Press, 1998.

Matier, Phil and Andy Ross. "UC Berkeley Chancellor Nicholas Dirks Announces Resignation." August 16, 2016. Available at sfgate.com.

Matthews, David. "Student Protests Trigger U-Turn in India over Scholarships." *Times Higher Education.* October 27, 2015. Available at timeshighereducation.com.

Mbele, Veli. "South Africa: The Fall of Cecil John Rhodes and the Rise of Black Power." April 2, 2015. Available at allafrica.com.

McKenna, Laura. "The Cost of an Adjunct." *The Atlantic.* May 26, 2015. Available at theatlantic.com.

Mineiro, Amelia. "Afrikan Black Coalition Petitions for Wells Fargo to End Association with Private Prison Industry." *The Daily Californian.* January 22, 2016. Available at dailycal.org.

Mulhere, Kaitlin. "The Million Student March Protesters Say They're Just Getting Started." *Time.* November 13, 2015. Available at time.com.

Napolitano, Janet. "President Napolitano's Letter to UC Community on Gov. Brown's Revised Budget Proposal." May 14, 2015. Accessed September 10, 2016. Available at ucanr.edu.

Nicolson, Greg. "Luister: The Viral Film Exposing South Africa's Ongoing Racism Problem." *The Guardian.* September 7, 2015. Available at theguardian.com.

Nixon, Rob. *Slow Violence and the Environmentalism of the Poor.* Cambridge, MA: Harvard University Press, 2011.

Nkosi, Bogani. "#FeesMustFall Takes Fight to Union Buildings." *Mail & Guardian.* October 23, 2015. Available at mg.co.za.

Open Stellenbosch Collective. "Op-Ed: Open Stellenbosch—Tackling Language and Exclusion at Stellenbosch University." *Daily Maverick.* April 28, 2015. Available at dailymaverick.co.za.

Onishi, Normitsu. "South Africa Freezes Tuition Fees After Student Protests." *The New York Times.* October 23, 2015. Available at nytimes.com.

Quma, Babalwa. "UCT Students Occupy Bremner Building." October 19, 2015. Available at livemag.co.za.

Pather, Ra'essa. "Rhodes Must Fall: The Movement after the Statue." *the Daily Vox.* April 21, 2015. Available at thedailyvox.co.za.

Patten, Eileen. "Racial, Gender Wage Gap Persist in U.S. Despite Some Progress." Pew Research Center, July 1, 2016. Accessed September 10, 2016. Available at pewresearch.org.

Pillay, Daneesha. "Parliament Committee Demands 'Full Report' on Alleged Rape of Teen at Montague Police Station." September 6, 2016. Available at timeslive.co.za.

Platten, Andrea. "UC Students Rallying for Worker Rights March to Dirks' Residence, Hop Gate." November 8, 2015. Available at.dailycal.org.

Poverty in the United States Frequently Asked Questions. (Ann Arbor, MI:Gerald R. Ford School of Public Policy National Poverty Center, 2015). Accessed September 10, 2016. Available at npc.umich.edu.

Ramamurthy, Sangeetha. "Fifth Floor of Mrak Hall Closes to Public after Fire Katehi Sit-In." May 31, 2016. Available at theaggie.org.

Roetman, Sheena L. "Royall Has Fallen: Harvard Law to Remove Slavery-Based Crest." March 15, 2016. Available at indiancountryto-daymedianetwork.com.

Roy, Ananya. "'We Are All Students of Color Now.'" *Representations* 116, no. 1 (Fall 2011): 177–88. Available at ucpress.edu.

Sacks, Jared. "Marikana Prequel: NUM and the Murders That Started It All." *Daily Maverick*. October 12, 2012. Available at dailymaverick.co.za.

Sakala, Leah. "Breaking Down Mass Incarceration in the 2010 Census: State-by-State Incarceration Rates by Race/Ethnicity." May 28, 2014, available at prisonpolicy.org.

Sanders, Sam. "California College Students Walk Out of Class to Protest Tuition Hikes." November 24, 2014. Available at npr.org.

Silber, Gavin and Nathan Geffen. "On Race and Crime in SA." January 11, 2010. Available at politicsweb.co.za.

Simonds, Bill. "Posters Linking Muslim Students and BDS Activists to Terrorism Appear on College Campuses in California and Washington, DC." *Mondoweiss*. November 19, 2015. Accessed September 10, 2016. Available at mondoweiss.net.

Skovos, Alexandra. "How Activists Improved the Handling of Campus Sexual Assault This Year." *Huffington Post*. June 2, 2015. Available at huffingtonpost.com.

Smith, David. "Lonmin Emails Paint ANC Elder as a Born-Again Robber Baron." *The Guardian*. October 24, 2012. Available at the-guardian.com.

Smith, Alex. "Union Leadership under Fire in South African Labor Dispute." June 29, 2013. Available at adn.com.

"South Africa: UCT Signs Historic Agreement to Insource Services," October 29, 2015. Available at allafrica.com.

Swaine, Jon. "Homicide Investigation Under Way in Ferguson after Body Found Following Night of Protest." *The Guardian*. November 25, 2014. Available at theguardian.com.

Teagle, Andrea and Sumeya Gasa. "'UCT Is Winning': Judgment with Costs Leaves RMF Protesters Demoralised." *Daily Maverick*. May 13, 2016. Available at dailymaverick.co.za.

Thompson, Derek. "The Scariest Student Loan Number." *The Atlantic*. July 19, 2016. Available at theatlantic.com.

"The Counted," *The Guardian*. 2016. Available at theguardian.com.

"The Ivory Tower Is Too White," *The Economist*. December 5, 2015. Available at economist.com.

"The June 16 Soweto Youth Uprising," May 21, 2013. Available at sahistory.org.za.

The Leadership Conference Education Fund. *Despite the Promise of the Fair Housing Act, the Rate of Housing Discrimination Remains High.* 2008. Accessed September 10, 2016. Available at civilrights.org.

Tracy, Marc and Ashley Southall. "Black Football Players Lend Heft to Protests at Missouri." *The New York Times*. November 8, 2015. Available at nytimes.com.

Trewhela, Paul. "A Corrupt Elite Is Fighting for Its Life," May 27, 2013. Available at politicsweb.co.za.

Tuitt, Frank, Michelle Hannah, Lisa M. Martinez, Maria del Carmen Salazar, and Rachel Griffin. "Teaching in the Line of Fire: Faculty of Color in the Academy." *The NEA Higher Education Journal* (Fall 2009): 65–74. Available at nea.org.

U.S. Department of Justice, Federal Bureau of Investigation. "Crime in the United States 2013, Expanded Homicide Data Table 6." 2014. Accessed September 10, 2016. Available at ucr.fbi.gov.

U.S. Department of Labor, Bureau of Labor Statistics. "Employment and Unemployment Among Youth Summary." Bureau of Labor Statistics Economic News Release, August 17, 2016. Available at bls.gov.

"UCT Rhodes Must Fall Mission Statement," March 22, 2015. Available at uncensoredvoice.blogspot.com.

University of California, Office of the President. "Chapter 7: Diversity," In *Accountability Report*. Accessed September 10, 2016. Available at accountability.universityofcalifornia.edu.

Vergara, Eva. "Chile Students Protest Corruption, Demand Education Reform." April 16, 2015. Available at salon.com.

Vogel, Cassandra. "Linda Katehi Resigns as Chancellor of UC Davis." *The Daily Californian*. August 9, 2016. Available at dailycal.org.

Wainwright, Oliver. "Apartheid Ended 20 Years Ago, So Why Is Cape Town Still 'A Paradise for the Few'?" *The Guardian*. April 30, 2014. Available at theguardian.com.

Williams, Anthony. "Afrikan Black Coalition Accomplishes UC Prison Divestment!" December 18, 2015. Available at afrikanblackcoalition.org.

Wilson, Valerie. "State Unemployment Rates by Race and Ethnicity at the End of 2015 Show a Plodding Recovery." February 11, 2016. Available at epi.org.

Wong, Alia and Adrienne Green. "Campus Politics: A Cheat Sheet," *The Atlantic*. April 4, 2016. Available at theatlantic.com.

York, Geoffrey. "South African Tuition Protests Turn Violent as Police Use Stun Grenades on Students." *The Globe and Mail*. October 21, 2015. Available at theglobeandmail.com.

"Zuma, Ramaphosa Have Blood on Their Hands: UCT Students," August 18, 2015. Available at enca.com.

ON OBJECTIONS TO PLEDGING ALLEGIANCE

Zaina Alsous

mama's hijab wasn't given to God; she

layered scarf over soft hair

worn alongside polite smiles to strangers

to convince her children they were living

we woke up dead you see; ghosts

fermenting in an imperial continuum

an inescapable pageant

between the harem and the gun

did we choose death slow or sudden; what

did you give up phantom patriot

your own dark sisters?

your own tongue?

what flag did you swallow

SHAME:PRIDE :: INDUCED:FEVER

angry men with something to lose; terrified

pilgrims mark territory never discussing

distinctions between honor and theft

manhood is the saddest veil

i don't want to exist here; she

says to Gabriel and wise spiders

chewing on rose petals

at the edge of the world

on the cliff i see clearly; awake

sequence observing the burning below

envying ashes that blow in the wind

only believing in what comes after fire

---

daughter of Palestinian refugees. poems attempt to rewrite scripts levied upon displaced bodies as needing to be docile, useful, assimilated to empire. Instead i attempt to write to visceral rage, internal insurgency, inherited trauma, that spills out and holds empire accountable.

searchingfor-elsewhere.tumblr.com

CHECK ONE

Vincente 'SubVersive' Perez

I'll never forget the first time I took an in school survey
It was about drug use in adolescents
but the questions didn't bother me
The survey before it did

Age: 13
Sex: Male
Race: (Check one)

My heart drops

I raise my hand and whisper
"I don't want really wanna just check one"
Teacher reminds me, *Follow directions*
Check one.
I guess I should pick who I am today. . .

Today I am Mexican. . .
I wear my hair only 2 inches
Slicked back, gelled down so hard
Bullets would ricochet right off me

 I wanna make sure they get I'm at least Chicano
No puedo hablar español muy bien
Pero,
My last name is Spanish
I hope it counts for something.

Today I am Black. . .
Took the gel out my hair

Cause my step dad called me "Nigger"
I should braid it now
Fit "my role" right?

I'll never forget the first time somebody told me
"Yeah, you my nigga, but you not really Black"
It made my heart turn anchor
'Cause I gave up my Mexican side today
Hoping my black friends would pick me up. . .

Today I am Mexican. . .
The teacher sees my name tag and speaks to me in *Spanish*
Embarrassed, I say: I can't really speak it
But on the inside, I wonder if I should cherish this as a win
Because I was recognized as who I feel I am.

But, today I am nothing. . .
Because somebody asked me

What Are You?

As if my race preceded being human
Ran their fingers through my hair
To show me my body is not
My own.

I lose everything and nothing each time this happens.
When a teacher hands me a test tells me to check one
I refuse to answer. . .
This refusal is part of my Histories

You gotta think back then,
The shackles been taken off but niggas still think back then.

We are **Dread locked**,
Let me repeat that—I said **locked in dread**
We can't get "then" back cause our skin's black
I can't get "then" back 'cause my skin. . . **ain't.**

I can't take back the moment my *Abuelita* silenced her native
tongue

And painted my mom American
The same color my face gets when I'm approached by someone
Speaking with the same tongue that was taken from my mother
This color is embarrassment.

I cannot find my history in their textbooks
Every single one of my lands taken.
I want my "then" back but they keep telling me history is
    written by the victors,
But don't you know
My name comes from "conqueror"
My blood is from the *Yaqui* tribe.
I want my "then" back so that "Check One" boxes
Don't make my hand tremble and make me forget
The voice box that my "then" gives me now.

Now I rap and I rhyme 'cause I want time back,
Better yet, I want mine back.
Matter of fact, 2 times that,
'Cause even the time that we have now is their time halved.

This is to the haves and the have-nots
From the barrios to the cellblocks
I'm still learning how to pronounce my own name
I am learning my history
I am learning to take the weight of colonization
Off of my tongue
I am sharping it to check those
Trying to check-one me
Checkmate—I am future,
Without your history

As an activist, poet, musician, and more, I focus on the lived experiences of race in America through several mediums. My work centers on Black and Latinx experiences with a special emphasis on Hip-Hop, spoken word, narratives, and identity politics. Through a unique style of mixing political commentary, personal experience, and poetry, I do my best to challenge the idea that we live distinct political, social, and economic lives.

I believe that art and especially, writing, has the power to challenge popular narratives that structure peoples' lives. I spend a great deal of time exploring the themes of liminality, power, and the intentionally constructed narrative. I utilize liminal experiences as lenses that reflect back on the worlds that create these experiences. Instead of either/or world perspectives, I examine the multifaceted, complex world of "and." I ask and attempt to answer: what happens when we consider all of ourselves simultaneously rather than in isolated, limiting snapshots? How do the ways that we classify ourselves affect our agency in the world? Lastly, and most importantly, are the labels that are provided for us sufficiently capturing our experiences and if not, what do we lose when we accept these labels and all their baggage?

iamsubversive.com
twitter.com/iamsubversive
facebook.com/iamsubversive

ALL OUR COMMUNITY'S VOICES

UNTEACHING THE PRISON LITERACY COMPLEX

Michael Sutcliffe

SINCE THE PASSAGE OF THE ROCKEFELLER DRUG LAWS IN 1973, the United States has been in the business of incarceration. The number of people living in California has fluctuated with periods of immigration and exodus, yet the state's prison population has grown steadily and exponentially. According to a report compiled by *Huffington Post*, California's prison population has increased "eight times faster than the size of the overall population."[1] The state budget for criminal legal spending has adjusted accordingly. According to the report, "spending on California's prisons and associated correctional programs has skyrocketed by 436 percent" since 1980. California's other institutions were forced into crisis. In 2003, at the height of California's economic crisis, the legislature proposed budget cuts of $11 billion from K–12 education and $239 million from public universities while increasing prison spending by $40 million and moving forward with plans to build a new $595 million prison.[2] This increase was the only area of spending slated for increase on the 2003–04 budget. Rather than recognize the "direct relationship between how much money the Golden State spends on prisons and how much it spends on higher education," California's voters simply tried to outspend the prison population explosion.[3]

In the United States, illiteracy has long been associated with crime. Inherited notions of education and appropriate language

---

1. Aaron Sankin, "California Spending More On Prisons Than Colleges, Report Says." *Huffington Post*, September 8, 2012, available at huffingtonpost.com.
2. Prerna Anand, "Winners and Losers: Corrections and Higher Education in California," September 5, 2012, available at cacs.org.
3. Sankin, "California Spending More on Prisons."

use grew alongside the emerging economic and political climate in the colonial United States. Robert Johnson explains that the first jails appeared as populations increased and property within settled areas became a commodity. A shift in crimes away from person and morality and toward property and property owners (stakeholders tied intimately to the maintenance of government) resulted in an ideological shift as criminals were "seen more as pariahs who should be banished from society and less as wayward fellow citizens who were candidates for reform."[4] As the economic impact of crime became more politically significant, criminality was blamed on a deficient morality and worldview in need of correction, and criminals were marked for segregation. As incarceration became a formal response to social problems, clergy were charged with "last-hope" prisoner education through the facilitation of bible study and rigorously enforced quiet meditation. Education, and particularly literacy, served as the evidence of salvation or successful reformation.

This belief has persisted into our contemporary criminal legal system. According to Jonathan Messemer's history of correctional education, literacy levels among prisoners are difficult to evaluate, but conservative estimates suggest 40 percent of state prisoners and more than 45 percent of jail detainees do not have a high-school diploma or GED.[5] National studies of prison literacy offer a similar picture. *Literacy Behind Prison Walls*, a publication of the U.S. Department of Education, found "prisoners' basic literacy rates are significantly lower than their free peers and that thirty-six percent of inmates reported having at least one learning disability."[6] Moves to reform legislation and prison policy often focus on education as both a measure of criminality and a means by which to mitigate it.

In 1994, politics in the United States were characterized by partisan finger pointing over who was "soft" on crime and who

4. Robert Johnson, *Hard Time: Understanding and Reforming the Prison* (East Windsor, CT: Wadsworth, 1995), 56.

5. Jonathan E. Messemer, "The Historical Practice of Correctional Education in the United States: A Review of the Literature," *International Journal of Humanities and Social Science* 1, no. 17 (2011): 91.

6. Karl Haigler et al., "Literacy Behind Prison Walls," *US Department of Education* (Washington, DC: GPO, 1994), 31.

was "tough." Both Republican and Democratic Party leaders used legislation for political leverage. As a result, Congress passed the Violent Crime Control and Law Enforcement Act (VCCLEA) denying prisoners' eligibility for Pell Grants and other federal funding while simultaneously mandating federal prisons to provide basic literacy education. Federal law now both requires support for prisoners seeking a GED and prohibits state funding of postsecondary or supplementary instruction. This law not only closed programs run by state colleges, which had proliferated in the eighties and nineties, but also validated high-school equivalency as the threshold for functionality and placed blame for criminal behavior onto prisoners' lack of specific literacies.

Kirk Branch explains that the VCCLEA created an assumption that "illiteracy, or low literacy, causes crime. This assumption makes the provision of certain kinds of literacy education appear as a matter of some urgency, for to allow prisoners to leave prison without a basic education, often represented as necessary for post-release employment, fails to address an easily identifiable impetus toward a continuing criminal career."[7] Program administrators are positioned to see a specific, functional literacy as the "cure" for criminality. This view, or extension of the American "bootstraps" ideology, distracts attention from significant, systemic inequities that are directly related to criminality—advocates, teachers, and program administrators are encouraged to blame individual inmates when statistics show that entire populations are victim to the same "crimes" and overlook racism, poverty, drug addiction, and disenfranchisement as potential factors in inmate lives. These are seen as by-products of criminality rather than causes, and reform measures are authored accordingly.

The state has looked to educators to explain and then to reinforce links between criminality and illiteracy, seeking to explain those whose lifestyles fall outside normalized modes of production. Prison officials and policymakers alike routinely use academic measures as indicators of "progress" along an imagined linear path from criminality to social inclusivity, and parole boards often

7. Kirk Branch, *Eyes on the Ought to Be: What We Teach When We Teach About Literacy* (Cresskill, CT: Hampton Press, 2005), 59.

cite educational achievement as a sign of rehabilitation. In *Prison Literacy: Implications for Program and Assessment Policy*, Anabel Newman defines literacy as the ability to complete high-school equivalency courses, although the study recommendations are a bit more progressive, listing learner-driven designs and access to technology among its recommendations.[8] The report continues the project of masking questions that might disturb the status quo means of economic production and questions about our collective, communal complicity, and instead directs research toward questions about enacting educational counter-measures to criminality.

On April 9, 2008, the "Second Chance Act" became law. Intended to reduce recidivism by addressing the limited options available to undereducated prisoners, the law set aside federal money to be distributed by the Department of Justice in the form of research grants. The first of these was issued in 2010 to the RAND Corporation, which was tasked with comprehensively evaluating the effectiveness of correctional education programs. Drawing upon studies done over the preceding thirty years, RAND evaluated adult basic, adult secondary, vocational, and adult post-secondary education programs and specifically omitted life-skills programs and community-based programs that serve prisoners upon release. Calculating the average cost of prison based programming, RAND juxtaposed the result against the (financial) cost of incarceration and projected average cost of recidivating. RAND reported,

> For a correctional education program to be cost-effective, we estimated that a program would need to reduce the three year reincarceration rate by between 1.9 and 2.6 percentage points ... our meta-analytic findings show that participation in a correctional education program is associated with a 13 percentage point reduction in the risk of reincarceration three years after release from prison.[9]

---

8. Anabel P. Newman, *Prison Literacy: Implications for Program and Assessment Policy* (Bloomington, IN: ERIC Clearinghouse on Reading and Communication Skills, 1993), 47.

9. Lois M. Davis et al., *How Effective Is Correctional Education, and Where Do We Go from Here?* (US Department of Justice, 2014), available at rand.org.

The report does not attempt to explain the economic impact of education on policing or the court system nor does it attempt to evaluate the emotional costs borne by those involved; the RAND report does specifically mention victims of crime but makes no mention of costs incurred on victims of incarceration or their families and communities. In short, correctional education programs are, according to RAND, simply cost-effective.

The RAND report rhetorically reinforces the criminalization of illiteracy and the illiterate by associating literacy acquisition with a medical procedure stating future researchers will be tasked with "measuring program *dosage*, identifying program characteristics, and examining more *proximal* indicators of program efficacy."[10] Broken, illiterate prisoners will be taught how to think, learn, and problem solve; they will be "saved" through education. In other words, prison education programs are positioned to teach poor prisoners, mostly people of color, how to be more middle class and more white. Those that do not reinforce capitalist stratification by accepting a labor class role are seen in terms of threat and maneuvered out of influential positions in society. Their credibility is destroyed by a near-permanent identification as a convict.

Underlying the putative American Dream ideology is a belief in meritocracy and the equal opportunities that are supposed rewards of individual efforts. Consequently, education is believed by many to be a panacea for crime and a cure-all for hegemonic social ills. Politicians, parents, teachers, and most voters believe that a "good education" is a pass to social success and financial independence. Unlocking economic opportunity and lifting oneself upward from historically disadvantaged social stature is believed to be achieved through schooling and hard work. The evidence of material realities such as unequal distributions of wealth, property, health, and so on, is offset by an ideological investment in the idea that equality secures the opportunity to pursue these goods. As Jennifer Hochschild explains, "so long as we live in a democratic capitalist society—that is, so long as we maintain the formal promise of political and social equality while encouraging the practice of economic inequality—we need the idea of equal

---

10. Ibid., 82; emphasis added.

opportunity to bridge that otherwise unacceptable condition."[11] In America, equality is understood to mean opportunity, and poverty and crime evidence individual inadequacies or disinterest rather than an unequal system of distribution or access. Revoking widespread public support for incarceration means un-teaching some very entrenched beliefs.

Educational programs in prisons and jails largely exist to rehabilitate prisoners upon release, so they teach from the outside in. Even when designed with the intent of creating change, they almost always assume a mantle of instruction and, usually, remediation. Programs teach prisoners vocational writing or skills for specific trades; however, as Kirk Branch explains, "the pedagogic discourse of vocational education cannot be understood apart from the economic interests it serves, apart, that is, from its various sponsors."[12] The systems of economic distribution that maintain a compliant working class and an elite bourgeoisie are maintained by a pedagogical approach that, ultimately, does little more than make worker-prisoners more comfortable with their station. I suggest that these programs make up a "Prison Literacy Complex," as their attempt to re-enfranchise prisoners assumes a benign or benevolent system and culture waiting to accept wayward members back into the fold.

THE PRISON LITERACY COMPLEX

Literacy programs that serve incarcerated students have been largely built upon literacy research from secondary and postsecondary education, yet most scholarship on prisoner literacy reduces a complicated, contentious history to a single theory. The association of social status with an individual's ability to process symbols (read, write, and speak in a particular standardized dialect) is indicative of what Alec Webster, Brian Caddick, Malcolm Reed, and Karen Ford refer to as a linguistic-functional definition of literacy; literacy is understood to be "a set of mechanical skills

11. Jennifer Hochschild, "The Double-Edged Sword of Equal Educational Opportunity," American Educational Research Association Annual Meeting (Washington DC, April 22, 1987), 8.

12. Branch, *Eyes on the Ought to Be*, 95.

for encoding and decoding print, or 'cracking a linguistic code.'"[13] Through this lens, literacy is seen as a measure of one's ability to transmit a preexisting message by means of an autonomous coding system (an alphabet) that is independent from the rhetorical situation in which it is used. Written competencies like handwriting, vocabulary, and grammar as well as spoken competency in transforming coded symbols into phonetic sounds are thought to be teachable through rote practice and skill-and-drill instruction. Literacy, in this view, is limited to the transmission of preexisting meaning and messages, and programs exist to "equip adults with just sufficient competence to operate at the lowest levels of mechanical performance."[14] Learners are taught to memorize and repeat. Significantly, little attention is paid to where the "correct" versions come from.

Literacy, when thought of this way, is understood by most to be a nongradable adjective; one either is or is not literate with clear separation between, although there is some gradation allowed among the illiterate population. In other words, it is possible for one learner to be more literate than another, but educators and successful community members are simply literate. Once someone learns to read and write, they are no longer in need of literacy education. As a result, education (and authority) is understood to emanate from the educated while those deemed illiterate are seen as deficient community members in need of remediation. As Walter J. Ong explains, literacy, when thought of this way, is normative and suggests illiterates "are deviants, defined by something they lack."[15]

This belief in language use as an indicator of social standing is what Harvey J. Graff has termed the "literacy myth":

> The acquisition of literacy is a necessary precursor to and invariably results in economic development, democratic practice, cognitive enhancement, and upward social mobility . . . [and is]

---

13. Alec Webster et al., "Functional Versus Critical Literacy in the Rehabilitation of Offenders: A Survey of Probation Services in England and Wales." *International Journal of Lifelong Education* 18, no. 1 (1999): 50.

14. Ibid.

15. Walter J. Ong in Ellen Cushman et al., *Literacy: A Critical Sourcebook* (Boston: Bedford St. Martin's, 2001), 19.

invested with immeasurable and indeed almost ineffable qual-
ities, purportedly conferring on practitioners a predilection toward social order, an elevated moral sense, and a metaphorical
"state of grace."[16]

The literacy myth connects a puritan sense of predestined
morality with a demonstrable skill. Buttressed by Western notions of self-sufficiency and "bootstraps" meritocracy, blame for
illiteracy falls on the illiterate with laziness, disinterest, or social
nonbelonging effacing poverty, privilege, and limited access to education as exigency. Brian Street explains that literacy had "come
to be associated with crude and often ethnocentric stereotypes of
'other cultures' and represents a way of perpetuating the notion
of a 'great divide' between 'modern' and 'traditional' societies that
is less acceptable when expressed in other terms."[17] Despite good
intentions, a view of hierarchized literacies pathologized particular cultures, lifestyles, and dialects attaching literacies to race.
Through uses of language, people of color and people with non-
normative lifestyles were and are signaled as less economically
valuable. Prisoners are presumed to be inherently deficient. While
what is said is a deficiency in literacy skills, what is meant is a
deficiency in white middle-class-ness.

As a result, the prison has become the enforcement wing of a
sort of neoliberal checks-and-balances. As David Harvey explains,
the role of the neoliberal state is to advance economic security "by
liberating individual entrepreneurial freedoms and skills within an
institutional framework characterized by strong private property
rights, free markets, and free trade."[18] Neoliberalism creates institutional (and ideological) frameworks to protect private property rights
rather than public access and equity. State intervention should, according to this worldview, never countermand market signals and
should only occur when necessary to deregulate and privatize new

16. Harvey J. Graff, "The Literacy Myth at 30," *Journal of Social History* 43, no. 3
(2010): 635.

17. Brian Street, "The New Literacy Studies," in *Literacy: A Critical Sourcebook*, edited
by Ellen Cushman, Eugene R. Kintgen, Barry M. Kroll, and Mike Rose (New York:
Bedford, 2001; originally published 1993), 433.

18. David Harvey, *A Brief History of Neoliberalism* (Oxford: Oxford University Press,
2005), 2.

markets, such as recent efforts to privatize water for corporate retail bottling or land for timber sales and oil pipelines. Neoliberal economic policies have disappeared solvent employment and shredded state support services through deregulation, the dismantling of unions, and a progressive weakening of corporate restraints.

The process of legislating criminality perpetuates control and maintains the prison as a robust sorting mechanism. The police and the courts target not only specific actions but also specific groups of people while maintaining a myth of criminality as a violation of a shared, communal morality. As John Irwin explains, criminality is a mechanism by which to sort according to cultural capital: "The difference between crimes is not seriousness or prevalence; it is offensiveness, which is determined by social status and context."[19] Essentially, laws are discursive technologies employed to punish people for being offensively out of place. These "instruments," as Michel Foucault calls them, "render visible, record, differentiate and compare" populations both before and after intake into the criminal legal system.[20] Prisoners are classified into a sublabor "criminal" class in ways that "serve only to manufacture new criminals and to drive existing criminals even deeper into criminality."[21] Former laborers are removed from the workforce and (permanently) re-classed as unemployable criminals. Criminality, then, is both the means by which people are sorted (primarily along class lines) for incarceration and the result of incarceration. Incarceration is not simply a set of institutions, laws, and facilities, but is also "a state of mind."[22]

The prison reinforces neoliberalism's market primacy and the economic advantage of the wealthy by physically removing resistant people from society and preventing them from sharing testimony that could point to contradictions in the economic status quo. Rather than a poverty class disenfranchised by the state, the

---

19. John Irwin, *Jail: Managing the Underclass in American Society* (Berkeley: University of California Press, 1985), 17.

20. Michel Foucault, *Discipline and Punish: The Birth of the Prison* (New York: Vintage Press, 1995), 208.

21. Michel Foucault, "Prison Talk," in *Power/Knowledge* (New York: Pantheon, 1980), 40.

22. American Friends Service Committee, *Corrupting Justice: Primer for LGBT Communities on Racism, Violence, Human Degradation, and the Prison Industrial Complex* (Philadelphia: Justice Visions Publication, 2005).

criminal legal system protects neoliberalism by legislating their exclusion as poorly made personal choice. As a result, the white middle class largely looks away as neoliberal economic and social policies financed by the human suffering of incarceration leverage devastating results. Communities of color are stripped of working age men and women and repopulated with a criminalized class unable to gain or hold legal employment. As Loïc Wacquant has said, this process has "spawned a carceral continuum that ensnares a supernumerary population of younger black men, who either reject or are rejected by the deregulated low-wage labor market."[23] Younger and older women are most often left to tend to children and to pick up pieces of broken communities.

Educational programs for prisoners began as bible study sessions in the first American prisons. This coupling of religion with literacy education was founded on the notion that committing a crime was an independent, individual choice made as the result of a personal skills defect and a moral insufficiency. Despite a legacy of scholarship that demonstrates otherwise, most literacy programs that serve incarcerated students have inherited their mission from this belief and approach literacy instruction as reparative and transformative. Prisoners are supposed to learn new ways of solving problems by learning from successful, informed outsiders or former-insiders who have succeeded. I have termed this alignment of literacy programs as a "voices-in" orientation. Literacy programs are designed to bring instructor expertise, source texts, and problem solving methods *in* to prisoners. While these types of programs exist to help prisoners, they do so by validating normative values and systems of distribution and criminalization that lead to increased rates of incarceration. While prisoners may get some relief from the monotony of prison life, may learn some valuable workplace skills, and even learn to communicate in ways that suspend judgment and stigmatization, the next generation of prisoners is still being targeted by widespread public support for prison building, militarized policing, legislated racism, and the expansion of the criminal-legal apparatus.

---

23. Loïc Wacquant, "Deadly Symbiosis: When Ghetto and Prison Meet and Mesh," *Punishment & Society* 3, no. 1 (2001): 97.

VOICING OUT

The ideological reliance upon literacy as a mark of exclusivity and affluence does, however, mark a paradigmatic shift in literacy studies as scholars began to apply critical theory and ethnographic methods to literacy studies. Brian Street explains that scholars seeking to reveal the relationship between language use and systemic privileging of one group over another "have come to view literacy practices as inextricably linked to cultural and power structures in society . . . [and] paid greater attention to the role of literacy practices in reproducing or challenging structures of power and domination."[24] Literacy, according to Street, is intricately woven into the attribution of values, and the connection between language, thought (often in the form of judgment), and social access makes language acquisition inseparable from the ways we think of each other and ourselves. This ideological view of literacy reveals tensions around authority, power, and resistance that are products of language use but that also produce uses of language that mark social standing. Language, as a result, "can no longer be addressed as a neutral technology."[25]

Street, however, cautions that an ideological understanding of literacy should not be seen as a binary choice to autonomous, functional definitions. While some critics of Street suggest "unnecessary polarization," Street explains that the ideological model views technical skills and ideological processes as "encapsulated within cultural wholes and within structures of power."[26] The processes by which we code meaning foreground particular value systems as natural and given while denigrating others as acquired or chosen deviations. This thought process is itself ideological, and it is implicated in ideological reproduction and the reinforcement of existing power distribution. Further, when adopted by institutional decision-makers, these ideologies are repackaged as "common sense," particularly when legitimized by induction into pedagogy. According to Street, "the naturalization of ideologies, as though they were universal necessities rather than institutions for reproduction of the

---

24. Street, "The New Literacy Studies," 434.

25. Ibid., 435.

26. Ibid.

cultural and power bases of particular interests and groups, has been reinforced by the academic community as much as by those whose interests it serves."[27] The adoption of functional definitions of literacy as well as concepts like "cultures of poverty" position education against those hoping for improved socioeconomic mobility. Education, as an institution, thus becomes an ideological apparatus mobilizing the economic resources of the state in service of capitalism and the culture of the dominant. Despite the intent of teachers and administrators, education is not politically or ideologically neutral, yet literacy programs for incarcerated students are usually modeled on school pedagogies with little critical consideration of their political consequence or implication.

Street suggests it is not enough to point to a specific linguistic structure or speech act, but instead, a challenge to hegemony must historicize and interrupt an idea:

> Social change involves challenging a given form of (dominant) discourse and the production and assertion of other discourses within new material conditions . . . not at the level of abstract philosophical inquiry but in terms of the real social relations between historical forces and relations on the one hand and forms of discourse sustained or undermined by them on the other.[28]

By adapting our understanding of literacy to include the ideological, we can visualize relations of power and material resources. Social change, then, must use an analysis of discourse and context, what Shirley Brice Heath calls the "Literacy Event," as a lens through which to analyze the history of relations of power and the distribution of material and economic resources.[29] By understanding the formation of valorized forms of communication in context, we can, according to Street, understand the ways that valuation is ideologically informed.

Definitions, perceptions, and value judgments are opinions informed, when processed uncritically, by tradition, repetition, and

---

27. Ibid., 437.
28. Ibid., 441.
29. Shirley Brice Heath, "What No Bedtime Story Means: Narrative Skills at Home and School," Language in Society 11, no. 3 (1982): 50.

routine (ritual) rather than with observation and evaluation. Secular rituals, according to Henry Bial, seem natural and value-neutral as they "invoke the authority of some concept larger than the individual: the state, the community, tradition."[30] Rather than forcing an interruption of comfortable ways of living, ritual grants familiar ideas a sense of authenticity validating the preexisting and forestalling the new. The influence of the institution of incarceration works discursively through notions of fixed, ideal truths to power a rhetoric that allows dismissal of inventive thought. Considerations of "why" and "how" are overlooked or dismissed in favor of given, predetermined, state-sponsored values for "justice" and "crime." Over time, accepted ideas or truths coalesce to form ideologies that leverage influence over competing ideas suppressing those that would challenge their dominance; in short, they combine to form hegemony.

Andrea Mayr explains that in Antonio Gramsci's theorization of hegemony, power is not physical force but rather "one ruling class has persuaded subordinate classes to accept its own moral, political, and cultural values through concessions or ideological means. Power is therefore not exercised coercively but subtly and routinely."[31] In other words, it functions rhetorically. Central to Gramsci's theories of hegemony is this notion that consent is given because of a perception of mutual benefit. Or, as Gramsci says, the state or institution "educates this consent, by means of the political and syndical association."[32] Through the language of policy and media, institutions are recursively powered discursively. The state manufactures and remanufactures consent by establishing definitions and the *appearance* of common, shared experiences and interests. Thus, as Karl Marx once explained, winning control of the means of production secures the future arrangement of the means of production. At the behest of private industry, the state controls what we believe to be history.[33]

---

30. Henry Bial, "Ritual," in *The Performance Studies Reader* (London: Routledge, 2004), 77.

31. Andrea Mayr, *Prison Discourse: Language as a Means of Control and Resistance* (New York: Palgrave Macmillan, 2004), 16.

32. Antonio Gramsci, *Selections from the Prison Notebooks*, trans. Q. Hoare and G. Nowell-Smith (New York: International, 1971), 259.

33. Karl Marx and Frederick Engels, *The German Ideology* (Amherst, MA: Prometheus Books, 1998).

Street's understanding of literacy as ideological, then, gives us a way to understand power and access as distributed through systems rather than motives. Ideology carried by discourse (re)produces distributions of power independent of a speaker-writer's intent. In the context of prison literacy programs, facilitators often intend to do "good" yet ultimately validate the neoliberal exclusivity that drives incarceration. A system of educational programming for prisoners that reproduces rather than resists survives despite reform efforts because it works *with* the overarching ideological system. Advocates function as state agents as they address specific inequities (illiteracy) as the root cause rather than as signs of a more systemic problem. The system of blaming individuals and then sequestering them away into institutions marked by violence, militant authoritarian regimes, and disease "is considered so 'natural' that it is extremely hard to imagine life without it."[34]

As a result, many reformers accept incarceration as a generally sound concept that has just been poorly executed or overtaxed. They seem to believe that the criminal legal system is merely "broken" and in need of repair. Suggested policy revisions improve specific conditions but without substantive change to the sorting, or othering, or the numbers of prisoners. Further, the culmination of institutions ideologically aligned in support of isolating and segregating "offenders" lends tacit support and recursive ideological maintenance in a self-fulfilling prophecy. As Gramsci says, "every relationship of 'hegemony' is necessarily an educational relationship."[35] Incarceration is not simply a product of legislation, but it is a product of a culture of incarceration that is taught across many contexts. Churches, families, schools, media, and more make us complicit in the propagation of criminality, yet they simultaneously posit it as a simple, natural reaction to threats and deviance. This oversimplification masks or completely effaces the systemic from media analyses, from community memory, and, as a result, from legislative sessions and voter ballots. When shown only the arrest report of an incarcerated person of color, white voters largely (dis)miss the historical roots of racism and disenfranchisement

---

34. Angela Y. Davis, *Are Prisons Obsolete?* (New York: Seven Stories Press, 2003), 10.
35. Gramsci, *Selections from the Prison Notebooks*, 350.

and see only a behavior. The ways we conceptualize and evaluate uses of language reinforce cultural hegemony and offer immense comfort and stability to white educators and policymakers.

·RESISTANCE AND RE-MEMBERING

I believe we can disrupt and interrupt this sense of comfort and empower educational programs, and literacy programs in particular, to be agents of revolution. Victor Villanueva explains that changes to hegemony "occur when there is widespread socio-historical criticism. Voices of discontent look back to the roots of oppression and articulate the socio-historical precedents. . . . The voices seek to persuade all groups that everyone's needs could be better met if substantive changes were to take place."[36] By historicizing "common sense," Gramsci's "organic intellectuals" point to the rhetorical construction and constructedness of truths held as natural and immutable. In other words, what seems to be a seamless progression of common sense ideas is revealed to be politicized discourse in service of a dominant culture. To effect a real redistribution of resources, whether economic, material, or ideological, those who would spark social change must demonstrate that seeming truths are not true for all communities; they must demonstrate the untruthiness of truths. There is a possibility for change in the reinfusing or re-membering of resistant historical narratives into public discourse and community memory.

It is the definition and understanding of literacy itself that must be revised to begin a process of change, rather than the processes by which incarcerated students acquire or demonstrate their education or their literacy. The ways a program identifies and defines its goals informs its relationship with state sponsorship and its use of students' voices. When program administrators believe they are liberating but refuse to recognize their incarcerated students' experiences and expertise, they validate the systems that placed their students there in the first place. As Gramsci tells us, "one could say that ideologies for the governed are mere illusions, a deception to which they are subject, while for the governing they constitute a willed

---

36. Victor Villanueva, *Bootstraps: From an American Academic of Color* (Urbana, IL: NCTE, 1992), 23.

and a knowing deception."[37] Regardless of intent, the instructors take on the role of oppressors. According to Marx and Engels, the only possible means for liberation from this mechanism, once set in motion, exists in the possibility that personal "history becomes world history."[38] Liberation can only happen when the dominant population can finally "see" the antidemocratic systems by which inequity is historically and discursively produced.

Paulo Freire expressed a sense of "duality" among oppressed and colonized people through which they experience a constructed sense of self: "They are at one and the same time themselves and the oppressor whose consciousness they have internalized."[39] Echoing Antonio Gramsci's theorizations of hegemony and consent, Freire demonstrates not only the ways in which oppression elicits complicity from those it dominates—the oppressed do not see the mechanisms as those by which they are dominated but instead see them as mechanisms that would enable their success—but also the ways in which its actions are invisible even (or especially) to those most affected. Freire explains, "The very structure of their thought has been conditioned by the contradictions of the concrete existential situation by which they were shaped . . . . Their perception of themselves as oppressed is impaired by their submersion in the reality of oppression."[40] Hegemony exerts control by consent and even by enthusiasm. Those without access to resources and power often do not see themselves as oppressed but rather as just not quite yet fulfilled. To reveal the faults in common justice narratives, we all need to see their instability.

In other words, literacy must be explicitly mobilized as an agent of socioeconomic change, yet this change can only result if minds change *outside* the space of acquisition (whether classroom or prison cell) as well as in. Radical pedagogy suggests reversing the polarity of classrooms so that teachers become students of the learners. I am suggesting a trifold reorganization. The experts on criminalization (as well as the social problems that lead to it) are

---

37. Antonio Gramsci, *The Antonio Gramsci Reader: Selected Writings 1916–1935*, trans. by D. Forgacs (New York: New York University Press, 2000), 196.

38. Marx and Engels, *The German Ideology*, 27.

39. Paulo Freire, *Pedagogy of the Oppressed* (New York: Continuum, 2003), 48.

40. Ibid., 45.

not the instructors but rather are the instructed, and the students in need of socioeconomic literacy are not the incarcerated learners but rather the instructors and even more so the communities that send them inside. While language use is the subject matter in the room, the ultimate education, in my opinion, is most needed outside. Educational programs, inside and out, act as a mechanism for validating popular myths and beliefs. By drawing upon prisoners' voices and their experiences with racism, near-permanent poverty, gender norming, and homophobia, these programs can use what I call a "voices-out" orientation to cut against popular narratives of meritocracy through texts and acts that reach out to the public from incarcerated spaces. When authorized as expertise, narratives told by those on the inside point to the untruthiness of commonly accepted myths and "truths" destabilizing the ideologies that maintain hegemony and its prison system.

However, simply being told revolutionary ideas is seldom enough and an ineffective means of sparking social change. White working- and middle-class voters have the privilege of overlooking conflicting social narratives. They can dismiss troubling accounts of prisoner-writers. Rather than betray the values of their families, churches, and political leaders, many simply refuse to acknowledge contradictory narratives or alternative histories as their lives are comfortable and they see no pressing need. Instead, they rely upon social and economic privilege to provide de facto support for systemic forms of oppression that they purportedly reject. After all, as Victor Villanueva tells us, "there is more to racism, ethnocentricity, and language than is apparent . . . . There are long-established systemic forces at play that maintain bigotry, systemic forces that can even make bigots of those who are appalled by bigotry."[41] These processes are at work in prisons and have particular implications for prisoners. Textual artifacts are not enough to disrupt the massive ideological inertia of incarceration. Critical projects will need a mechanism to turn observers as well as participants into advocates with motive and intent. Abolition requires the personalization and ideological reorientation that happens through participation.

---

41. Victor Villanueva, "Hegemony: From an Organically Grown Intellectual," *Pre-Text* 13, nos. 1–2 (1992): xiv.

A WORK IN PROGRESS

While the majority of literacy programs available to prisoners remain entrenched in functional literacy, a few do now exist that recognize the validity of prisoners' existing literacies and expertise and complicate the academic linear model of expert-to-learner education. Tobi Jacobi explains that for a literacy program to successfully move beyond the discursive replication of dominant criminalizing ideology, it must promote "engaged dialogue on writing, justice, and life experiences by valuing incarcerated writers' voices."[42] In these programs, facilitators set aside notions of affluence as evidence of expertise and authorize authentic dialogue. Prisoners' voices are brought out from behind prison walls in what I call a "voices-out" orientation. These kinds of literacy programs can challenge the norming, silencing effect of the prison by orienting their activities toward bringing prisoners' experiences and expertise *out* from the prison to teach community members, voters, and policy makers about social problems from what is usually a very unfamiliar perspective. Literacy, then, becomes a process of validating expertise as evidence of political and economic problems and collectively unraveling layers of obscuring privilege and compartmentalization. To authentically perform critical literacy, literacy programs must value prisoners' experiences rather than trying to repress and reform according to an imposed set of status quo values.

Community programs that use direct-service volunteers in order to counter the judgment and ideological inertia around criminality are not new, although they are rare. In 1973, the Women's Options for Recovery, Transitions, and Health (WORTH) program was created by a group of women in response to a request for support for women made by a county sheriff in the Pacific Northwest; women incarcerated at the jail were not issued clothing or personal hygiene products and the sheriff asked the group to provide them. In the mid-eighties, WORTH began recruiting volunteer representatives from community service agencies to speak to participants about women's health issues, alcohol and drug recovery, negotiating and exiting abusive relationships, and workplace

---

42. Tobi Jacobi, "Slipping Pages through Razor Wire: Literacy Action Projects in Jail." Community Literacy Journal 2, no. 2 (2008): 70.

(re)entry skills.[43] I joined the program in 2012 after it lost its volunteer staff and initiated an overall redesign. In order to better engage the mission of the parent organization, we reoriented WORTH around activities intended to influence change outside of the jail while still providing access to community resource information and to volunteers' expertise. Sessions became participatory workshops focused on specific literacies, and organizers created an interactive series of training seminars that repositioned volunteers as learner-facilitators and incarcerated women as participant-teachers. Writing activities became a central component of each session, and volunteers began helping participants share their writing online and through public venues.

Because of institutional constraints, I am not comfortable sharing program participants' writing here. However, overall, responses to our changes were positive. Participants told facilitators they used to enjoy getting out of the pod, but they felt lectured and judged. Since the reorientation, participating women say that it feels as though they're letting people hear them who otherwise would never know what it's like to live their lives.[44] Community volunteers also report changed feelings about incarceration. One stated, "I have discovered that [prisoners] are simply community members—not evil villains out to commit heinous acts. They are our friends, coworkers, neighbors, and family members: sisters, aunts, grandmothers. Some hold master's degrees, many have children. They could be you or I [sic]."[45] Other respondents expressed similar changes in perspective, and subsequent conversations have been driven more by questions than by presumed "truths," and more volunteers have expressed an interest in engaging in direct service as a means to learn rather than as a means to help or to fix. More importantly, each volunteer is now, to some degree, an advocate for a changed response to social problems, and while some may still support incarceration, they do so with hesitation and consideration that they may not have the entire picture.

43. WORTH volunteer, interview with the author, February 17, 2015.
44. Ibid.
45. Ibid.

In my terms, WORTH participants "speak truth to power" through stories of struggle and trauma and tragedy that are underscored with authentic hope and chance. By revealing the unequal valuing of multiple, divergent literacies, learners outside prison walls begin to recognize the extent to which their values and assumptions are products of what they've been told more than what they have experienced. Juxtaposing memories that refuse to comply with popular narratives against those that do interrupts dominant ideologies long enough to see the ways that our understandings of community and criminality reflect our identities more than our choices. Hegemony's institutional apparatus pressures those without privilege into a limited set of options while offering tokenized exceptions as models for reform efforts that ultimately do little more than suppress would-be revolution. Given the urgency of the inhumane treatment of those living behind prison walls, the pervasive intrusion of surveillance and incarceration into public life, and the privatizing nature of our neoliberal, capitalist hegemony, it is clear that we, as a society, need to hear from those of us who are most oppressed by these mechanisms and institutions. An authentic pursuit of social justice must take seriously the abolitionist commitment to ideological, social, and economic alternatives by bringing voices normally silenced by incarceration and isolation into conversation with those who would otherwise remain contently oblivious.

As Keith Gilyard reminds us, with regard to racism, any action that seeks to upset the norming power of systemic oppression must explicitly take that oppression as its object and the performance of resistance as its mode.[46] In order to interrupt the homophobic and racist notions upon which incarceration and its neoliberal hegemony are built, programs attempting to enact real change—a redistribution of material and economic resources across marginalized communities—must interrupt the epistemologies that privatize and normalize gender and race in the language of public life. Or, as Bruce Herzberg explains, real ideological critique is dependent on community members' ability to

---

46. Keith Gilyard, ed., *Race, Rhetoric, and Composition* (Portsmouth, NH: Boynton, 1999), 83.

"transcend their own deeply ingrained belief in individualism and meritocracy."[47] Engagement with texts or reports is not enough; they must be able to see the cuts where narratives patch their values together to make constructed truths.

I believe that we will only achieve systemic, widespread change by designing and implementing community programs that bring the personal experiences of those whose lives (not necessarily their motives) are resistant into conversation with those who are blinded by the myths of hegemony. Rather than teaching-in, we need conversations-out. In the documentary film *Visions of Abolition*, Angela Y. Davis and Ruth Wilson Gilmore call for a political ideology of prison abolition that is nuanced and multifaceted.[48] Rather than attempting to abruptly reverse the past four decades of prison expansion with a single vote or action, they suggest public education that results in support for incremental moves toward the deconstruction of mass incarceration. To move forward, the public must not only comprehend but also personalize the anti-democratic nature of incarceration and seek ways to deincarcerate and solve problems as a community rather than ways to police, punish, and fragment. While not a complete solution, an ideological interruption may provide a gap through which to historicize and activate. As Lois Ahrens explains, "everyone, not just those with fancy educations, can and must understand the complicated politics and economics underlying prison expansion if we are to stop [it]."[49] Or, to put Tobi Jacobi into conversation with Victor Villanueva and Ahrens, we all need to "trouble" our "truths" so that we can shape a comprehensive, historicized, nuanced understanding of the very "real costs" of incarceration.

---

47. Bruce Herzberg, "Community Service and Critical Teaching," *College Composition and Communication* 45, no. 3 (1994): 312.

48. Setsu Shigematsu, director, *Visions of Abolition: From Critical Resistance To A New Way of Life* (United States: Visions of Abolition, 2011).

49. Lois Ahrens, ed., *The Real Cost of Prisons Comix* (Oakland, CA: PM Press, 2008), 19.

REFERENCES

Ahrens, Lois, ed. *The Real Cost of Prisons Comix*. Oakland, CA: PM Press, 2008.

American Friends Service Committee. *Corrupting Justice: Primer for LGBT Communities on Racism, Violence, Human Degradation, and the Prison Industrial Complex*. Philadelphia: Justice Visions Publication, 2005.

Anand, Prerna. *Winners and Losers: Corrections and Higher Education in California*. California Common Sense, 2012. Available at: uscommensense.org.

Bial, Henry, ed. *The Performance Studies Reader*. London: Routledge, 2004.

Branch, Kirk. *Eyes on the Ought to Be: What We Teach When We Teach About Literacy*. Cresskill, CT: Hampton Press, 2005.

Cushman, Ellen, Eugene R. Kintgen, Barry M. Kroll, and Mike Rose. *Literacy: A Critical Sourcebook*. Boston: Bedford St. Martin's, 2001.

Davis, Angela Y. *Are Prisons Obsolete?* New York: Seven Stories Press, 2003.

———. "Prison Industrial Complex." Audiobook. Chico, CA: AK Press, 2001.

Davis, Lois M., Jennifer L. Steele, Robert Bozick, Malcolm V. Williams, Susan Turner, Jeremy N.V. Miles, Jessica Saunders, and Paul S. Steinberg. *How Effective is Correctional Education, and Where Do We Go From Here? The Results of a Comprehensive Evaluation*. Santa Monica, CA: RAND Corporation, 2014. Available at: rand.org.

Foucault, Michel. *Discipline and Punish: The Birth of the Prison*. New York: Vintage Press, 1995.

———. "Prison Talk." In *Power/Knowledge*. New York: Pantheon, 1980.

Freire, Paulo. *Pedagogy of the Oppressed*. New York: Continuum, 2003.

Gilyard, Keith, ed. *Race, Rhetoric, and Composition*. Portsmouth, NH: Boynton, 1999.

Giroux, Henry. *On Critical Pedagogy*. New York: Continuum International Publishing Group, 2011.

Graff, Harvey J. "The Literacy Myth at 30." *Journal of Social History* 43, no. 3 (2010): 635–61.

Gramsci, Antonio. *The Antonio Gramsci Reader: Selected Writings 1916–1935*. Translated by D. Forgacs. New York: New York University Press, 2000.

———. *Selections from the Prison Notebooks*. Translated by Q. Hoare and G. Nowell-Smith. New York: International, 1971.

Haigler, Karl, Caroline Harlow, Patricia O'Connor, and Anne Campbell. *Literacy Behind Prison Walls*. Washington, DC: US Department of Education, 1994. Available at: nces.ed.gov.

Harvey, David. *A Brief History of Neoliberalism*. Oxford: Oxford University Press, 2005.

Herzberg, Bruce. "Community Service and Critical Teaching." *College Composition and Communication* 45, no. 3 (1994): 307–19.

Herzing, Rachel. "What is the Prison Industrial Complex?" *Defending Justice*, 2005. Available at: publiceye.org.

Hochschild, Jennifer. "The Double-Edged Sword of Equal Educational Opportunity." American Educational Research Association Annual Meeting. Washington DC, April 22, 1987.

Irwin, John. *Jail: Managing the Underclass in American Society*. Berkeley, CA: University of California Press, 1985.

Jacobi, Tobi. "Slipping Pages through Razor Wire: Literacy Action Projects in Jail." Community Literacy Journal 2, no. 2 (2008): 67–86.

Johnson, Robert. *Hard Time: Understanding and Reforming the Prison*. East Windsor, CT: Wadsworth, 1995.

Kaeble, Danielle, Lauren E. Glaze, Anastasios Tsoutis, and Todd D. Minton. *Correctional Populations in the United States*. Washington, DC: Bureau of Justice Statistics, 2015. NCJ 249513.

Law, Victoria. *Resistance Behind Bars: The Struggles of Incarcerated Women*. Oakland, CA: PM Press, 2009.

Marx, Karl, and Frederick Engels. *The German Ideology*. Amherst, MA: Prometheus Books, 1998.

Mayr, Andrea. *Prison Discourse: Language as a Means of Control and Resistance*. New York: Palgrave Macmillan, 2004.

Messemer, Jonathan E. "The Historical Practice of Correctional Education in the United States: A Review of the Literature." *International Journal of Humanities and Social Science* 1, no. 17 (2011): 91–100.

Newman, Anabel P. *Prison Literacy: Implications for Program and Assessment Policy*. Bloomington, IN: ERIC Clearinghouse on Reading and Communication Skills, 1993.

Sankin, Aaron. "California Spending More On Prisons Than Colleges, Report Says." *Huffington Post*, September 8, 2012. Available at: huffingtonpost.com.

Shigematsu, Setsu, director. *Visions of Abolition: From Critical Resistance To A New Way of Life*. United States: Visions of Abolition, 2011.

Street, Brian. "The New Literacy Studies." In *Literacy: A Critical Sourcebook*, edited by Ellen Cushman, Eugene R. Kintgen, Barry M. Kroll, and Mike Rose, 430–42. New York: Bedford, 2001. Originally published 1993.

Villanueva, Victor. *Bootstraps: From an American Academic of Color*. Urbana, IL: NCTE, 1992.

———. "Hegemony: From an Organically Grown Intellectual." *Pre-Text* 13, nos. 1–2 (1992b): 17–34.

Wacquant, Loïc. "Deadly Symbiosis: When Ghetto and Prison Meet and Mesh." *Punishment & Society* 3, no. 1 (2001): 95–133.

Webster, Alec, Brian Caddick, Malcolm Reed, and Karen Ford. "Functional Versus Critical Literacy in the Rehabilitation of Offenders: A Survey of Probation Services in England and Wales." *International Journal of Lifelong Education* 18, no. 1 (1999): 49–60.

REVOLUTION AND RESTORATIVE JUSTICE

AN ANARCHIST PERSPECTIVE

Peter Kletsan (pseudonym)

INTRODUCTION

Restorative justice has been popularized in recent decades as a respectful and humane alternative to state-sanctioned, retributive incarceration. Abolitionists and reformists alike have praised this model of retroactively addressing harm as a way of challenging the monopoly of the state on the concepts of accountability and justice. Restorative justice sets important goals for its processes, which center on the victim and offender moving beyond a tragic situation. Restorative justice has no doubt been a positive new development in critical thought around crime. However, I want to posit some distinct limits of this approach that anarchists and abolitionists should be particularly concerned with.

The goal of restorative justice is to facilitate a space for direct engagement between the victims and perpetrators of a crime that includes the community in which a crime takes place. According to a popular advocate it is "an option on doing justice after the occurrence of a crime which gives priority to repairing the harm that has been caused."[1] It is beneficial to those involved because it offers a unique line of communication that privileges the voices of the individuals most affected by a crime. It is uniquely powerful because it holds its aim to be the healing of all parties rather than the pain of one and the retributive satisfaction of the other. This transformative process is in practice at San Quentin, facilitated by organizations like the Insight Prison Project (IPP) and its Victim Offender Education Group (VOEG). Late last year IPP was visited

---

1. Lode Walgrave, "Restoration in Youth Justice," in *Why Punish? How Much A Reader on Punishment*, ed. Michael Tonry (New York: Oxford University Press, 2011).

by a delegation of justices from Nepal interested in implementing a similar program there. Incarcerated people at San Quentin reported to the delegation that the restorative process was highly transformative in that it allowed them to be forgiven by those who they had harmed and cultivated in them an ability to forgive themselves.[2]

The dialogical process that is facilitated by restorative justice also incorporates the voice of the community. The notion that one's community is a "stakeholder" in the restoration of a harm is central, and theorists of restorative justice recognize that the state's acting as the voice of community in judicial processes erases the voices of actual community members who experience harm as a result of particular crimes.[3] This insight has motivated anarchist communities to incorporate restorative justice into practices of dealing with conflict internally, thus building more capable communities and undermining the state's insistent narrative of punishment and rehabilitation. Writers like Coy McKinney and Duane Ruth-Heffelbower have gone so far as to label restorative justice as the definitive "anarchist criminology." Like most people interested in critical criminology, I have very little criticism to offer of restorative justice in itself. I would not presume to challenge its practitioners who largely extol the transformative power that this process has had in their own lives.

However, a narrative persists that carries the promise of restorative justice to an overreaching conclusion. Increasingly critics of mass incarceration are confident that restorative justice is an alternative that will slowly replace or reform the state's monopoly on "justice." It is particularly of restorative justice as an "alternative" to state retribution that I remain skeptical. To my eyes, restorative justice has within it no revolutionary power remotely sufficient to undo the embedded ideology of retribution, nor does it bear any promise of truly challenging the material power of the state and the prison industrial complex. Restorative justice is a powerful, therapeutic practice that creates healing for individuals and exposes the stark failure of the state's rehabilitative enterprise. However, we

---

2. Kevin D. Sawyer, "Delegation from Nepal Courts Looks at San Quentin in Search of Restorative Justice," *San Quentin News*, December 2015. Vol. 12. No. 2.

3. Howard Zehr and Ali Gohar, *The Little Book of Restorative Justice* (Intercourse, PA: Good Books, 2002), 11–16.

must cease to see it as a structural alternative that will take the place of incarceration. Though it is a useful tool for undermining the retributive narrative of the state, it is insufficient to meet the challenges of ever-encroaching state legality and mass incarceration.

IS RESTORATIVE JUSTICE "ANARCHIST CRIMINOLOGY?"

I want to situate my concerns by directing them toward anarchist criminologists who are pinning their abolitionist hopes on restorative justice. Coy McKinney gives a compelling argument that restorative justice is the ultimate anarchist criminology. In this section, I will outline McKinney's argument while suggesting that it is an increasingly common treatment of restorative justice in critical circles.

McKinney's criticisms of the status quo open space for the alternative conception of justice that is offered by restoration. McKinney begins his argument by demonstrating that the state derives much of its power and perceived legitimacy from the consent or complicity of the general public. "Part of the state's existence and legitimacy is due to the mental recognition we assign to it. If everyone were to shift their thinking to a worldview in which the state was undesired, and instead, looked to live without its authority, the state's power and existence would be critically undermined."[4] To divest our consent from the state, then, is the principle recourse that anarchists and autonomists have against it.

This vision of political action, according to McKinney, saves anarchism from its perennial misfortune of being seen as a subculture that advocates "violence and mayhem." Anarchists like McKinney believe that the state may be defeated by spreading models of community-based accountability and by placing our collective power and energy in things other than direct confrontation and antagonism.

One of the ways that we can divest from the state is by practicing and advocating restorative justice. "The criminal justice system will continue to work the way it has, as long as we continue to consent and participate in it. If we collectively take a stand and

---

4. Coy McKinney, "An Anarchist Theory of Criminal Justice," *The Anarchist Library* (2012), 14.

withdraw our consent from the system, and instead redirect how we deal with conflict to a restorative approach, the criminal justice system will become irrelevant."[5] In order to disempower the state, and free ourselves, all that is needed is the collective divestment of consent from its structures and operations. In other words, violent confrontation with the state is unnecessary and often counterproductive, but creative alternatives that limit our dependence on the state are our greatest revolutionary tools.

Restorative justice is a method by which we divest consent from state institutions, in this case, namely courts, judges, and prisons. It proves that accountability and community integrity can be achieved more effectively and with greater humanity without the state. By doing so, restorative justice becomes an alternative to mass incarceration. It seeks to undermine the state's monopoly on justice and accountability. Having this power at its core is what, for McKinney, makes restorative justice the definitive anarchist criminology. In what follows I will raise a series of concerns about this view.

RESTORATIVE JUSTICE AND REVOLUTIONARY POSSIBILITY

McKinney is not alone in his affinity for restorative justice. Conflict resolution specialists like Duane Ruth-Heffelbower also describe the restorative process as an essentially anarchist criminology. Angela Davis suggests that restorative justice will play a large part in filling the void that is supposed to be left by the abolition of the prison industrial complex.[6] Critical Resistance, perhaps the foremost abolitionist organization in the United States, advocates for restorative and transformative justice processes as a strategy for changing the retributive narrative.[7] As mentioned above, incarcerated people are benefiting from practices of restorative justice inside San Quentin.

McKinney represents the persistent danger of overstating the power of restorative justice at the structural level. The mistake is in pinning to it the promises of abolition and the end of state

5. Ibid., 17.

6. Angela Y. Davis, *Are Prisons Obsolete?* (New York: Seven Stories Press, 2003), 113.

7. Cat Willett and Jordan Thompson, "Restorative Practices as an Attack on the Prison Industrial Complex," *The Abolitionist*, 24th ed., 2015.

legality. In his quasi-anarchist discussion of restorative justice, Ruth-Heffelbower betrays the reality that there is nothing essentially anarchist or antiauthoritarian about restorative justice:

> While organized by the central authority and operated by agents of the central authority, the restorative practices of New Zealand are still anarchist. The central practice used in New Zealand and most other places by RJ practitioners is a victim offender dialogue led by a facilitator with other stakeholders present. The decisions made by the group in working to meet the needs of the victim and providing the offender with an opportunity to be accountable to the community do not reference law, nor is enforcement by the central authority a key feature. Only when the offender refuses to be accountable to the group does the central authority stand ready to enforce laws by punishing the offender.[8]

What have we gained from restorative justice if we rely on the state, if not to facilitate it, to stand by and enforce its practice? This vision is what we open ourselves to when we advocate for restorative justice as a new state or structural apparatus. Not unlike education generally, restorative justice is a powerful enterprise that is by no means immune to state co-optation.

Restorative justice is revolutionary in exactly and only this sense. Restorative justice cultivates the power of individuals and strengthens social connections between them. In doing so, its practitioners assert their own humanity and recognize the humanity of someone they have harmed or one who has harmed them. Incarcerated people have their guilt reified every day by their material conditions and the narrative that surrounds and justifies those conditions. Restorative justice is a mode by which incarcerated and criminalized people can salvage their self-respect from a system that is consistently robbing them of it. Thus, the possibility is opened up for them to salvage their agency as political actors. But all of the empowerment and salvation that is offered by restorative justice is contingent on its participation not being forced or coerced.

---

8. Duane Ruth-Heffelbower, "Anarchist Criminology: A New Way to Understand a set of Proven Practices" (2011), 6–7.

Restorative justice can save the subjectivity of its practitioners from the mechanisms of guilt and social death, but it is not the weapon by which those mechanisms can be destroyed. It is not a revolutionary praxis in its own right. It is powerful in what it offers to those who practice it. However, there is nothing embedded in a practice like this to constitute a direct challenge to the material powers of the prison industrial complex and the American police state.

PROBLEMATIZING THE CATEGORIES OF CRIMINALITY

One crucial reason that abolitionists should be suspicious of restorative justice as a structural alternative becomes more obvious in light of the proportions of various crimes for which people are incarcerated. According to 2012 data, 53.8 percent of inmates incarcerated in state jurisdictions were charged with crimes classified as violent. Only 26.2 percent were serving time for charges of murder, sexual assault, or manslaughter.[9] These are crimes that we uncontroversially think of as very serious, as they are interpersonal in nature and create harms that are irreparable in material terms. If we include "aggravated and simple assault" in our category of very serious interpersonal crimes, the proportion increases to 37.3 percent. Furthermore, what is important about this minority of offenses is that they are ostensibly not complicated by property relations. These interpersonal offenses are the sorts of crimes that restorative justice is most concerned with. To quote its founding theorists, "Restorative justice is not primarily intended for 'minor' offences or first time offenders. . . . Experience has shown that restorative approaches may have the greatest impact in more severe cases. Moreover, if the principles of restorative justice are taken seriously, the need for restorative justice is especially clear in these cases."[10] In strictly numerical terms, we have here a reason to be concerned about the potential for restorative justice to be an alternative that would replace incarceration. The sorts of offenses for which restorative justice

9. U.S. Department of Justice, Office of Justice Programs, Bureau of Justice Statistics, "Prisoners in 2013," 15.

10. Zehr and Gohar, *The Little Book of Restorative Justice*, 9.

has been developed and on which it continues to be focused account for less than half of the incarcerated population.

The numbers, however, are much less significant than the relations that are implicit in these categories. The above figure does not account for robbery (13.7 percent), nor does it reflect nonviolent crimes relating to property (18.8 percent).[11] So, according to the state's data, 32.5 percent of people incarcerated at this time are charged with crimes for which property was the central factor. The remainder of crimes are drug crimes and crimes of "public order."

In "Law and Authority," Peter Kropotkin hands down to us an influential anarchist criticism of property and points out the hierarchical relations inherent in this majority of so-called crime. He centers his criticism on the claim that after the fall of feudalism the task of lawmaking was transferred to the bourgeoisie. Thus he observes, "the major portion have but one object—to protect private property, i.e., wealth acquired by the exploitation of man by man." He further notes that the remainder of laws serves the secondary function of maintaining and reinforcing state power and control.[12]

These secondary laws include those that criminalize direct challenges against the social order: laws regarding nuance and obstruction of space, perhaps laws that govern the use of and sale of drugs, and certainly laws that specify the power and often the immunity of governmental bodies including the police. Kropotkin sees the function of these laws as secondary because they aid in the achievement of the chief function of law. That primary function is the maintenance of the dominance of property owners and the hierarchy created by economic relations under capitalism.

Jeff Ferrell suggests a way of thinking about our understanding of criminality in light of this seminal observation; "anarchist criminologists argue that the political (and politically inequitable) nature of state law and state criminalization means that acts of crime under such a system must also carry some degree of political

---

11. Bureau of Justice Statistics, "Prisoners in 2013," 15.

12. Peter Kropotkin, "Law and Authority," 2009, available at theanarchistlibrary.org.

meaning."[13] Ferrell thus suggests that we rethink the distinction that we assume between political criminality and standard or apolitical criminality. Ferrell's examples are those that already have political texture and are generally familiar to anarchist scenes, "graffiti writing, 'obscene' art and music performances, pirate radio broadcasts, illegal labor strikes, curfew violations, shoplifting, drug use, street cruising, gangbanging, computer hacking."[14]

However, why should we stop there? Implicit in the anarchist critique of capitalism, exemplified here by Kropotkin, is the recognition that property relations are power relations that reinforce class hierarchy, and property law exists to protect those relations in service of the dominating class. In this way, I submit that at least 32.5 percent of the incarcerated population is made up of political prisoners if for no other reason than that their "offenses," regardless of their inception or intent, were direct challenges to the property relations that are created by and enforced in service of the bourgeoisie. To engage in restorative justice in these instances is problematic, even hypocritical, for anarchists. To do so is to attempt to *restore* the very relations of domination that we oppose.

Restorative justice is more obviously inapplicable in the latter cases of drug crime and crimes of "public order" for which the state is the supposed victim. So, from an anarchist perspective, restorative justice is only a way of handling offenses that is appropriate for a minority subsection of people who have been classified as criminal. And even in those cases restorative justice, if we continue to hope that it will structurally replace the prison industrial complex, runs the risk of being corrupted by the state's force or coercion or to the state's benefit.

RADICAL PRIORITIES: CONFRONTATION WITH THE STATE

If restorative justice, as noted above, is being practiced to the benefit of victims and offenders alike, then why should we be so suspicious of its expansion, even if that involves some compromise

13. Jeff Ferrell, "Against the Law: Anarchist Criminology," *Social Anarchism*, no. 25 (1998).
14. Ibid.

in terms of state oversight or enforcement? Perhaps, if restorative justice flourishes as a structural alternative then increasingly only those offenders for whom it is appropriate would be the targets of incarceration. This is neither the anarchist's nor the abolitionist's vision, but it would have to be admitted that this would constitute a great stride in that direction.

To belay this legitimate impulse toward compromising in service of greater goals requires some discussion of what the state is. Though McKinney well recognizes the grave injustices of the state's punitive enterprise, he insists that its power is derived from our consent. He argues that the collective withdrawal of that consent is sufficient to bring about its demise.

To press the point of consent, allow me to briefly discuss two opposed ideas on this concept from the so-called enlightenment. McKinney is following a long tradition of liberal political philosophers who assert a causal or justificatory relationship between the *consent of the governed* and the organization and behavior of those in power. Indeed John Locke, in one of the formative articulations of liberalism, proposes this very same understanding of the origin of governmental power. This understanding of power rests on the idea that consent can be given tacitly; the liberal idea is that we offer our tacit consent to governing powers by continuing to live within their ostensible jurisdictions.[15] It is thus prudent to remind ourselves of the importance of a robust conception of consent.

In his criticisms of Locke's ideal of government, David Hume posits two criteria for a more genuine conception of consent that will prove instructive here. Hume says, first, that consent is only present when one is empowered to make a choice. One would not say, in Hume's example, that anyone consents to obey the laws of gravity. Whatever feelings we may have about this physical phenomenon, we have no choice in the matter, so there is no consent. Second, beyond the mere possibility of choice, Hume asserts that consent is genuine only in the presence of viable alternatives. Someone who wakes up aboard a ship that they were brought aboard without their knowledge always has the option of flinging

---

15. John Locke, *The Second Treatise of Government*, ed. Richard Cox (Wheeling, IL: Harlan Davidson, 1982), 73–74.

themselves into the sea.[16] Their not doing so would constitute tacit consent to be aboard the ship in Locke's sense. However, this is not how we think about consent in any real world application.

Alternatively, what McKinney may be suggesting is that the state's authority, like all authority, is only as real as the collective group recognizes it to be or allows it to be. However, this fails to recognize all of the material and ideological mechanisms that perpetually operate to maintain power. The very discussion of restorative justice stems from the reality that nearly 2.3 million people are currently incarcerated in U.S. facilities, the United States has an extremely militarized police force domestically, and a staggering military presence throughout the world. This is not a hegemon that will disappear as a result of our collective will to stop recognizing it. At best, this observation may be a crucial step in a network of diverse tactics and strategies for antagonizing and disempowering the states hegemony.

Ferrell's critiques provide further guidance here in explicating the nature of the state as an entity that is essentially antithetical to consent. First, he observes that state legality is, in some sense, a self-propelled wheel, ever extending and justifying its own expansion, "state legality constitutes a sort of bureaucratic cancer that grows on itself, that produces an ever-expanding body of bureaucratic and legal sycophants employed to obfuscate and interpret it."[17] Law grows and continues to grow in most cases with only the faintest pretense of participation by the governed. As this expansion progresses, greater proportions of social life begin to fall under the prescription and determination of law. Furthermore, as is pointed out in Noam Chomsky's *Manufacturing Consent*, recent developments in communication technology and media have created a situation in which the illusion of choice has become especially powerful.[18] Thus, given the increasing ubiquity of state legality, tacit consent is easily retained while the possibility of genuine consent, in Hume's sense, is foreclosed.

16. David Hume and Eugene F. Miller, *Essays, Moral, Political, and Literary* (Indianapolis: Liberty Classics, 1987).

17. Jeff Ferrell, "Against the Law: Anarchist Criminology."

18. Edward S. Herman and Noam Chomsky, *Manufacturing Consent: The Political Economy of the Mass Media* (New York: Pantheon Books, 1988).

So, the state is not an inert structure that can be readily disempowered by the divestment of popular consent. It is rather a living and dynamic force that, colluding with the interests of capital, continues to colonize the human experience. It must be opposed in a way that is equally active and dynamic. Restorative justice gives anarchist communities a tool for building relationships of power and accountability without the state, and gives victims of state violence a way toward rehumanizing themselves. Restorative justice may well be a powerful tool against the prison industrial complex, but it is *not* an alternative. As a structural alternative to the prison industrial complex, restorative justice is at best a way for the state to repackage its oppressive profiteering and sell it back as progress. Restorative justice is good and beautiful and human only so long as it is outside the power structure.

In the settler's history on the continent, none but a very few have consented to the power and expansion of the state and its colonial domination. To collectively say no to it now is a passive gesture where an active force is needed. It is to add voices to a chorus of resistance that is centuries old. *Anarchist* is the orientation toward the world that recognizes this essentially corrosive aspect of state power, and for some hierarchy in principle. The response that is needed is radical and militant organization, not only against prisons but also against all the oppression and domination of the neocolonial-hetero-patriarchal-white-supremacist-capitalist power-er structure. It is the duty of the anarchist and all radicals to stand against by prioritizing the dismantling of these cages. We ought to be spreading propaganda by word and deed until everyone is angry enough to fight. It is the anarchist's job to live against the world we are in for the dream of the world that we want. May we be ever watchful of anything that asks us to compromise, to slow down, or to work within. Liberation begins in ideas and abstractions, but it must become a material fight brought to bear against concrete enemies.

REFERENCES

Carson, E. Ann. "Prisoners in 2013." Bureau of Justice Statistics. 2013. Available at bjs.gov.

Davis, Angela Y. *Are Prisons Obsolete?* New York: Seven Stories Press, 2003.

Ferrell, Jeff. "Against the Law: Anarchist Criminology." Social Anarchism, no. 25 (1998). Available at library.nothingness.org.

Herman, Edward S., and Noam Chomsky. *Manufacturing Consent: The Political Economy of the Mass Media.* New York: Pantheon Books, 1988.

Hume, David, and Eugene F. Miller. *Essays, Moral, Political, and Literary.* Indianapolis: Liberty Classics, 1987.

Kropotkin, Peter. "Law and Authority." 2009. Available at theanarchistlibrary.org.

Locke, John. *The Second Treatise of Government.* Edited by Richard Cox. Wheeling, IL: Harlan Davidson, 1982.

McKinney, Coy. "An Anarchist Theory of Criminal Justice." 2012. Available at theanarchistlibrary.org.

Ruth-Heffelbower, Duane. "Anarchist Criminology: A New Way to Understand Proven Practices." (2011). Available at ruth-heffelbower.us.

Sawyer, Kevin D. "Delegation from Nepal Courts Look at San Quentin in Search of Restorative Justice." *San Quentin News,* December 2015.

Walgrave, Lode. "Restoration in Youth Justice." In *Why Punish? How Much? A Reader on Punishment,* edited by Michael Tonry, 319–35. New York: Oxford University Press, 2011.

Willett, Cat, and Jordan Thompson. "Restorative Practices as an Attack on the Prison Industrial Complex." *The Abolitionist,* 24th ed., 2015.

Zehr, Howard, and Ali Gohar. *The Little Book of Restorative Justice.* Intercourse, PA: Good Books, 2002.

UNTITLED

Tess Scheflan

My work is driven by a strong conviction that photography is a vehicle for social and political change. I believe photographs have the power to shape public opinion and raise awareness on issues that are largely ignored in mainstream discussions, and see myself as part of the struggles against all forms of oppression, racism and violations of the basic right to freedom. Throughout my career as a professional photographer, I have covered and documented conflict, social struggles and activism from LGBTQ+ rights movements to war.

I have worked as a staff photographer for Haaretz daily newspaper and as a staffer for various photo agencies and wires in Israel. I am a member of Activestills since 2006 and a founding member of Normal, a documentary photo collective based in Boston, MA. I have been commissioned and published by newspapers and magazines worldwide and am a recipient of multiple awards and recognition internationally.

(IN)VISIBILITY

Siku Allooloo

(In)Visibility

I used to think being invisible would protect me from harm
sometimes it can
sometimes it's the only safety you have
– but it's also the end point of domination,
the thing that maintains the tyrannical order.

Sometimes being seen is the safety net
a connecting point
a fulcrum.

Either way, it comes at a cost.
Either way, be careful.

They're keeping tabs in all the visible spaces
the non-visible too.
We are tolerated, but they want us in the ground
deeply buried in the ground
our memory erased
our presence, rightful claim to the earth, erased.
We are meant to be invisible.
Except when we are showcased
when we are the mirror
for their own distorted image.

So don't assume that time in their gaze gives us power.
Though they might ask politely,
consent is only heeded if we give it.
We don't get to be autonomous.

A young woman of the earth
sensuous, soft-hearted, outspoken
is a curiousity
an exotic, fleeting attraction
until she turns her cheek
tells them no
denies them access.
Then her autonomy is a threat to white alpha manhood –
something to be dominated.
Her sacred body becomes a site for reinforcing control
and she is disappeared
in death or death of spirit.

Just like her land
when her nation says they have never surrendered
it is not for sale
they have no jurisdiction
they cannot trespass.
That source of life becomes a battleground
until dissent is disappeared
or there is nothing left.

I've been invisible
out of fear and desperation:
visibility makes me a target
asserting autonomy makes me a target.
Those like me dare not defy white men
dare not deny them access
as we are only here so long as they allow it
or we can easily be not here at all.
Their choice – they hold all the power.
Some of us make it. Many of us don't.

I choose to be visible
out of fear and defiance, out of self-love:
visibility makes me a *target*
asserting autonomy makes me a *target*
because protecting our sources of life means
we can so easily be not here at all.

They hold all the power
but I am taking it back
we are taking it back.
Visible or not visible, we exist
we remember
we will continue on.

Visibility is a danger, a choice
a victory.
But what they can't see, what they will never see,
is our stronghold.

To whoever is keeping tabs:

I am an Indigenous woman.
We have always stood in your way.
We have always paid the price.

So see me, or don't see me –
you don't understand anyway.

I am of a collective truth
that beats in my heart and speaks through my voice.
I do not own it
and you cannot stop it.

What I am – to you, is a threat.
To my people, a beacon

Siku Allooloo is an Inuit/Taino writer and community organizer from Denendeh (Northwest Territories). Her work incorporates legacies of resistance, continuity and creative expression to support the revitalization of Indigenous communities. Siku holds a BA in Anthropology and Indigenous Studies from the University of Victoria.

LESSONS ON ABOLITION FROM INSIDE WOMEN'S PRISONS

Mianta McKnight

Additional contributions by Mychal Concepcion, Hakim Anderson and Christy Phillips, currently imprisoned at the Central California Women's Facility, Jane Dorotik, currently imprisoned at the California Institution for Women, and Misty Rojo, co-director at Justice Now and formerly imprisoned at the Central California Women's Facility.

WE LEARN EARLY ON IN WOMEN'S PRISONS THAT INVOLVING THE POLICE or prison officers to resolve conflicts won't make the situation any better. My friend and fellow abolitionist Hakim Anderson recently expressed, "We don't go to the cops most often in here. So what we try to do is resolve it in a way where really and truly the cops won't have to get involved. I think that the same thing can happen outside of prison."

Looking at the outcome of involving officers explains why we choose to avoid any police involvement: it makes things far worse. We often find that someone is wrongfully accused, abused, or victimized by the people that are supposed to be there to bring the peace. Their presence creates a hostile/dangerous environment for the person who contacted them for resolution. Their goal is not to seek peace. That is not what the prison environment is designed for.

Justice Now organizer Christy Phillips explains that "now that we're seeing all these incidents perpetrated by the police, people are starting to see that the police officers are not always working in the best interest of the people. And they're almost untouchable, meaning they can commit murder in cold blood and there will be no consequences for them. Most of the time they're not even charged with a crime."

Though some claim that additional training will decrease police harassment, officers often use the information delivered through their training to manipulate and control people in women's prisons through intimidation and violence. Justice Now board member Mychal Concepcion makes it clear:

> Custody [staff in prison] is trained in something called Gender Responsive Rehabilitation. It was to educate them so that they could treat us better, or treat the people in this prison better or in a more sensitive way. [But] they use this tool to educate themselves on how to scare or manipulate through threats of violence—and in some cases actual violence—to control the population here. So the people here who are actually supposed to be receiving rehabilitation from CDCR are actually being victimized by the same people.

Inside women's prisons, we have figured out how not to allow the police to further traumatize us. We have learned how to protect ourselves from their looming presence. We share these lessons with each other, and with new people who enter the prison system. We are seen as subhuman and at the mercy of the officers. This is why we put forth an extra effort to monitor ourselves. We do so out of a necessity to be safe. Cops apply the mentality of group punishment and everyone suffers as a result of one person's actions. It is not just one person's problem; it is a community problem. We come together to accomplish keeping the peace, and find resolution while handling situations in a way that doesn't further endanger us, especially in such a controlled environment.

We hold our community accountable using the respect earned by those who have been inside for a while to help. Misty Rojo, Justice Now co-director, remembers a time when an elder and well-respected peer inside stepped in and de-escalated a situation that would have resulted in police involvement.

> At that time everything made me fight. I was away from my kids, I had a ten-year sentence. I didn't give a fuck. One day I was on my way out of the unit to go and fight someone. Now I can't even remember what it was about, but I know I was really upset. It was during a time in the day when people could get

in and out of their rooms, go to appointments, etc. An elder, Madalin Bloxson, stopped me and physically diverted me from where I was going to. She rolled me a cigarette, and talked to me. She talked to me about our moms. She made me realize that all the anger I was holding, all the frustration I was feeling, was nothing to do with the situation I was about to get in. She kept me from getting a serious write up for violent acts, which would have gone on my file and added to the perception of me as a violent person. I would have lost my parole date. I would have lost the ability for me to call my kids. Besides the fact I might have got hurt.

According to Hakim,

They say it takes a community to raise a child. So if we had a village that was willing to be a closely knitted village where everybody was on the same page and in sync and willing to work together, we would never need the officers. I think that that's what a world without prisons would look like, is everybody getting involved and not just turning a blind eye and saying, 'Oh, that don't have nothing to do with me or my kids, so I don't care,' or 'that's not my woman' or 'that's not my man,' 'that's not my mom.' It's being involved; it's being proactive.

Justice Now board member Jane Dorotik shared,

What I would like to see, for all—but especially for women currently involved in the criminal justice system—is a lot more community support. I'd like to see a shift in thinking from a mentality that describes good and bad, right or wrong, to thinking that embraces the mistakes and learning from them. Or trauma recovery programs. Or a real belief in rehabilitation and the fact that people can change.

We want to share these lessons with people outside prison, these lessons that are ingrained in who we are and how our community functions. We can't rely on anyone else—or any other system—to problem solve for us. So many of us have suffered abuse and violence in our lives before we get to where we are in women's prisons. To survive the day-to-day violence of the oppressive environment we are in, we have to look after each other and use our resilience and creativity to stay safe. Being proactive in our problem-solving shows learning from our experiences, what we have seen take place around us, and knowing what has not worked in the past. Avoiding police and prison officer involvement proves to us that our voices do matter, our opinions do matter, and we have a choice in how we live even under those harsh circumstances of confinement.

Justice Now is an Oakland-based, grassroots activist-led legal advocacy clinic that works with people in the world's largest women's prisons. We are part of a strong movement for social justice and a world without prisons. We believe that it is possible to involve, empower, and honor people with direct lived experience of fighting and surviving the prison industrial complex, and that through long-term relationships with imprisoned leaders and activists, we can build programs and systems for critical education in the wider movement and wider society. Our work is designed to center the lived experience of people who are currently and formerly imprisoned.

AILMENTS

Jake Villareal

my psychiatrist prescribed me some medicine because
   there are things about my brain the world isn't prepared
   to accommodate
I remember watching Palestinian protesters in DC disappear
   into giant white police vans moving through the crowd like
   erasers
there was something about the way they thought, too, that the
   world couldn't handle
where does a word go when it's erased?
is it stuck in the eraser congregating with all the other
   disappeared thoughts, creating new, threatening, mistakes
   to be erased by people obsessed with white space?
mental health is feeling permanent
mental health is existing in the margins and at the center
my psych asks if I often feel like I'm being watched
I don't know whether to tell him I feel hypervisible, or
   invisible
he asks if I feel anxious
always.
anxious about what?
I remember the first time I was put in handcuffs
I felt like a mannequin: no agency, no identity, just a model
   for an officer to see that palette of silver on brown they're so
   fond of
an object to be arranged, displayed, or removed for others'
   comfort
mental health is taking up space
mental health is taking space back.

my psych asks me, are you prone to angry outbursts?
they're justified, I say
but that wasn't part of the question.
he asks, do you avoid public spaces, spend long periods of
 time indoors?
it's justified, I say
but that wasn't part of the question
he asks if I feel trapped
when police circle a group of protesters, then shrink the space
 to detain them indefinitely, it's called kettling
I guess that's because when you light a fire under a kettle, the
 water gets louder and builds pressure until it's either set
 free or erupts.
sometimes, mental health is erupting
always, mental health is having that eruption validated
my mental health is more than pills, it's an end to state
 violence
my mind can't be healthy if my body is constantly at risk

Jake Villarreal is a multidisciplinary artist and graduate student in
St. Louis, Missouri.

#RESISTCAPITALISM TO #FUNDBLACKFUTURES

BLACK YOUTH, POLITICAL ECONOMY, AND THE TWENTY-FIRST CENTURY BLACK RADICAL IMAGINATION

David C. Turner III

FIGURE 1. CHARLENE CARRUTHERS, NATIONAL DIRECTOR OF BYP 100 (CENTER) WITH OTHER
ACTIVISTS PROTESTING THE INTERNATIONAL ASSOCIATION OF CHIEFS OF POLICE (IACP)
CONFERENCE IN CHICAGO IN OCTOBER OF 2015
PHOTO CREDIT: BYP 100 TWITTER PAGE @BYP100

"Stop the cops, and FUND BLACK FUTURES!" "NO JUSTICE, NO PEACE! DIVEST FROM POLICE!" These chants echoed through the hall of a Chicago-based credit union for police officers from the counter, where organizers from the Black Youth Project 100 (BYP 100)[1] took over the main lobby of the bank in protest of state-sanctioned violence in Chicago, the most notable in recent memory being the release of the tape of the murder of Laquan McDonald. McDonald was allegedly armed with a knife, and was gunned down with sixteen shots by Jason Van Dyke, a white Chicago police officer who was bailed out of jail through the fundraising efforts of that same credit union. Wearing black sweaters with the phrase, "Fund Black Futures" emblazed across

---

1. byp100.org

their chests in red and green letters, the organizers made explicit connections to the financial investment in the policing of Black communities and the divestment from social services and education that had plagued the city of Chicago. Speaking about urban decay and what Joe Soss, Richard Fording, and Sanford Schram refer to as neoliberal paternalism,[2] in other words, the ways that poor Black people in urban cities across America are forced to be governed in a series of racialized policies and practices that shape a deficit oriented framework for their proximity to poverty, members of BYP 100, who were largely femme presenting and young, made connections to the political economy and racialized state-sanctioned violence. They used direct action to make their grievances explicit during MLK weekend in a tactful series of events to combat the ahistorical narratives of Dr. King that domesticate his views.[3]

THE TWENTY-FIRST CENTURY BLACK RADICAL IMAGINATION: ENGAGING A CRITICAL BLACK YOUTH POLITICS

When I was an undergraduate, one of my Africana Studies professors had us read *Freedom Dreams: The Black Radical Imagination* by Robin D.G. Kelley for an Africana Political Thought class in the spring of 2012. Trayvon Martin had just been murdered, the Marissa Alexander case was slowly gaining national recognition, and I was closing my second year out as the president of the Organization of Africana Studies, the student arm of the Department of Africana Studies at California State University, Dominguez Hills. We also had to read Michael Dawson's *Black Visions: Roots of Contemporary African American Political Ideologies.* In both of these works, Dawson and Kelley call for activists to move beyond one mode of analysis and mode of being, and adopt a multiplicity of political ideologies to gain freedom, with a center

---

2. Joe Soss, Richard C. Fording, and Sanford F. Schram, *Disciplining the Poor: Neoliberal Paternalism and the Persistent Power of Race* (Chicago: University of Chicago Press, 2011).

3. This story was in part assembled through a combination of corporate media accounts (the *Chicago Tribune*) and of Twitter accounts of the day, mainly from the twitter page of BYP 100: twitter.com/BYP_100.

on complete social transformation.[4] They encouraged us to dream and inspired us to work toward a radical future, not just to fight against white supremacy but to fight for something: to fight for us, our futures, our lives. This would become my introduction to the ideological framing of our current movement: The Movement for Black Lives.

I did not know it then, but three years later, I would be a doctoral student at UC Berkeley and knee deep in the Movement for Black Lives. The example that BYP 100 set for us during MLK Weekend reminds us of the radical potential of Black youth politics. Here you have folks—who are guided by a Black queer feminist lens—organize for redistribution with a thorough critique of the political economy and its connections to state-sanctioned violence. They see the connections to the investment in carceral technologies of violence[5] and the divestment in their lives through the neoliberal marriage between the state and public services.[6] I participated in BlackXMas actions, which were a series of events across six cities nationwide to disrupt the consumerist culture of capitalism and private complicity in the assault on Black lives. Members of the Afrikan Black Coalition, a Black youth-led organization made up of students from California's institutions of higher education, pressured the University of California system to divest twenty-five million dollars from the private prison industry, which represents the worst of racialized neoliberal capitalism.[7] In August of 2016, over fifty organizations came together to put forward an M4BL (Movement For Black Lives) Policy Platform.[8] In this platform, the common thread was a focus on state-sanctioned *and* funded models of violence, and they all became targets.

---

4. Robin D.G. Kelley, *Freedom Dreams: The Black Radical Imagination* (Boston: Beacon Press Books, 2002); Michael J. Dawson, *Black Visions: The Roots of Contemporary African-American Political Ideologies* (Chicago: University of Chicago Press, 2003).

5. Rashad Shabazz. *Spatializing blackness: Architectures of confinement and black masculinity in Chicago.* (Champaign: University of Illinois Press, 2015.)

6. Soss, et al., *Disciplining the Poor*; Loïc Wacquant, *Punishing the Poor: The Neoliberal Government of Social Insecurity* (Durham, NC: Duke University Press, 2009).

7. Anthony Williams. Afrikan Black Coalition Accomplishes UC Prison Divestment!" Accessed April 24 2017, available at afrikanblackcoalition.org.

8. policy.m4bl.org/platform.

Within the social movement repertoire of this new generation, the digital literacy of young activists was activated in order to spread a coherent message about the need to divest monies from oppressive entities and invest them in the growth of our communities, which can be seen in Figure 3.[9] In conjunction with the assault that Black students took on their universities across the country, we are witnessing something that is otherwise unprecedented: the radical potential of Black youth organizing and politics.

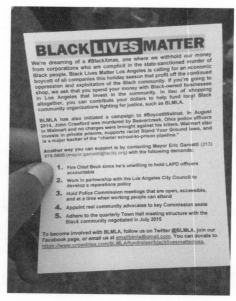

FIGURE 2. PHOTO OF THE LEAFLET THAT MEMBERS OF BLACK LIVES MATTER LOS ANGELES PASSED OUT DURING A BLACK THEMED "CHRISTMAS CAROL" EVENT AT THE GROVE, AN AFFLUENT SHOPPING CENTER IN LOS ANGELES, IN DECEMBER 2015. PHOTO CREDIT: AUTHOR.

---

9. Charles Harlod Frederick Davis, "Dream Defending, On-Campus and Beyond: A Multi-sited Ethnography of Contemporary Student Organizing, the Social Movement Repertoire, and Social Movement Organization in College." PhD diss., University of Arizona, 2015; Michael J. Dumas, "A Cultural Political Economy of School Desegregation in Seattle," *Eric* 113, no. 4 (2011): 703–34.

FIGURE 3. MATERIAL FROM THE MOVEMENT FOR BLACK LIVES'
INVEST-DIVEST CAMPAIGN, EMPHASIZING THE NEED TO INVEST IN
YOUTH, PARTICULARLY BLACK GIRLS
PHOTO CREDIT: M4BL POLICY TEAM

I call this moment, and the general frame for the movement "Critical Black Youth Politics." Critical Black Youth Politics serves three major purposes, which are situated in 1) intersectional analyses of power, oppression, and hegemony; 2) radical participatory praxis; and 3) collective resistance and healing. I do not pose these as tenets of a new theoretical model. I do, however, offer these as a way to engage the types of politics that Black youth are engaged in and committed to practicing.

INTERSECTIONAL ANALYSES OF POWER, OPPRESSION, AND HEGEMONY

The term "critical" in Critical Black Youth Politics serves a specific function, and that function is rooted in an analysis of the ways that hegemony, dominance, and social stratification shape our everyday lives. This particular segment of Critical Black Youth Politics is predicated on the idea that power has an influence in our collective life outcomes, and that by naming the ways that this power operates, one can work to transform the context where power is situated. Without that analysis, specifically of race, class, and gender, one can be motivated by social justice to try and create change, but not have a critique of social oppression, which Daniel Solorzano and Dolores Bernal call "conformist resistance."[10] Without being critical of oppression, one can potentially reinforce respectability, and reinforce the standards of "who" gets to be advocated for and who gets to be a political actor.

RADICAL PARTICIPATORY PRAXIS

The Ella Baker model of leadership, even though it can be difficult and long, has become the central model for organizing among Black youth.[11] This is rooted in the notion that the people who are the most impacted by interlocking systems of oppression are the experts in their own experiences, that they have the knowledge to liberate themselves. This tradition of participation and inclusion fueled the Mississippi freedom movement and organizations like the Student Nonviolent Coordinating Committee (SNCC),[12] which are being adopted today by organizations such as the Black Liberation Collective,[13] the national organization that helped to coordinate the #StudentBlackout movement.[14]

COLLECTIVE RESISTANCE AND HEALING

In a memoir with Eve Tuck and K. Wayne Yang, Pedro Noguera recounts his personal connections to youth resistance and activism.[15] Through a critical reflection on youth studies and his own growth as an activist, Noguera recalls how he learned to organize, the methods used to organize, the campaigns he either launched

---

10. Daniel G. Solorzano and Dolores Delgado Bernal, "Examining Transformational Resistance Through a Critical Race and Latcrit Theory Framework: Chicana and Chicano Students in an Urban Context," *Urban Education* 36, no. 3 (2001): 308–42.

11. Barbara Ransby. *Ella Baker and the Black freedom movement: A radical democratic vision.* (Chapel Hill, University of North Carolina Press, 2003).

12. Chares M. Payne, *I've Got the Light of Freedom: The Organizing Tradition of the Mississippi Freedom Struggle* (Berkeley: University of California Press, 2007).

13. For more information on Black Liberation Collective, see blackliberationcollective.org.

14. Black Liberation Collective, "On Urgency, Frustration, and Love: A Love Letter to Black Students," December 10, 2015, accessed April 19, 2016, available at blavity.com.

15. Eve Tuck and K. Wayne Yang, eds., *Youth Resistance Research and Theories of Change* (New York: Routledge, 2014).

or took part in, and the state of youth resistance studies now. Noguera warns young scholars not to conflate all forms of opposition with "resistance," or what Solorzano and Bernal will call "self-defeating resistance." Noguera suggests that agency should not be: "My school is bad, so I'm going to cut school"; Noguera asserts that if we are to think about resistance as a precursor to building social movements and as agency, it should be a student "organizing a walk out." The tension point, in this case, is what we actually count as agency, and what gets to be resistance. Collective resistance and healing is dedicated to two aims. First, it is dedicated to resistance that seeks to build movements that can change the material conditions for everyone in their respective communities. Second, it posits that resistance to systems of domination and oppression are learned skills that can help one heal from the impact of systemic oppression.[16] Critical Black Youth Politics takes all forms of resistance into account, and suggests that riots are just as important for democratic repair as nonviolent civil disobedience.[17]

AGAINST THE NEOLIBERAL TURN IN BLACK (YOUTH) POLITICS

Even though Black youth are positioned in civil society as amoral, deviant, and in need of state intervention, young Black people across the country are engaging in a new wave of intersectional Black organizing that has not been seen on such a popular scale in this country. These young people—my generation—are currently providing a counter to the cultural matrix that some scholars use to examine the plight of young Black people without seeking the transformation of the context that caused said plight.[18] This deficit model of understanding fails to capture political agency, and presents Black youth as merely static in our conditions. However, for some scholars, engaged Black youth are not enough. Technologies of control are the only interventions that come from scholarship

16. Shawn A. Ginwright, *Black Youth Rising: Activism and Radical Healing in Urban America* (New York: Teachers College Press, 2010).

17. Juliet Hooker. "Black Lives Matter and the Paradoxes of US Black Politics: From Democratic Sacrifice to Democratic Repair." *Political Theory* 44, no. 4 (2016): 448-469.

18. Orlando Patterson, ed., *The Cultural Matrix: Understanding Black Youth* (Cambridge, MA: Harvard University Press, 2015).

that focus on our "decisions" to buy fast food and not catch the bus, without questioning the structural conditions that lead to such decisions.

The political and intellectual left, even with claims to social justice and social change, still cannot reconcile the call of Black people to make their lives matter to a state that is literally invested in their demise.[19] The unsettling notion of Black Lives Matter highlights a fundamental flaw in racial equity reform logic: that Blackness cannot be reconciled in an anti-Black state with a political economy built on their backs and indigenous land. This is why claims to "reform" are largely absent from the rhetoric of Black youth organizers in this movement. We recognize the failures of attempting to be incorporated into a state dependent on our suffering, and that is why we are calling for abolition, redistribution, and intervention into the settler colonial project of expendable Blackness.[20] We also recognize what Lester Spence refers to as the neoliberal turn in Black politics.[21] As corporations and the privatization of activism have invested interests in our continued racialized suffering,[22] we have largely rejected the calls of "efficiency" and "participation" in a polity where marginalization is its only frame of reference.[23]

MOVING FORWARD:
ENGAGING CRITICAL BLACK YOUTH
POLITICS AND THE POLITICAL ECONOMY

While a critique of capitalism is not new at all to radical Black organizing,[24] it certainly is not one of the most popular frames of reference when thinking about racial justice. Yet, even with a

19. Anthony Williams. "The Road to Private Prison Divestment." *Boom: A Journal of California* 6, no. 2 (2016): 98–103.

20. Jared Sexton, "Unbearable Blackness," *Cultural Critique* 178, no. 90 (2015): 159–78; Eve Tuck and K. Wayne Yang, "Decolonization Is Not a Metaphor," *Decolonization: Indigeneity, Education, & Society* 1, no. 1 (2012): 1–40.

21. Lester Spence, "The Neoliberal Turn in Black Politics," *Souls: A Critical Journal of Black Politics, Culture, and Society* 14, no. 3–4 (2013): 139–59. Available at tandfonline.com.

22. Michael J. Dumas, "'Losing An Arm': Schooling as a Site of Black Suffering," *Race Ethnicity and Education* 17, no. 1 (2013): 1–29. Available at tandfonline.com.

23. Charles W. Mills, *The Racial Contract* (Ithaca, NY: Cornell University Press, 1997).

24. Joshua Bloom, and Waldo E. Martin. *Black Against Empire: The History and Politics of the Black Panther Party.* Berkeley: University of California Press, 2013.

slew of Black activists who have been influenced by radical leftist thought such as Bayard Rustin, Ella Baker, Huey P. Newton, and others, somehow liberal racial integrationism finds its way to the center of analysis for scholars who are interested in justice, either through critique or through endorsement. While the conflating of Black power with Black capitalism has been analyzed as a point of departure for radical Black movements,[25] our new generation of activists are well aware of the mistakes of their predecessors. Young Black people, who have lived through events such as Hurricane Katrina,[26] the "Great Black Depression," and America's first Black president, have all but abandoned traditional social movement frames of political participation and incorporation. As Eddie Glaude writes in his new work, *Democracy in Black: How Race Still Enslaves America's Soul,* he states, "They came of age politically with President Barack Obama in office and now they bathed in the intense rage of Ferguson. In so many ways, these young people were unprecedented."[27] Black youth are engaging in forms of activism that deeply connect systems of oppression, especially how these systems are monetized, and no singular theoretical analysis can possibly capture all of it. Our youth are giving us new ways to reimagine and think about the world: it's about time we pay attention.

25. Robert L. Allen, *Black Awakening in Capitalist America: An Analytic History* (Trenton, NJ: Africa World Press, 1992); Noliwe C. Rooks, *White Money/Black Power: The Suprising History of African American Studies and the Crisis of Race in Higher Education* (Boston: Beacon Press Books, 2006).

26. Vincanne Adams, *Markets of Sorrow, Labors of Faith: New Orleans in the wake of Katrina* (Durham, NC: Duke University Press, 2013).

27. Eddie S. Glaude, *Democracy in Black: How Race Still Enslaves America's Soul* (New York: Broadway Books, 2016), 4.

REFERENCES

Adams, Vincanne. *Markets of Sorrow, Labors of Faith: New Orleans in the wake of Katrina*. Durham, NC: Duke University Press, 2013.

Allen, Robert L. *Black Awakening in Capitalist America: An Analytic History*. Trenton, NJ: Africa World Press, 1992.

Bloom, Joshua, and Waldo E. Martin. *Black Against Empire: The History and Politics of the Black Panther Party*. Berkeley: University of California Press, 2013.

Davis, Charles Harlod Frederick. "Dream Defending, On-Campus and Beyond: A Multi-sited Ethnography of Contemporary Student Organizing, the Social Movement Repertoire, and Social Movement Organization in College." PhD diss., University of Arizona, 2015.

Dawson, Michael J. *Black Visions: The Roots of Contemporary African-American Political Ideologies*. Chicago: University of Chicago Press, 2003.

Dumas, Michael J. "A Cultural Political Economy of School Desegregation in Seattle." *Eric* 113, no. 4 (2011): 703–34.

———. "'Losing An Arm': Schooling as a Site of Black Suffering." *Race Ethnicity and Education* 17, no. 1 (2013): 1–29.

Ginwright, Shawn A. *Black Youth Rising: Activism and Radical Healing in Urban America*. New York: Teachers College Press, 2010.

Glaude, Eddie S. *Democracy in Black: How Race Still Enslaves America's Soul*. New York: Broadway Books, 2016.

Hooker, Juliet. "Black Lives Matter and the Paradoxes of US Black Politics: From Democratic Sacrifice to Democratic Repair." *Political Theory* 44, no. 4 (2016): 448-469.

Kelley, Robin D. G. *Freedom Dreams: The Black Radical Imagination*. Boston: Beacon Press Books, 2002.

Mills, Charles W. *The Racial Contract*. Ithaca, NY: Cornell University Press, 1997.

Patterson, Orlando, ed. *The Cultural Matrix: Understanding Black Youth*. Cambridge, MA: Harvard University Press, 2015.

Payne, Chares M. *I've Got the Light of Freedom: The Organizing Tradition of the Mississippi Freedom Struggle*. Berkeley: University of California Press, 2007.

Ransby, Barbara. *Ella Baker and the Black freedom movement: A radical democratic vision*. Chapel Hill: University of North Carolina Press, 2003.

Rooks, Noliwe C. *White Money/Black Power: The Suprising History of African American Studies and the Crisis of Race in Higher Education*. Boston: Beacon Press Books, 2006.

Sexton, Jared. "Unbearable Blackness." *Cultural Critique* 178, no. 90 (2015): 159–78.

Solorzano, Daniel G., and Dolores Delgado Bernal. "Examining Transformational Resistance Through a Critical Race and Latcrit Theory Framework: Chicana and Chicano Students in an Urban Context." *Urban Education* 36, no. 3 (2001): 308–42.

Soss, Joe, Richard C. Fording, and Sanford F. Schram. *Disciplining the Poor: Neoliberal Paternalism and the Persistent Power of Race.* Chicago: University of Chicago Press, 2011.

Spence, Lester. "The Neoliberal Turn in Black Politics." *Souls: A Critical Journal of Black Politics, Culture, and Society* 14, no. 3–4 (2013): 139–59.

Tuck, Eve, and K. Wayne Yang. "Decolonization Is Not a Metaphor." *Decolonization: Indigeneity, Education, & Society* 1, no. 1 (2012): 1–40.

———, eds. *Youth Resistance Research and Theories of Change.* New York: Routledge, 2014.

Wacquant, Loïc. *Punishing the Poor: The Neoliberal Government of Social Insecurity.* Durham, NC: Duke University Press, 2009.

Williams, Anthony. "Afrikan Black Coalition Accomplishes UC Prison Divestment!" 2015. Available at afrikanblackcoalition.

Williams, Anthony J. "The Road to Private Prison Divestment." *Boom: A Journal of California* 6, no. 2 (2016): 98–103.

I SEEN SOMETHING

Max Parthas

I seen something in South Carolina.
I seen something all across America.
Yes I seen something and I've got something to say.
I'm here now. What's more is I've been here before-
At the capitol where the confederate flag flies every day.

Prison is our top industry.
It's infinitely more profitable for the populace than mom and
   pop stores.
That's how it is here in my state and it may be the same in
   yours.
Check it, I mean it, and let me know when you've seen it.

The police here are big bruisers and have a sport where they
   "bump" young black men with their cruisers as they
   recklessly chase them through their community like deer.
Like Marlon Brown they will run you down and our people
   live in constant fear.

You know who they are.
The People Eaters.

I seen something and I know you seen it too
because when I was there I was talking directly to you
at the SC state capitol on numerous occasions
Using every method of poetic persuasion I have
when speaking to the community
as an abolitionist.

As a witness to this monstrous atrocity
at the same place
for the same reasons my forebears spoke in 1850
in the very same city.
After another black mother's child died
and no one wanted to say why.

I marched with babies and beside the young men so they
   could all see it too and know what to do when they see
   it again.

I have personally witnessed from courtrooms in a state of fury
as my black fathers, mothers, sons and brothers
were unjustly tried and incarcerated by all white
or near all white juries. . .

On purpose! In fact it's accepted tactics.
That's just how they do.
No polls or graphs needed to convince me it's true.
I seen it. . . and you seen it too.

With my own eyes I seen lawyers manipulate the structure
   of a jury by race.
By the color of someone's face.
I suggest you go see it take place. . . personally.
No reason why you can't.
For all intents and purposes our courts
looks just like a CCA or GEO corporate product processing
   plant.

I seen it. You'd see it too if you ever looked around.
You would know. . .

"There's "Something In The Way Of Things (In Town)"
So don't ask me why I'm so intense these days
because if you felt what I'm feeling
there would be more blood on this page.
And if you know like I know. . .

**"To be black and conscious in America
is to be in a constant state of rage." —James Baldwin**

So I'm not trying to hear about what's "legal" or politically
    correct.
This is not some problem that can be solved with a check.
Have you forgotten what was said about a man named Dred?
**". . . that colored persons of African descent have no rights
that white men are bound to respect"**

Here's a finger for your feelings.
Maybe even two. You know how I do.
I'm trying to be honest.

I don't give a damn about what ever laws
you think we need to change
and which politician you vainly claim
can superman our lives out of bondage. . .

A mission of petitions seems meaningless in this madness.

As Taylor Mali predicted.
**"And somewhere in Florida. . . .
Votes are still being counted"**

I'm trying to say *I seen it.*
You seen it too.
You all know it's true.
Every genocide is considered legal
by the people
doing the killing, enslaving,
exploiting and raping.
They never stop taking.

Till your eternal spirit is drained
and your soul left stained
by feelings of shame and guilt so old and ingrained
that you can't even *name it*
Until all that is left is the overwhelming urge
to protect and serve
The men who enslaved you and made you in their image.

There in the mirror of your soul!
Do you see it?!

Yes. . . I believe that you do.
That's why I said I seen. . . something.
I seen it.
And I know you seen it too.

© Max Parthas
Dedicated to Amiri Baraka. 1/12/2014.

Maximus Parthas (born in 1964 in Paterson, NJ) is a modern-day abolitionist, activist, spoken word artist, and mentor. He is a visionary who doesn't mind speaking his mind and facing the ugly truths of modern-day slavery head-on via the use of public platforms such as social media, broadcast radio, spoken word poetry, and videography. Parthas endeavors to enlighten and educate his audiences by gifting them with poetic images that leave them searching for truth.

His "in your face" honesty and passion act as a double edged sword that will force you to open your eyes and see the world for what it is (minus the rose-colored glasses); especially when it comes to the topic of modern-day slavery and the prison industrial system. He has won numerous awards and accolades and is well-respected in the spoken word industry, both nationally and internationally. He has appeared on stage with poetry giants, Emmy, Peabody and Grammy award winner(s), Hollywood actors and Hip-Hop artists alike. His work has appeared in anthologies, CDs, and numerous publications.

Maximus Parthas currently resides in Columbia, SC.

REFLECTIONS ON WHITE SUPREMACY

Jaan K. Laaman

RECENTLY A SMART, PROGRESSIVE, RETIRED ENGLISH PROFESSOR remarked, "How can it be that in late 2016, police are routinely shooting and often killing Black people with almost no legal consequences?" Police in the United States have been killing Black and other people of color just like this for twenty, thirty, fifty years and more. Back then they used to totally get away with it and today, not much has changed.

One big difference now is that many of these killings are caught on phone cameras and put online and thus, seen by millions. In the last few days, we are again witnessing footage of police murdering Black people making the national news, and new protests and resistance are erupting as a result of these murders. Nonetheless, cops are rarely charged with any wrongdoing and even when they are, very few are ever convicted of any crime. For example, in April 2015, Freddie Gray Jr., a twenty-five-year-old Black man, was arrested by police in Baltimore. Freddie Gray had three fractured vertebrae and a crushed voice box, which he suffered during transport in a police van. While in the police van, Gray fell into a coma and subsequently died; his death was due to injuries to his spinal cord. Although six officers faced charges related to the murder of Freddie Gray, they were all ultimately let off without any convictions.

An even more typical example of police killing with impunity is the decision of the prosecutor and grand jury in Cleveland not to charge the two white cops who shot and killed a twelve-year-old Black boy named Tamir Rice. In 2014, Tamir Rice was playing with a toy pistol in a park outside a recreation center near his home. Two Cleveland cops drove up and within two seconds, one cop repeatedly shot him. They left him lying on the ground, not even attempting to give him first aid. Tamir died of the gunshot wounds. The Cleveland prosecutor said, "it was a tragedy," but the police did not break any laws or regulations and a grand jury absolved them of any wrongdoing.

POLICE VIOLENCE TODAY

Life in the United States includes white cops routinely, that is, on a daily basis, killing people of color. The government and legal authorities always have and continue to rule almost all of these killings as lawful and acceptable actions of the state. So how can this be, that in the 21st century in a country supposedly based on law, Black people and other people of color can be routinely abused and even killed by agents of the state?

It's not a mistake and it isn't about Republicans or Democrats. It is a historical and ongoing reality that people of color face institutional disparity and discrimination from all aspects of the U.S. state apparatus. On a human individual level, a large percentage of white people have at least some prejudicial attitudes towards people of color. It is true that throughout history, especially in the 20th century, great leaders and massive popular struggles confronted and challenged institutional discrimination and racist practices. Marcus Garvey, W.E.B. Dubois, Malcolm X, Rosa Parks, Martin Luther King Jr., Cesar Chavez, Fannie Lou Hamer, H. Rap Brown, Huey P. Newton, Assata Shakur, all these and so many more outstanding reformers and/or revolutionary leaders and activists, contributed significantly to the struggle for justice, freedom, and equality for Black people and all people of color in the United States.

Yes, progress has been made. Barack Obama, the first Black man to be president, was twice elected. Yet everywhere we look, right on the surface and especially if we dig deeper, institutional discrimination, prejudice, and racist practices and abuses continue in all aspects of life in the United States.

In 2016, the United States is a majority white country. The United States comprises 5 percent of the world's population, but incarcerates 25 percent of the world's prisoners. The majority of prisoners across the United States are people of color. And on a daily basis Black men, women, and even children are shot and often killed by mainly white cops, who almost always are cleared of any wrongdoing.

These are the indisputable realities in early twenty-first century life in the United States. If we look back historically we can see even more blatant and vicious racist abuses and practices in all areas of life, directed against all people of color. This began with the earliest European contact and conquest of the Americas. Genocide, land theft, slavery of Indigenous people and the African slave trade, this was the origin of all the modern countries in North, Central and South America.

RESISTANCE TO RACISM

From the early period of colonialism, when white supremacy was being constructed on lies, material benefits based on white skin privileges, and the super exploitation of Black labor, there also was opposition and resistance to this hateful thinking and practice. Native and Black people found many ways to resist and oppose slavery, from running away to burning down the plantation, sometimes with the slave owner still inside. From these earliest times of resistance, there were white people who supported and assisted with the escapes and uprisings. The "underground railroad" was operational for well over 100 years. Networks, often of white homes and farms, gave refuge and assistance to Blacks who escaped from slave plantations and traveled north, sometimes all the way to Canada, to seek freedom.

The Abolitionist movement actively worked for the end of slavery. It included many white activists and leaders. Although fewer in number, there also were militant white abolitionists like John Brown, who literally, with guns in hand, freed Black people held as slaves on plantations in Missouri and Virginia.

There have always been white people, often in leftist and revolutionary organizations and sometimes from religious groups, who have allied with and supported the freedom struggle and the National Liberations struggles of New African/Black, Native/Indigenous, Puerto Rican and Chicano people. White people were in the Civil rights movement, communists in labor and community struggles, and students, antiracists and anti-imperialist activists supported the Black Power struggles. In the eighties and nineties the John Brown Anti-Klan Committee actively organized against racist attacks and terror, whether the racists were in white robes or blue uniforms. Other antiracist formations, like the Partisan Defense Committee, which is still active today, organize large anti-Klan rallies in many cities. In 2016, we see the Movement for Black Lives mobilizing on a nationwide level, including the recent release of their comprehensive platform. We also see this movement gaining solidarity and support from a variety of white activists and organizations, as well as from other communities and people of color.

White supremacy, in theory and in actual racist practice, has always had opposition. This resistance has and does include white people acting as allies and supporters of nationalist organizations and working in multinational formations.

"FREEDOM IS A CONSTANT STRUGGLE"

Many changes have and continue to occur in U.S. society. Change, of course, is the only constant in all life and reality. But the question my sister, the English professor, asked, how can racial discrimination and racist murders of people of color still be happening every day, can only be understood and answered by realizing that the false and ugly ideology of white supremacy continues to exist. This false ideology was the underlying ideological foundation of what were the British colonies that transformed into the slave-owning U.S. republic, which grew into U.S. imperialism and that today exists as the main military and imperialist superpower in the world. Many changes have occurred, including progress and advances in human and public rights, but underneath it, the ideology of white supremacy still exists and corrupts the United States. This false ideology manifests itself in public acts and attacks, and in private thoughts and motivations.

White cops murdering Black children, millions of people of color facing discrimination in a myriad of ways, even while we have a president who is Black. So, a final point about the false ideology of white supremacy. The fundamental and necessary changes, that we the vast majority of people in the United States very much need and want, will only be achieved once we can unite and work together for our common good. Racism and prejudicial thinking has been the main weapon used against working people—common people, to break our unity and defeat our struggles for progress, justice, a better life, for a revolutionary future of hope and peace. Again and again strikes have been broken, community efforts derailed and sections of people have been misled and misdirected to act against their common interests because of racism and racial prejudice.

The false ideology of white supremacy has been the main weapon used against us, common people, working people, farmers, miners, teachers, shop keepers, unemployed people, and yes, even prisoners too. Most of us have had some direct experience dealing with the negative impact of white supremacist ideology. Whether at work, in school or in the community, it is likely that some of our struggles have come up short or were defeated, because we were unable to sustain our unity in the face of the old "divide and conquer" tactics, based on racist thinking and perhaps weak or racist leadership. Many decades of community activism and revolutionary organizing all across the United States, have made clear that no matter what the specifics of the struggle, unity is always necessary to sustain the effort and to actually win. As Mumia Abu-Jamal has famously stated, "when we fight, we win." The main weapon used against popular struggle is and has been, to divide us based on racism and playing to lies of white supremacist ideology. Unity is our strength and rejecting racism is necessary for unity. Racism will continue to be used against us, until we expose it and simply reject it, for the lies and fabrications that it is.

PLAGUE

Catherine Tafur

Painting is my method of mourning. Unbridled feminist rage, anger towards the evils of capitalism and patriarchy, and the emotional fallout of shattered expectations and broken belief systems are the fodder that drive the content and shape my aesthetics. The failures of our social and political systems have exposed humanity's incomprehensible capacity for violence. Witnessing such endless destruction leads to despair. The monster of late capitalist hegemony seems insurmountable, and modes of resistance begin to feel like Sisyphean tasks. Art is a method to wrestle with this disillusionment, to grieve for our loss of innocence, and to release collective anger in a visual scream. Here is painting as funerary object and conduit for rage.

Catherine Tafur is a Peruvian-born artist based in New York City. Tafur spent her childhood in Peru in a bicultural home with a Japanese mother and Peruvian father before relocating to the United States. The content of her work is informed by the experience of her youth as a queer, multiracial immigrant in American suburbia. Her drawings and paintings explore themes of death, violence, vulnerability, and loss of innocence. Her subjects are political and personal, feminist, and confrontational. Since studying at the Cooper Union School of Art on a full scholarship, she has had numerous group and solo exhibitions.

WHOLE FOODS

Eric Allan Yankee

Whole Foods

Put an organic apple
in your belly
with no attachment
to an outcome
of liberation.

Until we amputate
hellfire
from our governing mythology:
There is no harvest of peace.
There is no funeral for death.
There are no believers in natural truth.
There are only excess crooks
oiling the robots on grandpa's old farm.

Eric Allen Yankee is a member of the Revolutionary Poet's Brigade of Chicago. His work appears or is forthcoming in *The People's Tribune, CC+D, Crab fat, Sweet Wolverine, Overthrowing Capitalism: Volume 2, The Miscreant, Writing Raw, Ygdrasil, Between the Lines, Erbacce,* and *The Fem.* He is coeditor of *Caravel* (caraveljournal.org).

TOWARD AN ABOLITION ECOLOGY

Nik Heynen

On January 16th, 1865, Major General William Tecumseh Sherman issued *Special Field Order Number 15*. This short decree had vast, yet ultimately unrealized, emancipatory possibilities moving into *Reconstruction*. Had his order been carried out to its most egalitarian ends it might have changed the trajectory of rampant uneven development via the proliferation of racial capitalism in the aftermath of the U.S. Civil War. *Special Field Order 15* "reserved and set apart for the settlement of negroes now made free by the acts of war and the proclamation of the President of the United States . . . the islands from Charleston, south, the abandoned rice fields along the rivers for thirty miles back to the sea, and the county bordering the St. Johns River, Florida." As a result of its initial implementation, which included that "each family shall have a plot not more than (40) forty acres of tillable ground . . . in the possession of which land the military authorities will afford them protection, until such time as they can protect themselves, or until Congress shall regulate their title," by June of 1865 roughly 40,000 freed African Americans had begun to imagine and build a new society on 400,000 acres of southeastern U.S. land. This land *could have* been the start of a path toward reparations both of wealth and ecological self-determination for people long enslaved through the logics of white supremacist exploitation and oppression.

In the months prior to January 16th, 1865, Sherman's Army had both won the *Battle of Atlanta*—forever changing the fabric of the city and the urbanizing logic of the Southeast more generally—and completed their *March to the Sea*. When taken together, these penultimate events precipitated the end of the Civil War and helped secure the abolition of slavery. Through the *Battle of Atlanta*, which occurred in July of 1864, Sherman's forces crushed what had become the most important transportation and supply hub of the Confederacy, thus sending southern capitalism spiraling into deeper crisis. The capture and scorching of the "Gateway City of the South" was especially important for President Lincoln, as he was in a contentious election campaign against the Democratic opponent George B. McClellan. Given this, we can draw a direct historical connection between the destruction of Atlanta and the permanent abolition of slavery.

Two distinct moments foreshadowed Sherman's issuing of *Special Field Order 15*, which demonstrated the interrelated and interconnected tensions surrounding land and property in the immediate moments following emancipation. First, there was a calamitous, albeit easily preventable, event through which hundreds (some estimates say thousands) of recently freed African Americans drowned as they attempted to cross Ebenezer Creek while following Sherman's Army toward the coast. The large trailing column of freed people, having no resource base of their own to sustain their lives, were dependent upon Sherman's troops for both sustenance and security. The mass-drowning event happened because engineers disassembled a pontoon bridge once Union troops had crossed the creek to dissuade the newly freed people from trailing them in December of 1864.

The second moment that informed Sherman's proclamation of *Special Field Order 15*, and stemmed from the criticisms he received for the loss of human life at Ebenezer Creek, was a community meeting in Savannah on January 12, 1865. Present at this meeting were Sherman, Lincoln's secretary of war, Edwin M. Stanton, and twenty African American leaders from within the Savannah community, many of whom were ministers. The purpose of the meeting was to discuss enacting emancipation and the political realities that would provide the foundation for *Reconstruction*. When Secretary Stanton asked the group of twenty men, "State in what manner you think you can take care of yourselves, and how can you best assist the Government in maintaining your freedom," Reverend Garrison Frazier replied, "The way we can best take care of ourselves is to have land, and turn it and till it by our labor—that is, by the labor of the women, and children, and old men—and we can maintain ourselves and have something to spare." While the conversation continued from there, this question of land, property, and self-determination regarding both the physical and social reproduction of emancipated African American people was resolutely inscribed onto the national conscious yet again and forever more onward.

While uneven racial development produced much of the foundation for U.S. history, too many of these moments and episodes remain absent from our collective geographical and political ecological imagination when considering the interconnected ways property relations are directly enmeshed within the broader environmental politics that force ongoing harm and suffering through racial capitalism. The historical circumstances surrounding *Special Field Order 15*, as do the Hunkpapa Lakota and Yanktonai Dakota's contemporary direct action and broader circumstances surrounding Standing Rock, offer important insights about how we can build upon past colonial and white supremacist logics of property relations and the cascading connections between property and the sustenance of populations. Related to this, I want to draw on something George Shulman asserted in his book *American Prophecy: Race and Redemption in American Political Culture* to help make this point. Shulman said: "It is strange really: Theorists read Agamben or Arendt on a genocide that Americans did not cause or experience directly, but do not read [Frederick] Douglass, W.E.B. Dubois, [James] Baldwin, or [Toni] Morrison, who draw on prophetic idioms to address the racial holocaust that Americans caused and experienced directly, whose legacy still grips the life of each and all."[1]

Just as Marx's political narrative was greatly influenced by the revolutionary efforts to abolish slavery,[2] ongoing violence committed through racial capitalist logics compels contemporary scholars and activists to keep abolition at the core of antiracist, anticolonial,

---

1. George M. Shulman, *American Prophecy: Race and Redemption in American Political Culture* (Minneapolis: University of Minnesota Press, 2008).

2. See Robin Blackburn, Abraham Lincoln, and Karl Marx, *An Unfinished Revolution: Karl Marx and Abraham Lincoln* (London: Verso Books, 2011).

and anticapitalist politics.[3] However, given all we have learned, there also seems to be a range of ways we can imagine, articulate, and enact variegated abolitionist politics. From this more granular yet always interconnected perspective we can think more deeply about the abolition of prisons,[4] the abolition of police brutality,[5] but also abolitionist politics as they apply to property and environmental relations. Given that political ecology has largely evolved from insights about the interrelated and interconnected politics of property rights, commodification, and the configurations of social and environmental changes driven by and resulting from these dynamics,[6] it is peculiar how little attention has been paid to racialized property relations and the resulting ability of communities to not only survive, but thrive.[7] It is odd that Sherman's *Special Field Order 15* has been so little mentioned regarding the intense urbanization of Atlanta and the Southeast more generally, especially given the tremendous unevenness of these processes of urbanization regarding racial and income inequalities. The lack of attention to this moment is especially peculiar given that *Special Field Order 15* led to the clarion call of the reparations movement, "forty acres and a mule," even if Sherman did not mention the mule. That said, it is promising to see how much support and attention the mobilization at Standing Rock is receiving.

3. See Clyde Woods, "Life after Death," *The Professional Geographer* 54, no. 1 (2002): 62–66.

4. See Ruth Wilson Gilmore, *Golden Gulag: Prisons, Surplus, Crisis, and Opposition in Globalizing California* (Berkeley: University of California Press, 2007); Angela Y. Davis, *The Meaning of Freedom: And Other Difficult Dialogues* (San Francisco: City Lights Books, 2013); Jordan T. Camp, *Incarcerating the Crisis: Freedom Struggles and the Rise of the Neoliberal State* (Berkeley: University of California Press, 2016); and also Critical Resistance, available at criticalresistance.org.

5. Cassandra Chaney and Ray V. Robertson, "Racism and Police Brutality in America," *Journal of African American Studies* 17, no. 4 (2013): 480–505; and Campaign Zero, available at joincampaignzero.org.

6. Michael J. Watts, *Silent Violence: Food, Famine, and Peasantry in Northern Nigeria* (Athens: University of Georgia Press, 2013); Becky Mansfield, *Privatization: Property and the Remaking of Nature-Society Relations* (Oxford: John Wiley & Sons, 2009); and Scott Prudham, "Property and Commodification," in *The Routledge Handbook of Political Ecology*, edited by Tom Perreault, Gavin Bridge, and James McCarthy (London: Routledge, 2015).

7. See Katherine McKittrick, "Plantation Futures," *Small Axe* 17, no. 3 42 (2013): 1–15; and Levi Van Sant, "Plantation Geographies: Agriculture, Race, and Science in the South Carolina Lowcountry, 1865–Present." PhD diss., University of Georgia, 2016.

As historic and geographic insights into racial capitalism help illustrate, radical struggles for anticolonial and antiracist socionatural change have always required thoughtful political vision, strategic political organizing, and necessarily, forceful agitation to help spark consciousness and facilitate direct action and bring about legislative changes. W.E.B. Du Bois' discussion of "abolition democracy" offers important ways of continuing to think through revolutionary change as a driving force behind ongoing efforts for the idea of "abolition ecology." In *Black Reconstruction in America*, Du Bois illustrates how the freedom dreams underlying African American's fighting against the Confederacy were dashed through the collective recognition that the self-determination they sought would be implausible if the very democratic fabric of the United States was not also simultaneously abolished along with slavery given its inherently white supremacist logics and traditions. Du Bois calls this political vision "abolition democracy."[8] Joel Olson expanded upon Du Bois by suggesting:

> The abolitionists' principles and achievements make them an important, if underappreciated, source for new democratic politics for in the process of challenging slavery and racial prejudice they challenged white citizenship itself, thereby creating space for expanded democratic practices. There are three elements of abolitionist praxis that are particularly relevant for today: their model of the political actor as agitator, their emphasis on freedom, and their willingness to follow the radical implications of their demands.[9]

This more specific idea of abolition ecology, then, is rooted squarely within these ideals of W.E.B. Du Bois. This notion is to push forward through well-informed and deliberate organizing and continued theorizing against and about the continued existence of white supremacist logics that continue to produce uneven racial development within land and property relations.

---

8. W.E.B. Du Bois, *Black Reconstruction in America, 1860–1880* (New York: The Free Press, 1935/1998).

9. Joel Olson, *The Abolition of White Democracy* (Minneapolis: University of Minnesota Press, 2004), 135–36; see also George Lipsitz, "Abolition Democracy and Global Justice," *Comparative American Studies* 2, no. 3 (2004): 271–86.

How can abolitionist ideals inform contemporary political ecological struggles around air quality, soil quality, water pollution, inadequate shelter, food insecurity, and hunger that continue to ravage communities of color and poor communities? Because the formation of the United States is territorially based in forms of oppression and violence against indigenous nations and communities of color, there are indeed many sources of insight to look to for connections between colonial and racist ideology and environmental contradictions.

A driving notion of abolition ecology builds on direct action traditions that began in the abolitionist movement against slavery, were core tactics during the Civil rights movement, and continue today through Black Lives Matter—because as human history shows rights are seldom just granted; they are won through struggle. Building upon Du Bois, moving toward abolition ecology is an effort to take abolitionist ideas created through hard-fought struggles so as to better organize around the racialized questions of who gains from and who pays for, who benefits from and who suffers from particular processes of political ecological change. While scholars and activists organizing around contemporary environmental problems continue to have episodic victories, there still is great revolutionary promise in fidelity to what is at stake in the 14th Amendment of the U.S. Constitution, and in bringing in the prefigurative abolitionist logic of direct action politics as a way to keep moving forward toward egalitarian political ecological goals.

I reflect on Sherman's *Special Field Order 15* in this brief essay to consider the prefigurative possibilities of what forms of social reproduction and political ecological politics might have transpired via the abolition democracy had Rev. Garrison Frazier's thoughts about land been woven into the democratic fabric of *Reconstruction*. While only referenced in one paragraph in *Black Reconstruction*, Du Bois is clear to make the point, "the government broke its implied promise and drove them [freed people] off the land."[10] Just as telling are the continued political ecological consequences of having those lands ripped from their possession as the order was rescinded in December of 1864 via President

---

10. Du Bois, *Black Reconstruction*, 393.

Andrew Johnson, who insisted confiscated lands had to be returned to former [white] owners. Racial capitalism won another victory when President Johnson suggested that despite losing their new lands, freed people occupying those lands should be offered contracts to work that land for the original owners (many instances their former masters), which was tantamount to a new form of wage servitude that quickly evolved into sharecropping.

Recalling this history is in line with Cedric Robinson's engagement with Du Bois, when Robinson says, "unless we continue to evoke a consciousness of the historical moment in which Du Bois was working, we have little chance of recognizing the nature of thought to which he addressed himself in *Black Reconstruction*."[11] From here, and keeping with theme, we could just as easily pivot to how in the late 1860s, after the Civil War, Sherman was responsible for ordering the killing of nearly five million bison in a strategic military effort to drive them into extinction as a way of containing First Nations' people living on the U.S. Plains and as a result, force them onto reservations. The possibilities of continued abolitionist progress will certainly be premised upon internalizing these histories and the agitation, clear articulation of freedom dreams, and ongoing fidelity toward the radical implications of abolition.

REFERENCES

Blackburn, Robin, Abraham Lincoln, and Karl Marx. *An Unfinished Revolution: Karl Marx and Abraham Lincoln*. London: Verso Books, 2011.

Camp, Jordan T. *Incarcerating the Crisis: Freedom Struggles and the Rise of the Neoliberal State*. Berkeley: University of California Press, 2016.

Campaign Zero: joincampaignzero.org.

Chaney, Cassandra, and Ray V. Robertson. "Racism and Police Brutality in America." *Journal of African American Studies* 17, no. 4 (2013): 480–505.

Critical Resistance: criticalresistance.org.

Davis, Angela Y. *The Meaning of Freedom: And Other Difficult Dialogues*. San Francisco: City Lights Books, 2013.

---

11. Cedric J. Robinson, *Black Marxism: The Making of the Black Radical Tradition* (Chapel Hill: University of North Carolina Press, 1983), 207.

Du Bois, W.E.B. *Black Reconstruction in America, 1860–1880.* New York: The Free Press, 1935/1998.

Foner, Eric. *Gateway to Freedom: The Hidden History of the Underground Railroad.* New York: W.W. Norton & Company, 2015.

Gilmore, Ruth Wilson. *Golden Gulag: Prisons, Surplus, Crisis, and Opposition in Globalizing California.* Berkeley: University of California Press, 2007.

Lipsitz, George. "Abolition Democracy and Global Justice." *Comparative American Studies* 2, no. 3 (2004): 271–86.

Mansfield, Becky, ed. *Privatization: Property and the Remaking of Nature-Society Relations.* Oxford: John Wiley & Sons, 2009.

McKittrick, Katherine. "Plantation Futures." *Small Axe* 17, no. 3 42 (2013): 1–15.

Olson, Joel. *The Abolition of White Democracy.* Minneapolis: University of Minnesota Press, 2004.

Prudham, Scott. "Property and Commodification." In *The Routledge Handbook of Political Ecology,* edited by Tom Perreault, Gavin Bridge, and James McCarthy, 430–45. London: Routledge, 2015.

Reed, Isaiah. *The Forgotten Act: General Sherman's Special Field Order 15.* Lexington, KY: Pyrite Press, 2015.

Robinson, Cedric J. *Black Marxism: The Making of the Black Radical Tradition.* Chapel Hill: University of North Carolina Press, 1983.

Shulman, George M. *American Prophecy: Race and Redemption in American Political Culture.* Minneapolis: University of Minnesota Press, 2008.

Van Sant, Levi. "Plantation Geographies: Agriculture, Race, and Science in the South Carolina Lowcountry, 1865–Present." PhD diss., University of Georgia, 2016.

Watts, Michael J. *Silent Violence: Food, Famine, and Peasantry in Northern Nigeria.* Athens: University of Georgia Press, 2013.

Woods, Clyde. "Life after Death." *The Professional Geographer* 54, no. 1 (2002): 62–66.

ABOUT THE CONTRIBUTORS

MUMIA ABU-JAMAL is author of *We Want Freedom: A Life in the Black Panther Party* (Common Notions, 2016) and ten other books written from deep inside America's gulag. He is an internationally renowned and acclaimed journalist and author whose case and writings have garnered him broad worldwide support. For more than twenty years his piercing weekly radio commentaries have been broadcast around the world.

RENÉE M. BYRD is an activist, scholar, educator, and community organizer, committed to building countercarceral knowledges in pursuit of a world without prisons. She is currently an assistant professor in the Department of Sociology at Humboldt State University. Outside of academia, Renée has worked as a legal advocate for women prisoners with Justice Now in Oakland, a family advocate for youth in the Juvenile Justice System and on broader campaign work aimed at building genuine human security. Her current book project, titled *Punishment's Twin: Carceral Logics, Abolitionist Critique and the Limits of Reform*, brings an abolitionist critique of reform to a wide audience.

ANDREW DILTS is associate professor of Political Theory at Loyola Marymount University, and is author of *Punishment and Inclusion: Race, Membership, and the Limits of American Liberalism* and co-editor (with Perry Zurn) of *Active Intolerance: Michel Foucault, the Prisons Information Group, and the Future of Abolition*.

JOSHUA DUBLER is assistant professor of Religion and Classics at the University of Rochester. He is the author of *Down in the Chapel: Religious Life in an American Prison* (FSG, 2013).

COLLEEN HACKETT is an educator and critical criminologist at Colorado State University in Pueblo. She organizes political education classes with incarcerated women, coedits an antiauthoritarian newsletter written by femme and trans prisoners called *unstoppable!*, and coedits *The Fire Inside*, a collection of re-port-backs and reflections from contemporary prison rebels.

NIK HEYNEN is a professor in the Department of Geography at the University of Georgia. His research utilizes a combined urban political ecology/urban political economy framework to investi-gate how economic, political and cultural processes contribute to the production of inequality and uneven racial development. His research interests relate to the analysis of how social power rela-tionships, including class, race, and gender are inscribed in the transformation of urban nature, space, and social reproduction.

PETER KLETSAN (a pseudonym) is trained in philosophy and is only peripherally an academic, sometimes teaching community college courses and devoting the rest of his time to local political organizing. Peter is an active member of the Oakland chapter of the Incarcerated Workers Organizing Committee.

JAAN K. LAAMAN is a long-held U.S. political prisoner, one of the original Ohio-7/United Freedom Front defendants. Jaan is the ed-itor of 4strugglemag.org, a primary voice of political prisoners in the United States. Jaan has two bachelor degrees, one in Sociology and one in Psychology, from Saint Mary College in Kansas. Jaan can be directly contacted at:

Jaan Laaman (10372-016)
US Penitentiary Tucson
P.O. Box 24550
Tucson, AZ 85734

VINCENT LLOYD is an associate professor of Theology and Religious Studies at Villanova University. He is the author of *Black Natural Law* (Oxford, 2016). Together, with funding from the American Council of Learned Societies, Dubler and Lloyd are completing *Break Every Yoke: Religion, Justice, and the End of Mass Incarceration*.

MIANTA McKNIGHT knows first-hand what the prison system is like, as someone tried as an adult as a juvenile. She served eight-een years and one day, growing up within the prison industrial complex. Mianta had just turned seventeen years old when she was arrested in 1995. As Justice Now's Director of Community Engagement, she is the most recent directly impacted person to transition from fellow to codirector. She is dedicated to challenging the inhumane conditions in women's prisons and being the voice for those unable to speak for themselves. She is a professional dancer and shares her gift of dance with the world, performing by using dance as a form of therapy and expression. Mianta is also striving to bring holistic health and massage to the social justice world and to the people coming home from women's prisons. The benefits of massage help empower others to embrace a holistic way of living, while healing the trauma of incarceration and its effects.

LENA PALACIOS is a tenure-track Assistant Professor in the Departments of Gender, Women's and Sexuality Studies and Chicano and Latino Studies (University of Minnesota-Twin Cities). Her research and teaching focuses on transnational feminist prison studies, Indigenous, Chicana and Latina, queer feminisms, race-radical and critical race feminisms, transformative justice and community accountability, media justice, as well as participatory action research.

ALEXANDRE PUBLIA (pseudonym) studied international relations, with a focus on civil disobedience and social change post-9/11. Their Master's and Bachelor's are both from public West Coast U.S. universities. Their research and passion is the achievement of human rights for all peoples, no exceptions.

SUJANI K. REDDY is an associate professor of American Studies at SUNY the College at Old Westbury. She is the author of *Nursing and Empire: Gendered Labor and Migration from India to the United States* (UNC Press, 2015) and a coeditor of *The Sun Never Sets: South Asians in an Age of U.S. Power* (NYU Press, 2013) Both books were also published by Orient BlackSwan in South Asia. You can listen to Who Makes Cents? podcast with Sujani Reddy on the history of nursing and empire.

ANASTAZIA SCHMID is an activist artist and graduate independent scholar in the higher education program at the Indiana Women's Prison. She received the 2016 Gloria Anzaldúa Award for her work in gender and sexuality by the American Studies Association, and received the Outstanding History Project Award presented by the Indiana Historical Society. Her work and interviews span multimedia sources including NPR and Slate magazine. She is the coauthor of the play The Duchess of Stringtown currently under production both inside prison and out. You can write to Anastazia via email with Jpay (enter Indiana for the state and inmate #122585) or via letter at:

Anastazia Schmid #122585
800 Msh Bus Stop Drive
Mcu Bsl-18
Madison, IN 47250-2852

MICHAEL SUTCLIFFE seeks literacies and uses of language that interrupt and subvert the (re)production of racist, heteronormative power drawing upon degrees in rhetoric and linguistics, a medical-technical writer vocation, and experience coordinating a re-entry program for women in a county jail.

BEN TURK is an anarchist from Milwaukee, Wisconsin. He is a coeditor of The Fire Inside, member of Milwaukee Incarcerated Workers Organizing Committee (IWOC) and the #closeMSDF Coalition (the campaign to shut down Milwaukee Secure Detention Facility), and long time supporter of the Lucasville Uprising Prisoners. He has also toured North America with abolitionist plays via Insurgent Theatre.

DAVID C. TURNER III is a PhD student in Social and Cultural Studies in Education at the University of California, Berkeley.

HARSHA WALIA is the author of Undoing Border Imperialism (AK Press, 2013) and is a South Asian activist, writer, and popular educator rooted in migrant justice, Indigenous solidarity, Palestinian liberation, antiracist, feminist, anti-imperialist, and anticapitalist movements and communities for over a decade.

INDEX

108n35, 127n5, 141, 143, 219, 228, 229, 241
Foucault, Michel, 24, 24n3, 179, 179n20–21, 239
Free Alabama Movement, 47, 47n70

G

Geertz, Clifford, 116
Gilmore, Ruth Wilson, 23n1, 32, 109n46, 191, 234n4
Gilyard, Keith, 190, 190n46
Gingrich, Newt, 23, 29, 32
Gordon, Avery, 93, 93n5, 113
Gottschalk, Marie , 31n20, 32, 33, 33n27, 34n36, 41n50, 42n52, 43n58, 48n75, 49n77
Grande, Sandy, 62, 62n16
Gunn Allen, Paula, 58, 58n2

H

Hartman, Saidiya, 59, 59n6,
Harvey, David, 178, 178n18
Heinrich, James, 85
Herzberg, Bruce, 190, 191n41
Holder, Eric, 30, 30n17, 38
Hume, David, 203, 204n16

I

ideology, 25, 49, 73, 103n21, 118, 173, 175, 184, 188, 191, 196, 236
Indian Removal Act of 1830, 36
Indigenous Action Media, 1n2, 17n4
insurgent politics, 12–21, 46, 166
Inuk, 60

J

Jackson, Andrew, 36
Jacobi, Tobi, 188, 188n42, 191
Jim Crow laws, 4, 9, 25, 26, 117, 148
Joshua, Deandre, 149

K

Kelley, Robin D. G., 65, 65n29, 128, 128n7, 218, 219n4

Kneebone, Elizabeth, 39, 39n46
Kropotkin, Peter, 201, 201n12

L

Landry, Andrea, 61, 61n10
Lee, Alexander, 28, 28n13
liberation, 17, 29, 100, 125, 126, 129, 131, 143, 155, 186, 205, 222, 230, 242
Linsey, Kate, 82, 87
Locke, John, 203, 203n15
Lopez-Aguado, Patrick, 38n42, 39n45, 48, 48n73
Lucasville Uprising, 45, 242
Lynd, Staughton, 8

M

Marikana Massacre, 140, 144, 150
Marx, Karl, 183, 183n33, 186, 186n38
Marxism, 25n6, 121, 237
mass incarceration, 9, 23, 26, 29, 30, 96, 116, 117, 118, 119, 120, 121, 156, 191, 196, 197, 198; carceral logic, 23, 92, 94, 116; decarceration, 23, 24, 28, 29, 31, 32, 35, 39, 40, 43, 48
Maynard, Robyn, 20, 20n5
McKinney, Coy, 196, 197, 197n4
Messemer, Jonathan, 172
Million, Dian, 58, 58n3, 59
Mohawks of Kahnawà:ke, 62
Moore, Tonya, 87
Murakawa, Naomi, 42, 43n57

N

National Black Feminist Organization, 63
Nehisi-Coates, Ta, 36, 36n38
New Democrats, 29, 32
No One Is Illegal, 12, 12n1, 15n3, 18, 19
nymphomania, 75–79

O

Ohio State Penetentiary, 45
Olson, Joel, 6, 235, 235n9

MORE FROM COMMON NOTIONS

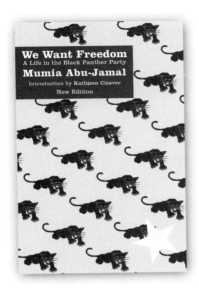

We Want Freedom: A Life in the Black Panther Party
Mumia Abu-Jamal
Introduction by Kathleen Cleaver

978-1-942173-04-5
$20.00
336 pages

"A moving, incisive, and thorough history of the Black Panther Party. This book is required reading for anyone who would seek to understand race, revolution, and repression in the United States."

—Amy Goodman, journalist and host of *Democracy Now!*

"Writing from the barren confines of his death row cell, Mumia Abu-Jamal provides a remarkable testament about the Black Panther Party. . . .an amazing book that illuminates the truth of what his membership in the Party was about, and reveals the extreme price extracted from him for having learned, and for now telling the truth."

—Kathleen Cleaver, from the Introduction

In the Name of the People
Liaisons

978-1-942173-07-6
$18.00
208 pages

The ghost of the People has returned to the world stage, claiming to be the only force capable of correcting or taking charge of the excesses of the time. This truly internationalist and collectivist publication boldly examines the forms of right and leftwing populism emergent in the fissures of the political world. Experimental in both form and analysis, *In the Name of the People* is the commune form of thought and text.

. . .

Writings From a Greek Prison: 32 Steps, or Correspondance From the House of the Dead
Tasos Theofilou
Translated by Eleni Pappa
Preface by Ben Morea
ΔΙΠΛΗ / DIPLI imprint

978-1-942173-12-0
$15.00
144 pages

Writings from a Greek Prison is a literary work of biting realism. Tasos Theofilou gives testimony on the brutality of prison life, and its centrality in contemporary capitalism, through a blur of memoir, social commentary, free verse, and a glossary of the idiom used by inmates in Greek prisons.

MONTHLY SUSTAINERS

These are decisive times, ripe with challenges and possibility, heartache and beautiful inspiration. More than ever, we are in need of timely reflections, clear critiques, and inspiring strategies that can help movements for social justice grow and transform society. Help us amplify those necessary words, deeds, and dreams that our liberation movements and our worlds so need.

Movements are sustained by people like you, whose fugitive words, deeds, and dreams bend against the world of domination and exploitation.

For collective imagination, dedicated practices of love and study, and organized acts of freedom.

By any media necessary.
With your love and support.

Monthly sustainers start at $10 and $25.

At $10 monthly, we will mail you a copy of every new book hot off the press in heartfelt appreciation of your love and support.

At $25, we will mail you a copy of every new book hot off the press alongside special edition posters and 50% discounts on previous publications at our web store.

Join us at commonnotions.org/sustain.

ABOUT COMMON NOTIONS

Common Notions is a publishing house and programming platform that advances new formulations of liberation and living autonomy. Our books provide timely reflections, clear critiques, and inspiring strategies that amplify movements for social justice.

By any media necessary, we seek to nourish the imagination and generalize common notions about the creation of other worlds beyond state and capital. Our publications trace a constellation of critical and visionary meditations on the organization of freedom. Inspired by various traditions of autonomism and liberation—in the United States and internationally, historically and emerging from contemporary movements—our publications provide resources for a collective reading of struggles past, present, and to come.

Common Notions regularly collaborates with editorial houses, political collectives, militant authors, and visionary designers around the world. Our political and aesthetic interventions are dreamt and realized in collaboration with Antumbra Designs.

commonnotions.org
info@commonnotions.org